CW01024535

LET NOT THE SUN
SET ON YOU

LET NOT THE SUN SET ON YOU

"Olibambe Lingashoni"

*A threatening Zulu proverb meaning
one must make sure that the sun does not set,
because if it does, one will not awaken
when it rises again.*

Kingsley Mamabolo

NOMAD
PUBLISHING

Let Not The Sun Set On You
Kingsley Mamabolo

Published by Nomad Publishing in 2024
Email: info@nomad-publishing.com
www.nomad-publishing.com

ISBN 978-1-917045-08-7

CIP Data: A catalogue for this book is
available from the British Library.

Dedication

I dedicate this book, first and foremost to my wonderful wife, Noreen, who has been by my side through thick and thin, encouraging and making sacrifices alongside me while allowing me to attain my career goals. She has been the ideal diplomat's spouse and an incredibly supportive and loving mother.

Secondly, to our children, Yolanda (Popi), Mahlatsi (Sam), Maloyela (Loyi) and Tawanda (Tawi). May the sacrifices we made give you the future we fought and aspired for. With sincere love to my siblings, Buti (Isaac), Ivy (Dineo) and Ashley, who loved me enough to keep the light on for me even when they did not know whether I was still alive and if I was, where in the world I was.

And to the memory of my father who was gone too soon and my mother who held on with dignity and gave us the grounding that we needed to survive and later thrive despite the odds.

CONTENTS

ABOUT THE AUTHOR

Kingsley Mamabolo left South Africa as a very young man armed with little beyond a fighting spirit and a desire for freedom and the dignity that comes with it. Decades later, having traversed the African continent in roles that would serve him well as a career diplomat, he returned to his family and home country.

His leadership qualities, evident very early on, had him tasked to lead his team from Angola to Germany for military training. His acute intuition enabled him to quickly appreciate the extent to which the regime would go in its attempts to silence opponents. He recalls how the organization that he served, the African National Congress (ANC), was, at regular intervals, flooded with 'agents' provocateurs who were sent to disrupt the well- run machine that was the ANC.

Responsibility weighed heavily on the young man, he always rose to the occasion, and on many of those, it was truly a matter of life and death. Deployed to the front-line in Zimbabwe and Mozambique, Kingsley became witness to atrocities committed by the regime, the constant attacks on individuals and communities. As a result, he has harrowing stories to tell of a tense life in exile where to survive, he and other comrades had to ensure that they were at all times, a step ahead of the agents of the regime.

A brief respite to the tension and fear of becoming a victim came when he and his family relocated to Cuba upon his appointment thereto as the ANC Representative in 1989. In Cuba, the hospitality of the People, who were themselves under siege from American Economic Blockade, was amazing. He marveled at the resilience of Cubans who survived and prospered against all odds.

In the new and democratic South Africa, Kingsley has played and continues to play a vital role. He has been appointed by and therefore, served all the presidents since the country attained the historic majority rule in 1994.

Nelson Mandela appointed him the first High Commissioner of the democratic Republic of South Africa to the Republic of Zimbabwe. Thabo Mbeki appointed him as the Ambassador to the OAU/AU, and High Commissioner to Nigeria, while Jacob Zuma appointed him as the Permanent Representative to the United Nations. Today, at the pinnacle of a great and illustrious diplomatic career, Kingsley is South Africa's High Commissioner to the United Kingdom and Northern Ireland, having been appointed by Cyril Ramaphosa. All these appointments saw him crisscross the globe representing his country and its people.

It was in Zimbabwe whilst he was still in exile that he met and married his sweetheart, Eleanor (aka Noreen) who was born and bred in South Africa but migrated to Zimbabwe with her family in later years.

He was South Africa's Ambassador to Ethiopia at the time of the transition of the OAU to the AU. This historic event was preceded by the adoption of the AU Charter. Kingsley witnessed and participated in interesting debates during the formative years of the organization that gave birth to, amongst others, the Peace and Security Architecture of the Continent, the Peer Review Mechanism, and the establishment of the Pan African Parliament.

He served as High Commissioner to Nigeria, a country he loves for the warmth and hospitality of its people, the beauty of its culture evident in their food, their fashion, and entertainment.

Kingsley has also served as South Africa's Permanent Representative to the United Nations and simultaneously, bore the additional title of Chairperson of the Group of 77 plus China (G77 and China), a diverse group of about a hundred and thirty-five small island states and developing countries within the broad family of the United Nations who come together to enhance their joint negotiating capacity in the one hundred and ninety-three member states of the global organization.

In 2015, as Chair of the G77 plus China, Kingsley led the group in negotiations at the UN that led to the adoption 2030 Agenda for Sustainable Development. His demeanor and personality are greatly suited to peace and conflict resolution as well as negotiations between warring groups.

In post-1994 South Africa, he has served in several roles where these qualities have been crucial. These include South Africa's Special Envoy to the Great Lakes, where he, amongst other tasks, deputized one of his mentors, former Minister Comrade Charles Nqakula, and together with others, facilitated the comprehensive ceasefire agreement between the Government of the Republic of Burundi and the Palipehutu – FNL. He also, together with other Envoys, got engaged in negotiations aimed at resolving the conflict in the Democratic Republic of the Congo (DRC).

He represented South Africa when the International Conference of the Great Lakes Region (ICGLR) was formed. Along with it, he and other envoys created the group constituting "Friends of the Great Lakes", which group is chaired by Canada and the Netherlands.

Appointed Special Envoy of the Secretary General of the United Nations and to the Chairperson of the African Union, Kingsley headed a Hybrid Mission of the UN/AU known as the United Nations Mission, African Mission in Darfur (UNAMID), reporting to Secretary Generals Ban Ki-moon, Antonio Guterres and Chairpersons Dr Nkosazana Dlamini- Zuma and Moussa Faki Mahamat, respectively.

Kingsley continues to serve his country and the African continent with diligence, patriotism and the wisdom that has guided him throughout. A loving husband, caring father and African statesman, this book adds one more title that he can and ought to be proud of: an Author!

LIST OF ACRONYMS

ACCORD	African Centre for the Constructive Resolution of Disputes
AFRC	Armed Forces Revolutionary Council
ANC	African National Congress
AK	Alexander Kalashnikov
APRM	African Peer Review Mechanism
AU	African Union
AUHIP for	African Union High Level Implementation Panel Sudan
BPP	Burundi Peace Process
CCM	Chama Cha Mapinduzi or Party of the Revolution
CIA	Central Intelligence Agency (Zimbabwean)
CIDA	Canadian International Development Agency
CIO	Central Intelligence Organization (USA)
CPLP	The Community of Portuguese Speaking Countries.
CPSA	Communist Party of South Africa
DA	Democratic Alliance
DC	Disciplinary Committee
DIA	Department of International Affairs
DIP	Department of Information and Publicity
DDR	Disarmament Demobilization and Reintegration
DDPD	The Doha Document for Peace in Darfur
DJSR	Deputy Joint Special Representative
ECOMOG	Economic Community of West African States Monitoring Group
ECOWAS	Economic Community of West African States
EU	European Union
FFC	The Forces for Freedom and Change (Sudan)
FNLA	Fronte Nacional de Libertacao de Angola or

	The Nacional Front for the Liberation of Angola
FAPLA	Forcas Armado Populares de Libertacaos de Angola for or People's Armed Forces for the Liberation of Angola
FAO	Food and Agricultural Organisation Phalipe Hutu
FNL	National Front for the Liberation of the Hutus
GDR	German Democratic Republic
GDP	Gross Domestic Product
GNU	Government of National Unity
GSEB	Group of Special Envoys for Burundi
GOB	Government of Burundi
G77 and China	Group of 77 developing countries plus China
HQ	Head Quarters
ICC	International Criminal Court
ICGRL	International Conference of of the Great Lakes Region
IMF	International Monetary Front
IDPs	Internally Displaced Persons
JSR	Joint Special Representative
MK	Umkhonto We Sizwe (The armed Wing of the ANC)
MPLA	Movemento Populares de Libertacao de Angola or the Popular Movement for the Liberation of Angola
MAP	Millenium Partnership for Africa' Recovery Program
NEC	National Executive Committee
NORAD	Norwegian Agency for Development Cooperation
NSSM	National Security Study Memorandum
NEPA	New Partnership for Africa's Development
MDGs	Millenium Development Goals
PAC	Pan African Congress
PLAN	People's Liberation Army of Namibia
OAU	Organisation of African Unity
RPC	Regional Political Committee
RENAMO	Resistencia Nacional Mocambicana or

	Mozambican National Resistance
RUF	Revolutionary United Front (Sierra Leone)
SADC	Southern African Development Countries
SDGs	Sustainable Developmental Goals
SACP	South African Communist Party
SWAPO	Southwest African People's Organisation
SOWETO	Southwestern Townships
SANDAF	South African National Defence Force
SIDA	Swedish International Developmental Agency
SOMAFCO	Solomon Mahlangu Freedom College
SSR	Security Sector Reform
TNT	Trinitrotoluene (Explosive)
TRC	Truth and Reconciliation Committee
SLA/AW	Sudan Liberation Army/ Abdul Wahid (Sudan – Darfur)
TMC	Transitional Military Committee (Sudan)
TGoS	Transitional Government of Sudan
UNAMID	United Nations African Union Mission in Darfur
USG	Under Secretary General
UDF	United Democratic Front
UK	United Kingdom
UNITA	Uniao Nacional por la Indipendencia Total de Angola or National Union for the Total Independence of Angola
UNSC	United Nations Security Council
USA	United States of America
USSR	Union of Soviet Socialist Republics
WB	World Bank
ZANU	Zimbabwe African National Union
ZAPU	Zimbabwe African People's Union
ZIPRA	Zimbabwe People's Liberation Army
ZBC	Zimbabwe Broadcasting Cooperation
ZBS	Zambian Broadcasting Services

FOREWORD

Kingsley Mamabolo's incredulous journey is absolutely riveting. From being one of the leaders the Tladi Youth Club to representing South Africa at the United Nations.

This memoir, "Let Not The Sun Set On You" will nourish readers from a wide range of backgrounds.

Kingsley gives us an insider's view of South Africa's struggle for freedom from a deeply patriotic perspective. At the same time, there is no attempt to falsely romanticize or gloss over the challenges and mistakes that inevitably took place.

What shines out of every chapter of the book are Kingsley's leadership qualities which were recognised every step of the way. He was decisive and quick to act, a trait that saved the lives of many people in many instances. Always willing to learn, he gained both knowledge and wisdom from those he served with and under. His humility has seen him live a life of integrity and compassion for others.

In detailing an account in which, as a 10-year-old he belittles an old man and becomes terrified that he might have been cursed, that Kingsley shows his own vulnerability. Indeed, it is from that experience that the title of the book arises.

Further, in a telling exposé, Kingsley shares the chilling effect of the way sadistic teachers used corporal punishment.

I first got to know Kingsley in Zimbabwe, in the 1980s, when he was the Deputy Chief Representative of the ANC. The responsibility for Information and Publicity came under his portfolio. I was part of a small committee that he led which produced a publication called 'Struggle Update to increase support for the liberation struggle in Zimbabwe'.

As a leader, when someone came to him with a problem, his approach was to always help as best he could. Given the circumstances, the security concerns and oftentimes, limited resources, Kingsley always went far beyond the call of duty. Further, and even more admirable was the fact that he gave his best whether he was responding to a call from people in leadership or those from the humblest walks of life. This is why he was greatly loved, as well as highly admired and respected.

At the time, I was a parish priest in the African township of Mbare as well as a member of the ANC. My friendship and relationship with Kingsley was invaluable to me and the work I was doing.

In the book, Kingsley recounts the night that the Zimbabwean intelligence warned the ANC of an imminent attack by the apartheid regime. Like the rest of the ANC, he told me to leave the priest's house immediately lest we were one of the targets. With brilliant command and military precision, he ensured the safety of so many of us and put shame to the callousness of the apartheid regime.

In 1985, Kingsley and I were both elected by the ANC comrades in Zimbabwe as delegates to the National Conference in Kabwe. It was at that Conference that the ANC voted, overwhelmingly, to open its leadership at every level including the National Executive Committee to people of all races. Hitherto, membership of the NEC was not open to white comrades. It was at this conference that Joe Slovo, who was extremely popular, was elected to the NEC. This decision was significant for me as a white person.

This decision was mirrored in Kingsley's own transition from wanting to kill all white people, to embracing non- racialism. On the other hand, Kingsley's poignant story of his beautiful friendship with Andre, his first white friend, and the impossibility of eating in a restaurant together, shows the impact of the regime's policy across board. Apartheid's tentacles permeated every aspect of life and tore apart the very fabric of our lives.

As a chaplain of the ANC, but also as a comrade and a friend, I had the great privilege of performing the marriage ceremony for Kingsley and Noreen. Since they are still together, I guess the glue I used must have been heavy duty.

In the marriage documents, we used his *nom de guerre* which in later years had to be rectified to make the marriage not only recognised in the eyes of God, but also valid in law. This one detail highlights, again, the clandestine lifestyle that was necessary for his security against the regime.

Kingsley is a natural raconteur, a gifted storyteller.

The book which has the makings of a thriller, takes us with him, on his rollercoaster journey punctuated by many hilarious and touching anecdotes.

Kingsley's account of his bittersweet return to South Africa, the precious moments spent with his dying mother, who would not die until her beloved son was home, illustrates the human cost of our struggle.

Towards the end of his brilliant diplomatic career, Kingsley fell afoul of envious, nefarious characters who were determined to bring him down just because of how much he was shining on the international stage. Because of his vast experience and expertise, the United Nations was quick to appoint him to head its peacekeeping-mission in Darfur, an assignment he carried out with his seasoned diplomacy, diligence and resolute.

The chapters about his work as a peacemaker in the conflict zones of the continent bring great credit to him personally and to South Africa, especially during the Mbeki years. He complemented the president's emphasis on Africa's renaissance.

To its credit, the South African government recognised that his worth, stature as a diplomat and his statesmanship made him the best person to represent his country as High Commissioner to the United Kingdom and Northern Ireland.

There is much to lament, be angry about and even ashamed of in the democratic Republic of South Africa today. Not so with the life and witness of Kingsley Mamabolo. As a nation, we have every reason to be immensely proud of what he has done for our nation, for Africa and the world.

Kingsley Mamabolo is a role model for every black child, for oppressed people and for people of goodwill everywhere. His story is one of endurance, of overcoming, and of triumph for him as an individual and for all of us as a nation, a people. It is also a challenge for us, a reminder that what he and so many went through, and were ready to die for, was freedom and dignity for all. Therefore, we must never take that political, economic and social freedom lightly for its price was extremely high. That price is detailed in this book and included the loss of life, loss of limbs, giving up families and one's home and country.

No Kingsley, you were not cursed. You were blessed and because of you, we are too.

Thank you, Kingsley, for sharing your wisdom and humanity with us.

Fr Michael Lapsley SSM
President - Healing of Memories Global Network

INTRODUCTION

The elderly man with the one arm is issuing orders in hush tones 'phansi majaga'- "down comrades" he calls out. His orders are firm, but he is careful not to make noise that will attract unwanted attention to our awkward-looking group. His voice is measured, and his tone is demanding of our attention. As soon as he barks the orders, we respond by taking cover and dropping to the ground like trees that have been felled. We lie still, breathing heavily and sweating profusely as we await the next command. He is conscientious and takes his time before giving the next set of orders; he does so only after he has scanned the terrain carefully.

We are down flat on our bellies, a respite for me as we'd already walked a long distance and my feet are burning. Perhaps that was compounded by the fact that we'd meandered in the thick bush on a tiny footpath, the fear of being discovered is our constant companion.

The bush is thick, and the uncovered parts of our bodies bear scratches from the prick of the branches and bites of the swarm of mosquitoes that seem to companionably follow us everywhere. Finally, we've reached the border, and as we rest on our bellies, the old man lies absolutely still in front of us. He is contemplating the best options for us to cross the border into Maputo, Mozambique, undetected.

From our high posts, we can see the Nomahashe border fence

between the then Swaziland, present-day eSwatini, and Mozambique, standing majestically before us. For us, it is simply another barrier standing between us and freedom. Just then, not far from the crossing where we intend to cross, a small formation of troops marches past, shortly after the old man's order for us to take cover.

How did he see them? I wonder, while looking at the old man's stern face as he concentrates, straining his eyes to pick any movement next to the border fence. I certainly did not see them coming and I am sure none of these new recruits in the group saw them either. I reason that it must be his sixth sense.

Undoubtedly, we are not the first group he is taking across the border illegally. This is his vocation evidenced by the ease with which he meanders through the trees in the thick bush, his movements confirming his familiarity of the area. Musing to myself, I weigh the situation and unintentionally let out the words, "He knows what he is doing." the words come out of my mouth loudly, my voice shattering the serene and uneasy silence. I do not realize that I am speaking aloud. I am thinking and, in the process, I uttered my thoughts.

The entire group looks sharply at me, all of them as anxious as I am. Nonetheless, they pause to digest my assurances. The relief on their faces on hearing those assurances makes it worthwhile to have uttered those words even though doing so had been completely unintended. My heart is pounding as I contemplate the soldiers we just saw marching past. I knew in my heart of hearts that they were the type that would shoot first and ask questions later.

Of some interest to all of us is this one-armed comrade called 'Baba Duma', a battle-scarred old veteran of the struggle and a campaigner for freedom from the KwaZulu Natal region. I came to learn later that his one arm was ripped off by a parcel bomb sent by agents of the apartheid regime.

Looking at Baba Duma, the conscientiousness in the execution of his leadership role, his commitment - he leaves nothing to chance –

makes me realize the depth and seriousness of the decision I took to join the ANC and go into exile.

If ever there had been any illusion, it had become clear to me that we were not on a 'joy ride'; this was not an adventure, rather it is a matter of life and death where men like Baba Duma were living examples of utter commitment to sacrifice for freedom. These people were ready to make the ultimate sacrifice for what they believed in and this is in justice and freedom for all. It felt great to be rubbing shoulders with these men and women of the soil.

Duma's conduct and persona tells a story - he has been around, through the vicissitudes of life and in that realization, he earned my respect immediately. Without a doubt, this comrade is a man of integrity!

I look across, trying to read from the anxious faces of all my friends from Tladi Youth Club who were in this group with me. Lying right next to me is Omry Makgoale (Phoisa), intent on keeping still and making sure that not even his muscles are twitching. Benedict Diphoko (Benny), his eyes bulging, is in front of us. Ephraim Meletse (Leba) and Elias Mataboge (Strike) are huddled together behind a shrub to our left. What would I not give to get to know what is on their minds at this very moment?

Seeing my comrades from Tladi Youth Club here with me fills me with pride. We are together, embarking on a historical, perilous journey that will ensure that we too, make our contribution to the noblest of causes – the liberation of our country. So far on this journey we've been there for each other. It's been a case of 'one for all and all for one.'

Did I call them comrades? If you had told me three months earlier that I would be referring to Benny, Omry, Leba and Strike as comrades I would have laughed my heart out in disbelief. The phrase was foreign but now, here we were, having joined the ANC. This also meant understanding the new struggle lexicon. For one to be called a comrade was the epitome of acceptance; it was tantamount to being awarded a badge of honour.

We felt that we richly deserved the honour considering that we had, after all, already taken a lot of risk on this journey to join the ANC. Surely that alone must make us deserving candidates, did it not? We now called each other 'comrade' with pride, sometimes overdoing it just for emphasis.

Besides identifying each other in that manner separated us from the rest, making us feel that we belonged. It was a form of differentiation from family and friends and all others, who did not ascribe to our values and outlook on life. We now understood that comrades are people on a mission, they are responding positively to the clarion call, the fight for the liberation of humanity. It is a title I take seriously and would never for granted, I wouldn't refer to anyone as comrade unless I had the trust and belief that I could literally put my life in their hands and have the confidence that my safety was guaranteed and secured.

In this group that Baba Duma is leading across the border into Mozambique, we, the Tladi Club members, constitute the core, but a few others joined us along the way. From Naledi Extension, where we had been hiding for about two weeks, we stopped briefly in Dube to pick up others who had been waiting for transportation. As we drove to a house in Dube where we had a brief stay, there were murmurs in the group. Apparently, someone had picked up information that we would be joined on this excursion by Tsietsi Mashinini, the student leader who had distinguished himself in the uprisings and was now in hiding. The comrades who were transporting us were not letting out anything, but the prospect of sharing this perilous journey with Mashinini was very exciting. When it turned out that Mashinini was not at the Dube residence and was nowhere to be found, I was a bit disappointed.

Cohesion in the group consisting of the Tladi Youth Club was strong. Even as we were integrated with others, we still found time to meet separately to strategize, to agree on the way forward on the decisions that were taken for and by the entire collective. We remained a cohesive group within the collective.

As Baba Duma leads us on our way to Mozambique, I note that it is not the first time we are in this kind of situation and suffering from anxiety. There have been a lot of close shaves on this journey so far. For instance, we'd already experienced the same anxiety and excitement when we crossed the Oshoek border post between South Africa and Swaziland.

CHAPTER 1

A JOURNEY TO THE UNKNOWN

*"The challenge of the unknown future is so much
more exciting than the stories of the accomplished past."*
Anon

We were fetched from our hideout in Naledi Extension in Soweto, by a lady comrade called Jeanette Ndhlovu and a tiny fellow called Roy. The journey from Soweto to Oshoek border post was laden with hurdles to cross, it did not help that Roy who was driving the car sometimes appeared edgy and reckless.

In one incident, as we started our journey from Soweto at around midnight, Roy who was driving the fifteen-seater 'Volkswagen' combi that was transporting the group, moved the car for a considerable distance without the headlights on. His action was inexplicable, but we dared not ask questions as we did not know better.

This was Roy being dramatic. There was absolutely no reason for him to drive the car, in the middle of Soweto, several hundreds of kilometres away from the border, without lights on. We were so far away from the border that there was no conceivable way, that our car could be associated with people intent on leaving the country illegally.

Consequently, driving the car without headlights and running the red light only served to draw attention to us. A police car driving from the opposite direction towards us, drove onto our lane with the intention of blocking us. We were heading towards Dube station and had just ran a red traffic light.

Luckily for us there was room for Roy to manoeuvre, there was a lot of space provided by the petrol garage on our side of the road, immediately past the traffic light and so the police car that had moved onto our lane could not block the space entirely. Given allowance by the ample space provided by the garage premises, Roy circumvented the oncoming police car, accelerated, and sped away. We were headed downward towards Phefeni in the direction of Orlando stadium.

Anticipating that the police car would make a U-turn and give chase, my body froze in fear. We were already jam- packed in the car with no space to move, and I was seated right at the back seat. My imagination was running wild, and I thought that if the police gave chase and started shooting, those of us on the back row would be the first targets.

The police cars that were frequently used during that period, were small, agile vans with long aerial communicating wires on the bonnet. They were notorious for their speed and agility. Agents of the regime relied on them to quell uprisings and demonstrations, and to give chase to runaway cars. There is no doubt that in any race the police car would outpace our VW by far.

What made this situation even worse was that we were heading in the direction of the Orlando Police Station, and if the police thought we were worthy of more attention they could have given chase, radioed the police station ahead to block our escape and rein us in. Fortunately, they did not think we posed a threat because they did not even bother to give chase as they moved on.

Their lack of interest in this awkwardly behaving group could be rationalized, being in the part of the country where we were, they could not have imagined that we were potential border jumpers. It was a Saturday in the early hours of the morning, and it is possible that the police dismissed this awkward group, travelling with no lights and passing through a red traffic, as revellers back from a party or a soccer team going back home after a match. Considering that they were specifically dealing with "riot" control, they might have felt that it is not their duty to pursue drunks in the townships.

Our journey to the border with Swaziland, took the entire early hours of the morning, punctuated by minor incidents. At one stage, we narrowly avoided plunging into a head on collision with a van driven by a white farmer that had failed to halt at a stop-sign. Our car that had been driving at high speed was forced off the road, skidded to a halt after moving uncomfortable for a considerable distance, up and down on the rough, bumpy and full grown with grass piece of land surface on the side of the tarred road, We were badly rattled when the car came to a stop as the farmer who nearly caused the accident drove into our road, turned, moved on unperturbed and without looking back. Leaving us wondering whether he was even aware that he was almost involved in an accident that would have had a catastrophic outcome.

When our car came to a halt, nobody moved or spoke, there was silence, the only sound that could be heard was the occasional tick and scratch of the fleeting grass, pebbles and dust particles that were coalescing into a mini storm after being disturbed and ruffled by the force of our fast-moving car. Long after the orange and red tail-lights of the farmers van had disappeared, our eyes, with all of us facing the same direction, remained transfixed, staring blankly into the pitch darkness on the spot where we last saw the farmers' van disappear. In that brief silence some of us even forgot of the pain that we were feeling after our heads had knocked repeatedly on the roof top of the car, as our bodies were juggled in an up and down motion when the car moved with speed on the rough terrain.

About fifteen kilometres before reaching the Oshoek border post, we pulled next to a covered truck that was transporting maize meal from South Africa to Swaziland.

After discussions with the driver of the truck, Roy and Jeanette instructed that all the boys in the group were to climb on top of the bags with maize powder and lie flat. This was the tiniest space left between the maize meal and the roof of the car. We scrambled into the opening and hid in the space created.

These trucks criss-crossed the border post daily, and the ANC activists that were recruiting and helping people flee South Africa had noticed that over a period, the guards and the drivers had grown accustomed to each other and were quick to exploit this situation in their favour. The guards and the truck drivers had come to know each other so well that they were on first name terms. The guards trusted the drivers implicitly and in most cases they did not search their trucks. It became apparent that Roy and Jeannette had reached an agreement with the drivers to transport us across the border possibly for a fee. Some of the drivers were committed to taking the risk because for them, doing so was their way of contributing to the advancement of the struggle against oppression.

As our truck rolled into the border gates, the sun began to rise, casting light and heralding the beginning of the day. The winter's sun slowly and lazily rose in its epic battle against both the pitch darkness and the freezing cold of the night. From atop the maize bags, I was lying facing what should have been the closed doors of the truck. However, the one door was, due to some earlier accident, bent a little. The doors were slightly ajar and could not close properly, leaving a small gap from the top to the bottom. A ray of sunshine coming through the gap, provided the only light in the pitch darkness inside of the truck.

The truck was held at the border post for about thirty minutes. For us inside the truck, those minutes were like hours. Occasionally a silhouette would flick past the slit on the door as the officers and the drivers chatted amicably, passing jokes, and teasing each other. We waited with bated breath, expecting the doors to swing wide open, and if they did, we would have been there for the picking. Eventually, after what appeared to be an eternity, the truck started moving and rolled past the border post into Swaziland.

We were safe! We had made it! We could not believe our fortune! and as the truck slowly rolled past the border gate into Swaziland, we held back our breath and kept still lest we give away the game in inadvertent gasps of excitement. I considered that it was perhaps sheer luck that on the day we were crossing while hidden in the truck, the officers at the border did not have police dogs with them. Undoubtedly, trained dogs would have easily sniffed us out.

The ladies in our group did not join us in the truck but proceeded to the border post with Roy and Jeannette, using the fake passports they'd been given to enable them to cross the border. We were all taken aback when we saw the documents and were even more surprised that they did not encounter any problems at all. The pictures on their passports were a far cry from those who carried them and even the age gap was glaring. The authorities simply stamped them without checking the person against the photo appearing on the passport. All that was quickly relegated to history once we safely crossed the border. There was no question as to the thoroughness with which the ANC had created the labyrinth that was to help make the dream of freedom a reality.

CHAPTER 2

OUT OF SOUTH AFRICA: OUR EXILE BEGINS

"Exile is strangely compelling to think about, but terrible to experience. It is the unhealable rift forced between a human being and a native place, between the self and its true home: its essential sadness can never be surmounted."
Anon

Once we were all safely across the border without a hitch, and reunited with the girls, we were overjoyed. We hugged each other and jumped up and down with excitement.

For all of us, this was the first time we set foot in an independent African nation. I was excited, but disappointed at the same time. Swaziland was not what I had envisioned in my romanticized picture of independent African nations. It was not as developed as South Africa, and there were visible signs of poverty everywhere, not least of all the poor infrastructure.

Before this journey I had only undertaken a few trips around South Africa that had been organized by my school And the Tladi Youth Club where I was a member. I had not travelled much and knew little of the world beyond our borders. At the age of twenty one, I had only done two major trips that I was proud of. These were excursions to Lesotho and Umtata/Transkei in the Eastern Cape.

The journey to Umtata was my first exposure to the sea. I

remember being totally mesmerized. Our geography lessons taught me that there are various large bodies of water on the earth, namely, the Indian Ocean, the Atlantic Ocean, and the Pacific Ocean. Of course, there are also lakes, major rivers and picturesque waterfalls. However, nothing in theory could possibly have prepared me for the reality that I saw spread out before me. The infinity effect of the water was indescribable. I stood for hours on the beach in disbelief, just gazing at the endless rolling waves that stretched far beyond the point where the sea on earth appeared to join the blue sky.

In Swaziland, we were received by Ntate John Nkadimeng and stayed at the ANC residence in Manzini. Comrade Nkadimeng and other ANC leaders taught us ANC politics. We had difficulty in comprehending the ANC 's position that 'South Africa belonged to all who live in it, black and white'. Coming from a black consciousness background, we found it difficult to understand why Africans were so forgiving and understanding. In short, Nkadimeng's teaching amounted to 'we are not fighting whites; the problem is not the colour, but the system.

The crux of our debate was centered around 'who is to blame for the deplorable conditions of blacks in South Africa?' Was it okay to live with a response that puts blame on a problematic and discriminating system only? Many of us countered the argument by saying that the system did not drive itself, white people were behind it.

We pointed out that such an argument is tantamount to arguing that a whip would be guilty of an offense whilst exonerating the hand that wields it.

From our point of view, the reality in South Africa was that whites were oppressing blacks. The picture of a white man or woman driving an open van in the mid-winter, with a black worker at the back whilst a cat or a dog was seating in the front seat next to the driver kept flashing past my mind. It was clear to me that these people put their pets ahead of black people.

There was also witnessed the increase of the influence of white supremacy and extremists who hated and feared blacks. They promoted and buttressed racism and were prone to use whatever was within their means, religion included, to justify their enslavement of black people. The survival and growth of this hate-filled phenomenon was dependent on an aggressive campaign of lies that instilled fear and insecurity. The bogeyman dangled before the white community was what the white Afrikaners referred to as "Die Swart gevaar" ("the black danger").

Ntate' Nkadimeng did not restrict our movements; we were allowed to go into the city, and we had the freedom to move about during the day. This gave us an opportunity to confer with our friends and former schoolmates who were not with us in the ANC. After June 16, Swaziland was abuzz with students who had fled our troubled country, some were in the ranks of the rival Pan African Congress (PAC) of Azania and other black consciousness entities.

The debate on race within the ANC and in the country is as old as the Drakensburg Mountains and has led to differences that resulted in breakaways of members of the ANC who went on to form their own parties such as the Pan African Congress (PAC) and the Group of Eight. This debate drags on even to date, and will, I believe, continue into perpetuity until a resolution is found with regard to the inequality and economic marginalization of the Africans.

After the Soweto Uprising, thousands of predominantly young people joined the ANC for a variety of reasons. The ANC had structures on the ground inside South Africa that were well coordinated. There were legally established formations such as the United Democratic Front (UDF) and trade unions that were aligned to the policy and outlook of the ANC. The contacts that existed of the internal and exiled structures made it easy to facilitate recruitment of cadres to join Umkhonto We Sizwe (MK) the armed wing of the ANC. The ANC was also able to recruit and ferry comrades out of the country, particularly those that were in danger of being arrested by the regime. It was also better organized than most of the other parties.

Over the years, the ANC had established good contacts in the international community and could therefore be relied upon to provide a home for the multitudes that were leaving South Africa, seeking refuge elsewhere. The leadership had developed an array of contacts in various countries and were better placed to provide adequate training for those that were eager to engage and fight for freedom. Oliver Tambo and his comrades in exile had, undoubtedly, developed an excellent network.

Faced with the realisation that the ANC was better equipped than any other party to provide the training we needed, we decided to stay, even though we did not accept the organization's position that South Africa belonged not only to the Blacks, but to the Whites as well. We reasoned that it was important to get the required expertise and weapons, then go back and massacre all the whites in the country indiscriminately. We told ourselves that when one is back home, alone with a gun, the ANC will not be there to direct as to who should be shot and who should be spared.

With our background and lack of history at the time, it was going to take some doing for the ANC to change our attitude and make us realize that consumed by our own experience and the hatred that we were subjected to in South Africa, we had in turn, unconsciously become racist ourselves. Our reasoning was restricted and shallow, but that was our life then.

Baba Duma led us across the Swaziland/Mozambique border undetected and delivered us into a big camp in a place called Nomahache on the Mozambican side. There were hundreds of new 1976 recruits, and lots of excitement as we met many friends and acquaintances who came from our part of the world and who had left the country much earlier. There were others too from various provinces that we did not know, and we made new friends.

Even though the ANC had established a well-coordinated network in exile, it had not anticipated such swelling numbers of people joining its ranks at once. The 1976 crisis had forced thousands of people, mainly students, to leave the country. There were some hiccups initially when it appeared that the numbers of new recruits were overwhelming. The ANC quickly adjusted and with the help of its contacts and international solidarity, it was able to provide food and shelter for all its members. I recall two incidents after our arrival that brought the reality to me that this was not going to be an easy journey.

In the camp in Nomahache, we made our own mugs out of empty condensed milk or jam tins. We cut them open nicely on one end and tied a wire around the mouth on both ends of the tin making sure the wire made a loop on the side which we then used as a handle. The mugs were used for drinking coffee or tea. The beverages were made in large three-legged pots and served to all of us while we lined up and awaited our turns. For breakfast we had a choice of coffee or tea already mixed with milk and sugar, and a round bread that the Mozambicans called 'Pao.'

Shortly after our arrival at the camp, an embarrassing incident happened one morning after breakfast. We queued for our breakfast, as usual, and got our coffee or tea served. Having received the beverage, one immediately joined another queue to collect a pao, one per person. Since the paos were counted to a person, there was therefore no allowance for seconds.

The night before, the whole camp had gone to bed without a meal, it was not clear why this was the case. It is possible that funds were not available for the purchase of food. Whatever the reason, when breakfast came the following morning, we were all very hungry.

We had just arrived and were thus not aware that the paos given to us at breakfast were counted to a person. And so, when one colleague, that obviously was still suffering from hunger pangs even after having had their share, joined the queue twice and helped themselves to the second pao, consequently another comrade was to go hungry. On realizing what had happened, the comrades in charge of the camp made us fall in line and tried to find out who had taken the extra pao, but no one came forward.

Most of the comrades were disgusted with this incident and publicly condemned this 'uncomradely' act. "How greedy can one get?" some of us remarked. These remarks were a demonstration for the benefit of others, to absolve ourselves from the guilt and at the same time to give assurance, that the true comrades we were, it would be inconceivable to entertain the notion that we could be capable of 'cheating others of their meal. The public acts, over-zealously displayed, concealed our inner-most emotional sentiments that superseded the repugnance of the deed. Tacitly we empathized with the thief since we, ourselves, were experiencing the same hunger pangs and understood the desperation that drove the comrade, whoever it was, to such an act.

Whilst the whole camp was baffled and trying to figure out who the culprit was, Strike from the Tladi Youth Club group tugged my shirt and whispered that I should follow him. Once we were out of hearing distance, he mentioned that he saw the person who queued twice. It turned out to be Comrade Benedict Diphoko who was one of our own, from the Tladi Youth Club.

When the hullabaloo was over, I convened a meeting of our group under a tree, far away from everybody. We confronted Diphoko who confessed, stating in his defence that he had been unable to stomach the hunger and could not resist the temptation. He had hoped this would go unnoticed because of the huge numbers of comrades in the camp. He was also blind-sided in that he was not aware that the Paos were counted to a person. The whole group reprimanded him, but we did not report him to the camp authorities.

Long after the incident, Comrade Lennox Langu, the ANC Chief Representative in Mozambique at the time, and his team came to interview us one after the other. The ANC presented each one of us with two options; the first one, was to go back to school if one so desired, the organization guaranteed to help plan for studies abroad. The second option was to join the armed wing of the people's army (Umkhonto we Sizwe). The militant ones among us opted to go for military training. We could not conceive how the struggle would be pursued and won if we all decided to go to school. There was peer pressure on those opting to go to school, and we immediately branded them cowards.

Most of the new members had no skills or formal education worth mentioning as we had abandoned our studies at pre-university level and some midway through their university education. In our enthusiasm and our eagerness to engage the forces of the regime, there was no time to think about education.

The results of the interview with Langu were kept secret, but somehow word got out and once we got know who opted to go to school, we teased them, asking the question, "If we all decide to go to school, who will shoulder the responsibility to take up arms and liberate the people?"

After the interviews we were dispatched group after group to various destinations, those who opted to go to school were flown to Dar Es Salaam and we were to go to Angola for military training.

CHAPTER 3

ANGOLA: LIFE IN A MILITARY CAMP

"We soon learned that we were not the only ones fighting for the liberation."
Kingsley Mamabolo

Before our journey to Angola, Langu was compelled to take me to Maputo, to buy some decent clothes. The clothes I had on me were in a bad shape and were not suitable for flying. I admired comrade Lennox' patience as we moved from one shop to another and could not find anything ideal. The bell- bottom trousers and high heeled shoes of the hippie era were in fashion, and I hated them, but unfortunately those were the only items available in the shops in Maputo then. Eventually I had no option but to settle for some moderate, high-heeled shoes and a slightly smaller bell bottomed trouser.

This was to be my first time ever in a plane and all my possessions fitted in a small paper bag that I'd carried from SOWETO and was now going to take with me all the way to Angola.

On arrival in Angola, we were taken to an engineering military camp in the capital city, Luanda. When we got there, we were shocked to see that there were hundreds of thousands of new recruits, many more than what we had seen in Nomahache. Engineering appeared to be the accumulation point of most of all the youth that had been leaving South Africa in huge numbers, through Botswana, Swaziland – Mozambique and Lesotho. It was also a transit camp that the ANC used as a short stop over for cadres going to other places for further training or those who had completed their training and were being infiltrated back into South Africa, while others were going to the front-line states. Some cadres from the Engineering camp were sent to the Soviet Union, some to Cuba, and others to ANC military bases in the interior of Angola itself.

We soon learned that we were not the only ones fighting for the liberation, the Angolan Government and people in their internationalist nature were supportive of other struggles on the continent as well. We met other fighters such as those of the People's Liberation Army of Namibia (PLAN), the armed wing of SWAPO (South West African People's Organization) and ZIPRA (Zimbabwe's People' Revolutionary Army) the armed wing of ZAPU (Zimbabwe People's African Union) who were also training in various camps in Angola.

Angola was in the throes of a civil war during this period. The overthrow of the dictatorship of Prime Minister Marcelo Caetano of Portugal on the 25 April 1974, was also a watershed opportunity for former Portuguese colonies of Mozambique, Guinea Bissau, Cape Verde, Sao Tome and Principe and Angola. The problems in Portugal precipitated a process of transition in the colonies. However, the Portuguese, pre- occupied with their own internal problems did not assist to ensure a smooth transition in the colonies.

Angola attained official independence on 11 November 1975 and the country's transition from Portuguese rule was beset with ethnic tensions combined with international pressures rendering Angola's hard-won victory problematic. Angola was left with both economic and social difficulties which translated into a power struggle between the three predominant liberation movements. The people's Movement for the Liberation of Angola (MPLA), formed in December of 1956 that had as its support base the Ambundu people and was largely supported by other African countries, Cuba and the Soviet Union.

The National Liberation Front of Angola (FNLA), founded in 1962, had its support mainly from the Bakongo people and was backed by the government of Zaire and (initially) the People's Republic of China.

The Ovimbundu people formed the base of the National Union for the Total Independence of Angola (UNITA), which was established in 1966 and founded by a prominent former leader of the FNLA, Mr. Jonas Savimbi.

The power sharing agreement that was reached between the ethnic groups collapsed in 1975, paving the way for a bitter atrocious war in the struggle for power. The conflict in Angola was compounded by the involvement of international forces where major powers fought against each other by proxy. The Angolan war ensued at the height of the cold war that pitted the United States of America (USA) against the Union of Soviet Socialist Republics (USSR).

In 1975, a year before my group arrived, Angola had been through a large-scale war that roped in the South African Defense Force in support of the FNLA. The South Africans were, in turn, enjoying the blessing of the USA. The MPLA defended the onslaught waged by the South Africans and gained the right to form a government of independent Angola.

The racist troops were thoroughly defeated by a combined Angolan and Cuban force in the town of Quito Carnavale. During the war, the Cuban force effectively used a soviet rocket launcher, that the western media derogatorily referred to as 'the Stalin Organ' because of its appearance, thus, holding the marauding force that was marching to Luanda on its tracks and in the process scuttling a well-orchestrated American imperialist plan to install a government of their choice with absolute disregard for the interest of the people of Angola.

We are eternally indebted to the Soviet Union for providing the Cubans with the "Stalin Organ" and to the Cubans for so much sacrifice, all combined to deliver a sweet victory over Pretoria. It was clear in our minds that had South Africa won the battle, not only the people of Angola, but the entire African continent would have remained forever captive to the whims of the vicious white minority regime and America's imperialism.

The outcome of that battle was a source of inspiration; it proved that the mighty South African army was not invincible.

Angola had all the visible signs that it was at war. Almost all buildings in the city were riddled with bullet holes and cracked walls. Soldiers in military camouflage driving Soviet-made military vehicle roamed the streets and had become a permanent and acceptable feature of the city. The ruling party did its utmost to inculcate patriotism through the media and propaganda in general. Angolan radio stations regularly punctuated their messages with the national anthem, and revolutionary songs, the slogan 'aluta continua', the struggle continues, reverberated throughout the country from morning till dusk.

Every single day for a few minutes, at 6am and 6pm, the city came to a standstill as the raising and lowering of the flag was observed. Angolans and foreigners were obligated to stand at attention. Those who continued driving or defied the order were at risk of been shot by soldiers or police who suspected that such people were being disrespectful of the national flag.

The people were mobilized to support the MPLA and its leaders, in particular the president, Comrade Agostino Neto. We were accustomed to hearing energized shouts from people appreciating their leaders, and of slogans such as "Viva o povo Angolano! Viva Camarada Presidente Agostino Neto!" The people were committed and, on the march, fighting and defending their hard-earned independence.

There was, at the same time, a deep-rooted hatred for what the ordinary folks referred to as 'racista Sul Africano'- racist South African. Most Angolans did not just theorize about the need to destroy the system in South Africa, many had personally witnessed the viciousness of the racists of the south. After all, some of their children had died in wars like those in Quito Carnavale and other raids conducted by Pretoria.

Comrade Joe Slovo, Secretary General of the Communist Party of South Africa frequently narrated a story of an incident he encountered. One day he visited a comrade friend of his, Comrade Lucio Lara at the MPLA party offices. At the gate of the office, Comrade Slovo was accosted by a security element that inquired, as it was accustomed to do, the details: "Who are you? Who do you want to see, and from which country do you come from?"

Comrade Slovo responded to all that, explaining that he represented the Communist Party of South Africa. The security guard rushed off to report that there was a 'racista Sul Africano' at the gate who wanted to meet Comrade Lara. It was apparent that as far as the guard was concerned, every white South African represented the racist regime.

Cuban People, Lovely People

The President of Cuba, Fidel Castro Ruz, had dispatched thousands of Cubans to intervene and defend the Angolan revolution. There were Cubans everywhere, a famous popular joke about the Cubans' love of 'puerco' (pork meat) narrated by Angolans was that 'when driving a car, one had to be careful if suddenly a pig crosses the street because a Cuban is probably giving chase.

The Cubans were loved by the people, particularly after their performance and victory in the battle against the South African troops in Quito Carnavale.

The support rendered by Cuba was very much appreciated in the camps of the ANC in Angola and elsewhere by the struggling masses inside the country. A popular song we sang in the camps and that also quickly could be heard throughout in protest marches in South Africa had a verse that stated:

"Cuban people, lovely people,
here we are far from home,
we shall need you; we shall love you,
for the things you have done for us."

Many cadres of MK had opportunity to stay with Cuban soldiers in various camps in Angola, we found them to be disciplined, but also easy-going, life-loving people who are not difficult to get along with. I did not know it then, but for me, getting to know the Cubans in this manner was a dress rehearsal, a preparation for the future because many years later, the ANC was to send me as its Chief Representative in Cuba.

Fidel Castro and Che Guevara were heroes, a great inspiration and role models for the kind of struggle that we needed to wage if we were to win and transform our society. The ANC was constantly attacked and put under pressure for its support and warm comradely relations with Cuba.

Immediately after his release, Comrade Nelson Mandela defended the relations that the ANC enjoyed with Cuba. An American journalist, Mr. Ted Koppel had tried to pressurize him into issuing a declaration condemning Cuba's so-called violation of human rights Mandela was unambiguous and emphatically declared that Cuba was a friend of the oppressed people of South Africa and that her contribution was invaluable. The response was pleasing to Cuba and its friends internationally.

Internally, Angola was bleeding because of the on-going war. There were attempts by insurgents to subvert the revolution and undermine the forward march to independence. In May 1977, a prominent leader of the ruling party, their first Interior Minister under the MPLA government, Mr. Nito Alves attempted a *coup de tat* to overthrow the leadership of President Agostino Neto.

Neto was a committed revolutionary, soft spoken, poet who believed in the ability of Angolans to liberate their country. One of his poems, entitled *We shall return*, beautifully encapsulates Neto's dream. The poem symbolizing the freedom fighters' return from exile, a return to liberty also talked to the freedom of immigrants who ran away from their country. It reads as follows:

We shall return
to our mines of diamonds gold, copper, oil
we shall return
to our rivers, our lakes
our mountains, our forests we will return
to the shade of the mulemba to our traditions
to the rhythms and bonfires we shall return
to the marimba and the quissange to our carnival
we shall return
to our beautiful Angolan homeland our land, our mother
we shall return
We shall return
to the houses, to our crops, to the beaches, to our fields, we shall
return
to our lands red with coffee
white with cotton
green with maize fields
we shall return
to liberated Angola independent Angola.

(translated to English by Marga Holness)

As part of the plan to overthrow Neto and his government, Alves had planned carefully. He had arranged for food supplies to the military camps to be withheld for long periods of time, worked with collaborators to hoard the salary of the troops, and attempted to organize rolling mass action and protests in the streets. He had worked very hard to install his supporters in key positions at provincial and district levels. All these measures were intended to deepen the crisis and to portray the government of Neto as incompetent and therefore not capable of governing the country.

On the 27th of May, hundreds of criminals at the Sao Paulo

prison, including imprisoned UNITA and FNLA combatants, as well as British and American mercenaries were released by Alves. At about 08.00am, the radio station was captured, and announcers urged the masses to congregate in large numbers outside the palace and demonstrate against Neto's government. Seven members of the central committee of the MPLA were summarily executed.

Chaos ensued; the country slid deeper into socio- economic crisis where poverty was almost palpable. The Angolan currency tumbled, inflation shot sky high, and ordinary Angolans struggled to put food on the table. Unemployment reached alarming heights as companies were forced to shut down and retrench workers, but the black-market economy thrived.

A typical feature of the black market is the drastic devaluation of the local currency, money laundering and the irrational increase in the prices of essential goods and services. Just watching a popular movie would cost three times the normal price. Tickets would not be available at the movie house where it would be illegal to sell them at such a ridiculous price. Cinemagoers were forced to buy those tickets on the streets as that would be the only place where they were available.

Suddenly on the streets of Angola, I witnessed the epitome of a nation in economic crisis, a picture I had seen in other African countries. Angolan women could be observed sitting on the pavements with piles of the worthless currency trying to eke a living from foreign currency exchange with the few foreigners or would-be travellers. Nonetheless, there was something admirable in that we, South Africans, could not even begin to fathom a scenario back home where people could brandish cash so openly without concerns of criminals descending upon them.

In the barracks throughout Angola, the mutinous environment encouraged by Alves was taking root. The soldiers were becoming undisciplined and disobeying orders as food became scarce. When we arrived, the Popular Forces for the Liberation of Angola (FAPLA) and the ANC's Umkhontho we Sizwe (MK) shared the Engineering camp. We were, therefore, witness to the deteriorating situation within the FAPLA. The situation in the camps became intensely dangerous considering that those aggrieved soldiers were armed.

One day, Solly Ngobese, real name Lazarus Chiloane (a friend, former schoolmate and colleague of mine) and I, had a harrowing experience with an armed FAPLA soldier. We were together in one of the rooms of the barracks. A FAPLA soldier who was dressed awkwardly came in. We learned later that he had some mental health problems. Whispering to Solly I made some comments, and he in turn, burst into laughter which was in keeping with his character. The FAPLA combatant took offense and assumed that we were making fun of him.

The soldier was agitated, he pulled out a hand grenade and threatened to release the safety pin. Solly and I later found out that the hand grenade that he threatened us with was the defensive type, used mostly by soldiers in a trench or thrown by people behind a hard cover. They are said to have a potential radius of lethality that is greater than the distance that can be thrown by the average soldier and are much more effective than the ordinary hand grenade.

With a crazed appearance, the soldier screamed at us, shouting expletives in Portuguese. We did not understand a word he was saying. Solly and I, standing some distance away from the soldier and realizing the imminent danger, took turns to plead for our lives in broken Portuguese. Fuming and frothing at the mouth, the agitated soldier completely ignored our plea for mercy.

Eventually a colleague of his saw what was happening and spoke to him through a window as he had locked the door. He calmed down and when he opened the door, Solly and I left the place hurriedly. We were really traumatized and realized that we were lucky to have escaped alive. My friend Solly died many years later, his diagnoses was that he had gall stones in his liver and despite medication he could not be cured.

With indiscipline so rampant in the army and at the engineering camp, the new MK recruits who were sharing the camp with FAPLA were caught in between. We cooked separately and thus had different queues at mealtimes. One day whilst queuing, MK cadres were told there was no food. It transpired that some FAPLA soldiers had, at gun point, taken pots with the food meant for MK soldiers and served it to the FAPLA soldiers.

Amid the difficult and prevailing situation, the ANC leadership tried its best to instill and maintain discipline within the ranks of MK. Frequently leaders came to address the soldiers. It was in that period that I first got to know Comrade Joe Modise, the Commander of the army. A pleasant father-figure leader easy to socialize but could also switch and be a different person when he was angry. His face and posture changed when extremely angered, there could be no mistaking the state he was in when he lost his temper.

On the day I first got to know who the Commander of the army was, we were assembled and made to march section by section past Modise who was inspecting and made us repeat if we did not perform well. Due to the training of many cadres in the Soviet Union, the march we were taught was what we called the goose-step march like the one performed by Russian soldiers. It is a beautiful march performed during formal military parades, with troops moving in unison.

One can only imagine a company of about thirty people followed by others making the same moves, the legs straightened and outstretched at the same time in a movement that symbolizes a person kicking an imaginary soccer ball, as they march lifting the left and then the right leg. And at a command by the commander of each company that marches past the podium "eyes right" all members of the company turning their heads, whilst still goose-stepping in the direction of the principal who is taking the salute.

Each time the straightened leg, once lifted is brought down to land with a thud and the more the people the greater the legs stomping the ground in unison produces a "RATA A TATA! RATA A TATA...! sound of the heavy boots. The drill is a pleasure to watch, and the beauty is in both the visual effect and the booming rhythmic sound. Somehow, properly done, such a drill talks to the discipline of the army. With Modise barking orders and complaining about our performance, we spent half a day trying to perfect our drill. The lines needed to be straight and not slanting.

Beyond Modise's anger and the screaming of the military commands and the tension and stress that accompanied the exercise, I learned something on that day, and that lesson is that what appears to be simple and easy to one is not necessarily the case with someone else. My Comrade and friend, Bruce Moeketsi also known in MK as Captain had a serious problem of coordination. Normally when we march, 'left right, left right,' this becomes a simple action of coordinating and ensuring that your right hand moves forward with the left leg at the same time and as these rest, the same action is undertaken by the left hand with the right leg thus creating movement forward. Captain was struggling to make this coordination and instead moved the right hand at the same time with the right leg followed by the left hand and leg thus creating an awkward movement forward.

I had known Bruce for a long time, we were in the same classroom in Naledi High School completing matric. He was one of the most intelligent people I have known, which made this inability to coordinate his march even more inexplicable. Together with Bruce, Benny Diphoko, Popo Molefe, a well-known figure and respected Comrade in the struggle, Patrick Molaosi and others we constituted the debating team. The debating team in Naledi High School was well respected in the entire SOWETO region, our fiercest opponents were Morris Isaacson High School, whose debating team was led by the popular and renowned Tsietsi Mashinini.

Bruce was our first speaker; he was eloquent and could in a concise manner give the crowd a clear exposition of the topic of the day and the position to be argued by his team. The first speaker, in most cases

Bruce, and the last speaker, always at all times Popo Molefe were given equally more time than the rest of us, as they had the difficult task of introducing and summarizing the topic of the day. Bruce was popular, he was even made more famous by a phrase that he used all the time when rebutting the opposition's arguments which was "Ladies and gentlemen, I nearly jumped out of my skin when my opponent stated that... or made the assertion...." Despite the difficulty of coordinating his movements and the fact that he was made to repeat so many times in that parade inspected by Modise, Bruce rose within the ranks to become a highly respected leader within the organization.

During this time, at the engineering camp, and with the increase of new recruits we were becoming too many and it was becoming congested and unbearable to live in. The unstable situation in South Africa, particularly after the June 16 uprisings, resulted in a steady flow of new recruits that kept pouring into Angola. To reduce the numbers and to decongest the Engineering camp, the ANC began sending groups of cadres for military training abroad, to the Soviet Union, German Democratic Republic (GDR). Eventually the hundreds that remained were all transported to the South of Angola to a camp in Novo Katenge.

All of us desired to leave Engineering, I was eagerly awaiting nomination to go for training abroad and was elated when I was informed that I would be part of a group that would leave shortly for the German Democratic Republic (GDR). Not only was I nominated to be in the group, I was also chosen to be the commander of the group of thirty individuals. At this stage, the Tladi Youth Club group was breaking up. With Omry and I heading to the GDR, we were leaving Benny, Molebatsi and Strike behind. We had been such a solid group and ideally it would have been preferable for us to be kept together.

CHAPTER 4

MILITARY TRAINING IN THE GERMAN DEMOCRATIC REPUBLIC

"With the fearful strain that was on us, both day and night,
If we did not laugh, we would have died."
adapted by Kingsley Mamabolo

On a cold January afternoon in the then German Democratic Republic (GDR) at a training session,
I crawled, slowly and quietly with my belly flat on the ground. The coordinated movements of my hands and feet edged my body forward, swaying slightly to the left and then to the right. My deliberate moves were gentle, inaudible, and almost motionless. The only audible sound was the wind hissing through the tall trees that peculiarly had thin trunks of the German forest trees. The forest trees with a greyish whitish colour clustered together forming a thick bush that could conceal an entire platoon of soldiers.

The thick bush completely cut off the sun rays that were struggling to make an impact on a cold winter afternoon. It was daylight, and yet below and under the thick tall tress the shade had brought night fall prematurely.

Taking advantage of the poor visibility in the dark, I moved myself forward painstakingly, going through the same motion repeatedly as I approached the target. In the cool winter breeze, my face is dried up, and my cheeks hardened. I crawled, advancing towards the enemy, my lips tasted the wet sand on the ground. The effect of this scenario on my imagination was magical. The taste of sand is proof that one belongs to the earth. The force that holds all things in place has made room for me and my kind. Regardless of the hate and inhumanities of my fellow man, I belong here on earth. To keep my space and that of my kind, I am prepared to fight.

The target is in sight, my intention was to shorten the distance between the upright stationary sentry and myself. Then from a comfortable distance, I would gently lift my body from the ground and charge with great speed, hoping and praying that the element of surprise would gain me sufficient time to silence the guard before he realized that he was under attack. My success in that expedition depended on the momentum gained to catch the sentry off-guard, grab him from behind with my left arm around his neck and using the dagger in my right hand to stab him repeatedly, targeting certain parts of the body to ensure instant and noiseless death.

His death would be quick and hopefully in no time the whole sordid debacle will be over, and the poor bastard would never get to know what hit him. It is important that this is done well, with as little commotion as possible as any noise would alert the enemy camp of the attack.

For the operation to be successful, I had to execute everything with precision and accuracy.

When I was entrusted with the task of silencing the sentry, it was a proud moment; I dared not fail. My comrades, the entire platoon waited with bated breath, and would only act after I had given a signal.

What I have just described could have been a scene in a popular war film with the audience holding their breath, willing the hero to succeed in the risky venture. It was not. This scene described is from a training session and no one was intended to die. The German instructors were preparing us for a possible encounter in future.

This was no fantasy; the conscientious German instructors were conditioning our bodies, souls, and minds for what could be a likely scenario in a real battle, where a silly mistake or a momentary lapse could result in certain death or capture and possible imprisonment.

Renowned for their thoroughness and efficiency, the German instructors where uncompromising as they took us through the paces, they were ruthless in execution. Many of us were not accustomed to such rigorous training and had come to believe that these instructors were almost like machines; they never appeared to tire as they ran alongside us during exercises, they were simply put, truly the embodiment of the endurance of the human body through physical fitness. They barked instructions in voices that brooked no nonsense, voices that made it clear that failure to perform was unacceptable and would not be tolerated. They pushed one to the edge, almost to the point of breaking down. The echoes of the voices of Dieter and Gunter our instructors, 'Schneller Comrade! Schneller' (faster Comrade! Faster) still ring in mind to this day.

We shared rooms, there were two of us in each, and my roommate was a chubby fellow we called Ishmael (real name Tebello Motapanyane), the Commissar of the group. With each passing day after rigorous training, Ishmael would, almost in tears, his mouth hissing curses and obscenities, throw himself on the bed and plead with me to pull off his heavy boots, complaining bitterly that the kind of training we were subjected was not feasible. Every day he threatened to lodge a complaint with the leadership of the ANC that were responsible for our presence there in the first place, to ask that the group be pulled out of Germany and be returned to Africa.

He would argue that it was impossible to match the resilience of the German instructors, stating:

"Don't forget, my friend," he would cry excitedly, "for many years before being finally defeated by the combined might of the allied forces, Germans proved their resilience and perseverance to the entire world."

On this particular day at the training field, while lying on the ground with my body slightly embedded in the thickness of the pure white snow, I could feel the soft crunching sound of the snow as it crumbled under the weight of my body. The snow created a thickness that served as a cushion against the rough surface of the earth. The stillness was overwhelming, not even the bush nearby which at that time was covered with snow rustled with any sound. Nothing moved other than the white snowflakes that were gently falling in a disciplined formation on the ground, creating layer upon layer of snow, gradually transforming the landscape.

My soul engaged this tranquil moment, my thoughts wondered despite the chilly winter and the cold breeze hardening my cheeks. At the same time, in a flash, thoughts and pictures of my life flooded through my mind, including the significance of the exercises I was undergoing in Germany fused with the pictures of my childhood until our arrival as a platoon from the transit camp in Angola. In simple ways, I started to feel a sense of faith again. Here we were, a small group of thirty enthusiastic young men, being trained to be professional and ruthless killers in the name of freedom, committed to fight for the justice of a cause.

For some with Christian backgrounds and upbringing, the training posed a challenge, it became difficult to reconcile the Godly fear we have of taking a human life and accepting a training that is preparing us for that eventuality. We had to accept the inevitable reality that in the pursuit of freedom and justice, one should be ready to do whatever it takes, to kill or even to be ready to pay the ultimate sacrifice if necessary.

We were young, strong, highly motivated and inspired. We read a lot about other revolutions and heroes of other struggles. Most of us were admirers of the Cuban revolution, and exchanged whatever reading material we could lay our hands on revolutionaries such as Jose` Marti, Fidel Castro, Che Guevara, and other Latin American personalities. We had read a lot of books by great Russian authors such as Maxim Gorky, Lev Tolstoi and Alexander Pushkin.

There is a novel by the Russian author Nicolai Ostrovsky, titled `How the steel was tempered` that was like a point of reference for us. Nicolai Ostrovsky was born on 29 September 1904 in the small Ukrainian Village of Viliya into the family of a labourer and a cook. It was easy for many of us to relate to his humble beginnings. Biographers state that he joined the Red Army and participated in the civil war between the Red Army and the monarchist White Guard. In 1920, Ostrovsky was seriously wounded in the back, and then demobilized. Ostrovsky was a blind invalid when he wrote the novel *'how the steel was tempered'*. Our particular interest in the book was the passage about dedicating one's life to the liberation of mankind that states:

> *"Man's dearest possession is life. It is given to him but once, and he must live it so as to feel no torturing regrets from wasted years, never know the burning shame of a mean and a petty past; So, live that, dying he might say: all my life, all my strength was given to the finest cause in all the world – the fight for the liberation of mankind"*

It was these kinds of messages that motivated us, inspired us to have an understanding that nothing must stand in the way of genuine freedom.

We learned through studying 'liberation theology' that even the highly religious and pacifist need not be bystanders. We were persuaded that in the face of the inhumanity and cruelty of the barbaric apartheid system and its perpetrators, even our Lord Jesus Christ would have been supportive of the measures we were pursuing to rid humanity of the curse.

Our highly respected and renowned President, Comrade Oliver Tambo argued in many of his messages, that: -

"The leadership of the ANC had for many years sought peaceful methods of resolution of the conflict in South Africa. The leadership had knocked and knocked, pleading, and begging for an end to an inhumane system that treated its overwhelming and oppressed majority as third-class citizens.' these pleas were met with a hardened rebuttal from an obstinate white minority, determined to perpetuate white domination at all costs."

As we were training, we understood perfectly that violence was necessary to end apartheid. We could not continue talking peace when all avenues of reason were shut by a desperate white minority regime. In the words of Oliver Tambo;

"We had turned the other cheek so many times that there were no more cheeks left to turn"

The turmoil in my head notwithstanding, I was not an unwilling participant. I was more than ready to take the bull by the horn and possibly to decapitate it.

There were thirty of us who were being trained by the Germans, twenty- eight had come from Angola, and we were joined by two comrades who were recruited in London. I was the commander and Ishmael was the commissar. Comrade Arthur Sidweshu was the overall supervisor and the link between the military Head Quarters in Angola and the German authorities.

At different intervals and as part of the curriculum, Comrades Aziz Pahad, Pallo Jordan, and Ronnie Kasrils came to GDR to teach the history of the ANC. Kasrils wrote of his impression of the platoon that I commanded in his memoir, 'Armed and Dangerous', as follows:

"I was curious to meet the new recruits, to compare them with my generation – the Umgwenya of the 1960s.
That generation (the umgwenya) had received their experience in

the non-racial politics of the congress movement. This generation
was unacquainted with the ANC which had been outlawed most
of their lives. They were young and grew up in a political void.
The only whites they had known were arrogant, school inspectors,
township supervisors and swaggering thugs in uniform.
Now they were receiving instructions from the German army
officers and were being catered for by a staff of elderly white
women."

It took some time for us to settle down in the GDR and to become
accustomed to being catered for by a staff of elderly white women.
We arrived in winter and were provided with appropriate clothing
for the weather, this included the white underwear with a long sleeve
vest and underpants that reached at the ankles. We immediately
referred to these after the Portuguese explorer, Mr. Vasco da Gama.

We were under strict orders not to wash any of the clothing
ourselves, and in the military, there is no accommodation for
defiance. Huge baskets were placed around where we were expected
to throw any of our dirty linen that was to be washed by the elderly
white women, and that included our underwear.

Coming from apartheid South Africa, we were uncomfortable
with such an arrangement, the prospect of white women washing
our underwear did not go down well.

At 9pm the alarm would go off, lights would be switched off
signalling that it is time for bed. Woe unto those walking about and
not in bed after the lights were switched off. I recall an embarrassing
moment when, after the alarm had gone off, I found myself in our
big communal bathroom violating an order to be in bed. Once it
was dark and I thought everybody was asleep, I snuck out to the
bathroom with soap and my underwear.

As I was quietly washing my underwear in the dark, I heard some
movement behind me and on checking, I found that it was Jungle and
Bob who were doing exactly what I was doing, washing their underwear.

Our group was lively, there was Sidwell Moroka (Omry Makgoale) my friend and comrade from the Tladi Youth Club, a strict disciplinarian, who had adjusted very quickly to requirements of the training by the German instructors. Part of the training was intended to teach respect for the rank of higher officials. I struggled a bit to fit in my new role as a commander partly because one of the requirements for the group was that, whenever a high-ranking person passed by a group of trainees, the most senior in the collective at the time must quickly call for attention. I guess it is my nature, but it felt awkward to see these colleagues, some of whom my friends were, freezing into attention each time I passed by and this would happen wherever they were relaxing or playing games.

Solly Ngobese was also part of the group, but unfortunately illness caught up with him and made training difficult. We also had Comrade Jungle who was humorous. His jokes helped to keep the spirit of the group up. Dick Gatsheni (Sipho Mthembu) was the no-nonsense commander of the first section of the platoon; he, together, with Jackson Mba (Samora) the Commissar of the section oversaw their group. Others such as Moss Thema (Mbulelo Musi), Robert Dladla (Lehlobi Rantsatsi) contributed one way or the other to the cohesion of the collective.

One of the comrades joining us from London was a character we called Ibrahim. He was a so-called coloured from Cape Town, a reclusive who kept to himself. He was also a devoted Muslim who uncompromisingly followed Islamic protocol and routine. He made it clear that he had to pray five times a day, facing the direction of the Mecca. When it was time for prayer, Ibrahim would dump whatever he was doing, even if we were in the middle of a training session at the shooting range or any other military activity.

The German instructors, whose country was pursuing Socialism and Communism, were careful not to be seen as being insensitive and not respecting religious needs of those whose faith was different from their belief. They did not want to be seen as being dismissive either, so, despite the disruption to the training, Ibrahim was allowed to scamper away to a secluded place to pray whenever he wished to do so and at the appropriate time.

While we all took notes when the German tutors were teaching, Ibrahim was fastidious about his note-taking. In addition, he wrote his notes in Arabic, claiming that he needed to practice and learn as required by his religious faith. None of us could read or write Arabic, so we were not in a position to know what Ibrahim was recording.

One cold afternoon, as part of our training, we received instruction that we should all be ready to move, as a platoon, to a far-off location. We dressed accordingly and took the necessary equipment that was required. We walked in military formation the whole night, from 6pm to 6.am with very few stops in-between.

Midway, Ibrahim collapsed and was, supposedly, unconscious. The instructors made it known that we could not leave a comrade behind. We quickly made a make-shift-stretcher by cutting the branches of the trees in the forest and tied canvas material to support his body. We then took turns carrying the heavy burden all the way to our destination. Ibrahim was about six feet tall and lean, but he had heavy bones. Carrying him under those conditions was an exercise that tested our endurance to the limit. As we carried him, we quietly muttered expletives and questioned, "Why was he not man enough? We were all faced with the same conditions, and we didn't collapse, and incidentally, we were still on our feet."

Our misgiving of Ibrahim's non-existent resilience escalated into anger and loathing when later after our training in the GDR we learned that Ibrahim was in fact planted by the apartheid agents, presumably to inform on the content of the course the Germans were providing. We did not know this until the end of the training course. In fact, we only found out all this when Ibrahim disappeared, never to be seen again.

Upon completion of the training, arrangements were made for Ibrahim to go back to London from where he had been recruited. At that stage it was assumed that people in South Africa only knew that he was in the UK studying and were not aware that he'd travelled to the GDR to receive military training. The intention of the ANC was to send him back to South Africa from London unnoticed, a chance to infiltrate a highly trained cadre of *'Umkhonto we Sizwe'*.

Ibrahim was seen off at the Schoenfeld Airport, the East German International airport, on his way to London where ANC officials were waiting for him. However, he never showed up in London. It became apparent that he got off at the airport in Holland where the plane made a transitional stop. It is assumed that from Holland the apartheid regime re-routed him to South Africa for a debriefing.

I have not seen Ibrahim since then, but I have bitter memories of the stress he caused us and we were forced to endure when he collapsed at the training in East Germany. I also suspect that he was probably faking his status and pretended that he was unconscious. It is also clear that the notes he was recording in Arabic during our training were a report of the content of the course that he was preparing for the benefit of the apartheid agents.

CHAPTER 5

RETURN TO ANGOLA
'ALUTA CONTINUA'

"A luta continua; vitória é certa":
"The struggle continues; victory is certain"
Samora Machel

We finished our course and were sent back to Engineering camp in Angola. This time around there were no FAPLA soldiers, and MK occupied the entire camp which was almost empty. The majority of the hundreds of the June 16 cadres that we left behind had gone for training in Nova Katenge in the south of Angola. I was immediately appointed Camp Commander and Moss Thema became the Commissar. There were practically no activities at the camp. However, there was constant movement in and out of the camp with people arriving on transit either to other camps in Angola or vice-versa from the camps to the frontline states and inside South Africa.

The intention of the leadership was that the engineering camp would eventually be shut down. A large contingent of troops including myself were all moved to a camp in Quibashe town, North of Angola. Our departure left Omry (Mhlongo), who was chief of staff at the time, managing the engineering camp. This camp was also known, among the ANC, as 'camp thirteen'. It was a long journey requiring both mental and physical preparation. We had a big truck that was used to transport the soldiers. We moved in a convoy led by

61

a Land Rover which ferried the leaders from the ANC headquarters in Luanda who were accompanying us. As Camp Commander I rode with them.

Comrade Obadi (Motso Mokgabudi) was driving the Rover, but he was not relaxed and appeared tense. I thought that he was probably a nervous, inexperienced driver or that he was anxious with having to drive the leadership of the army through the tortuous, winding, narrow roads that were climbing up the mountains on the way to the north. In the Landrover, Comrade Mzwai Piliso sat next to Obadi on the front seat. At the back I was joined by comrades Andrew Masondo, and Cassius Make (Job Thabane). In the boot of the car was a bag full of TNT explosives. These were supplies to be utilized for training of new recruits at the Quibashe camp.

We picked up speed and before long, we had reached the mountain range. The roads were in good condition, but the long and winding road uphill was undoubtedly intimidating. On one side of the road was a wall of rocks and soil, and on the other side was a sharp-edged escarpment and a deep gorge going all the way down to where the mountain began.

To navigate safely, all that Obadi had to do was to keep his cool and stay on the smooth curving road up the mountain. There was no doubt that if we fell over the cliff, our car would crash below and there would be no chance of survival. With a cold trickle of sweat trickling down my spine, I imagined how rescuers would struggle to pull our bodies that would probably be crushed beyond recognition, out of the mangled wreckage.

On approaching one of the myriad curves, the fear of edging too close to the cliff made the nervous Obadi suddenly swing the car in the direction of the rising wall of rocks on the opposite site. The car lost control and was heading for a crash, but Obadi swung it again to keep it on the road. This resulted in the car tumbling and ending with its roof on the ground with the wheels still rotating, facing the sky.

The overturned car caused a huge billow of dust on the side of the road. Peasants residing in the neighbourhood came running to the scene either to rescue us or out of sheer curiosity. Surprisingly, with no injury at all, I managed to pull myself out of the upside-down car, past a shocked Masondo who, having come out, was inspecting his body for any injuries. The impact of the force of the accident ejected Obadi from the car and threw him far from the vehicle. Curiously he came back to the scene approaching the car in the mix of the bystanders, creating an impression, if one did not know otherwise, that he was one of the many rushing to the rescue. Comrade Cassius was also lucky to come out without any scratches, only comrade Masondo had a big gash on the side of his body that was not life-threatening.

The three of us, later joined by Obadi, scrambled to rescue Comrade Mzwai who was trapped inside the wreckage, unable to move. Curiously, he had shifted position and was trapped between the steering wheel and the driver's seat as if he had been the one driving the vehicle. As we were trying to extricate him, my mind raced frantically to the explosives in the back of the vehicle. With a mind filled with fear, I wondered how it was that there had not been an explosion? If the explosives had gone off, we would have been pulverized; it would not have been possible to talk about rescuing anybody, all of us would have been discarded as dust in the dustbin of history.

Eventually, with the help of the peasants we carved open a bigger space on the driver's side of the vehicle and were able to pull Comrade Mzwai to safety. I have told this story of the explosives that did not go off to many comrades, and because of their understanding as trained cadres that TNT's are sensitive, some are dismissive and find it difficult to perceive that an impact such as that which was created by the overturning vehicle did not trigger the explosives. The reality, however, is that no matter the impact, the TNT's cannot explode if the tiny blasting caps that must be embedded in them for an explosion to occur are nowhere near the explosives. The decision not to bring along the blasting caps saved our lives.

With all of us safe and accounted for, and Comrade Masondo attending to his gaping wound, the large group of soldiers in the truck that was following arrived. Upon seeing the overturned car from a distance, they assumed that the leadership was attacked by the enemy. The highest in command of the soldiers gave orders and the troops alighted from the truck, took positions and with guns ready, approached the scene of the accident. After verifying that it was a genuine accident, the truck picked us all up and we proceeded to Quibashe.

We were all relieved and considered ourselves lucky to emerge from the incident with minimal injuries for it could have been much worse.

Camp Thirteen was situated in a beautiful, bushy area. There was a stream flowing nearby that was used by the camp for bathing and washing clothes. We were always warned to look out for crocodiles which were said to be very deceptive. It was said that they could leave the water from a different point, quietly move behind a person and come rushing to sweep one into the river.

The green vegetation provided good camouflage almost concealing the entire camp. There was a lot of wildlife which ensured sufficient meat supply to the cadres, and over time, comrades talked about eating pythons and hunting buffalos. Stories abound about following a wounded buffalo, which can be tricky and dangerous. A wounded buffalo can also be devious; it will pretend to be heading in a certain direction around a corner, only to turn back unseen, hide behind a tree and wait for its pursuer to approach. Taking advantage of the element of surprise, it will then charge when the distance has been reduced, completely surprising its pursuer.

We always ensured that we went to the river accompanied by others to ascertain that we had each other's back. One day, I went down to the river accompanied by Comrade George Lucky Mahlangu who had just returned from the front. George, a tall, handsome and pleasant comrade, had a fascinating story to tell and I cherished the opportunity to listen to him. He and his comrades had made a big headline story in the local newspapers. Comrade Mzwai had already addressed us relating the story of the comrades and extolling their bravery and readiness to sacrifice.

On 11th June 1979, in South Africa, comrades George, Solomon Mahlangu and Monty Motaung, carrying some parcels, were accosted by a suspicious policeman whilst trying to board a taxi at a rank on Diagonal Street in the center of Johannesburg. As they were passing the policemen, one of them was suspicious and grabbed one of the suitcases they were carrying; it fell to the ground and a Soviet-made Kalashnikov gun (AK 47) together with a hand grenade fell to the ground.

Pandemonium ensued with all three of them fleeing with the police hot on their heels in pursuit. George ran in one direction and Solomon and Monty took the other. The police cornered Solomon and Monty at a nearby factory, they in turn were firing their guns to pave their escape route. Messrs. Rupert Kessner and Kenneth Welfendale were killed in the ensuing battle.

Eventually Solomon and Monty were arrested, convicted and hanged in 1979. Monty had been severely beaten by the police and was declared unfit to stand trial. George was fortunate, the police focused on pursuing his comrades which enabled him to escape through Swaziland and was later flown to Angola.

What saddened me about George's situation was that not everyone at the camp welcomed the fact that he had eluded and slipped through the fingers of the enemy. As can be imagined, the regime had laid out a massive network to capture him. Comrades, including some in the group of instructors who should have known better, posed questions such as why he, unlike the other two was not arrested? They were insinuating that he had cowardly abandoned his colleagues who remained fighting bravely.

All the three comrades, including George had demonstrated remarkable courage just by agreeing to be operatives in an extremely dangerous environment. It is sad that they were arrested, but it was grossly unfair to begrudge George for escaping the clutches of the murderous regime when we should have been thankful that he'd managed to do so. Today we honour Solomon Mahlangu who is, indeed, undoubtedly one of our heroes. We should, however, also accord Monty and George the respect and dignity that they deserve.

Unfortunately, not much is heard of the two. There were many comrades that were infiltrated back into the country, some sacrificed their lives, many were arrested, hundreds of others accomplished their mission. Every single one of them deserves our respect.

How do heroes like Solomon Mahlangu, Barney Molokoane and others distinguish themselves? These were ordinary people that we grew up with, they were our brothers and sisters, and some were trained with us in Angola and elsewhere. I came from the same area with Barney, one of our heroes; his elder brother Pheko Molokoane is a personal friend of mine. When we were growing up, Barney was a youngster that we did not take much notice of. No one could have imagined that he would display such incredible bravery and become a hero.

In Quibashe, I became a firearm instructor and taught new recruits. My lectures on arms earned me a nickname the 'bolt and bolt carrier', which was how the new recruits referred to me when speaking among themselves.

I joined a group of instructors which included Francis Malaya who taught strategy and tactics. The commissar of the camp was a one-eyed fellow called Faro, who wore a black patch that resembled Moshe Dayan's, the former Israeli Défense Minister. Faro also taught political education. Our group of instructors was joined by comrade ANC Kumalo (Ronnie Kasarils) who I last saw in the GDR when he had come to lecture us on the history of the ANC. Comrade

Kumalo was vibrant and inspired many. He had a deep knowledge of the ANC and was well respected. He also wrote poetry. There was one that we all liked that made him popular in the camps. It is called 'Embers of Soweto'. I share the poem here that you might get a glimpse of the intensity of that period in time.

EMBERS OF SOWETO

Out of the crucible Warrior army of new age
Despising gas, batons, bullets Defying centuries of slavery
Advancing without care on armoured cars Striking metal with clenched fists Warrior cry "Amandla"
Rising in every throat Despising death
Under muzzle of machines Under muzzle of butcher
Teenagers and the eight-year-olds
Advance into the hail of lead and weight of centuries
And tumble — in an instant tumble Freeze tumble and sprawl
Like rag dolls in the dust Collapsing under barbed wire eyes
Butchers chorus baying "Vrystaat"! "Vrystaat"! These the embers of Soweto
Igniting the eyes of Mamelodi Enflaming the heart of Gugulethu Burning like flowers in Bonteheuwel. Winging with the incandescent embers Warrior cry whirls and soars
with collapsing child ignites the triumphant freedom gun
Mother! children! father! People! Listen! The cry "Vrystaat" dries on assassins' lips.

Comrade Parker was the Camp Commander; he was of the older generation and belonged to a group that we called 'Umgwenya which had left South Africa in the sixties. He was a gentle soul, always a voice of reason who preferred mediation and accommodation rather than confrontation. His Commissar, the one-eyed Faro, was a devious character, who reminded me of Squealer in George Orwell's 'Animal Farm'.

Faro was also of the older generation, eloquent and had over the years accumulated a wealth of knowledge of philosophies and theories. He used to quote Karl Marx and Lenin with confidence, whilst most of us were in the dark struggling to decipher what he was talking about. I developed a habit of attending his classes with the hope that I would learn something, but I soon realized that Faro was not teaching but advertising his talent. One was never the wiser after attending his classes, his way of teaching was such that one learned nothing but emerged even more confused. We would, however, come out of his classes full of praises for his unequaled knowledge of the subject.

One afternoon I found Faro encouraging a lady comrade recruit to launch a complaint against the Commander. Parker had apparently promised to bring her a present on his way back from Luanda where he visited regularly to consult with the HQ. Parker kept his word and brought back a gift. Unfortunately, his choice of a gift was ladies underwear. She was offended and felt that the gift represented a message, was suggestive and offensive.

I was upset with Faro Because I discovered that Faro had been briefed by someone, investigated and then actively pursued the matter. The lady comrade had indeed the right to take the matter further if she perceived that Parker was sexually harassing her. However, even though she was offended, personally, she had absolutely no intention of pursuing the matter and only changed her mind after being nudged by Faro to do so. It became clear to me that Faro had seen an opening and seized the opportunity, his intention being to embarrass Parker and to settle some score.

At this stage my unit from the GDR remained intact, gradually-one after the other-members of this unit were send and infiltrated inside South Africa or to operate in machineries in the Frontline States. There was generally a recognition that the unit from the GDR was well trained, and consequently highly regarded, thanks to the rigorous training we received from the Germans, which included lessons in explosives. I was confident that we would be infiltrated back inside the country to fight. Most importantly, I had high hopes that as the commander of the unit, and given the experience and skills I'd garnered in the GDR, I'd be amongst the first to be considered for deployment inside the country.

Clearly, the ANC leadership had other ideas, and appointing me as a Camp Commander at the Engineering post meant that there were no plans for me to leave Angola any time soon. I still held on to a slim chance that I would be considered. One by one my comrades from the platoon were leaving to the operating machineries in the frontline states of Swaziland, Mozambique, Zimbabwe, and Botswana. Many of them crossing into South Africa, I tried hard to follow their exploits inside the country.

Comrades Mzwai Piliso, and the national Commissar, Andrew Masondo, members of the military leadership, kept us abreast of activities of MK cadres inside South Africa. As members of the National Executive Committee of the ANC, they had access to information and knew exact details of operations inside the country from the reports received. Successful operations of our comrades inside the country were received in the camps with joy and celebrations. There were many inspiring achievements of MK, such as the Silverton attack, the raid at the Moroka Police Station and many more.

The reports on the progress of MK units that we received regularly from Mzwai and Masondo would get us all fired up, our moral would be very high, and we would end up singing revolutionary songs long after the stories had been told. The songs would be interspersed with some war chants, the most popular one being one that the MK cadres learned from ZIPRA forces that we lived with in some camps in Angola. Interestingly, these chants spread like wildfire and were ultimately performed in marches and demonstrations throughout the width and breadth of South Africa.

The chants usually followed the same format, an inspiring central voice barking orders or praises and a chorus of voices backing up the lead. The lead voice would say whatever came to mind, as long as it was inspirational, and the inspired crowd would then respond in a manner similar to that of backup singers to a famous lead singer.

I followed the progress of my comrades of the GDR unit, who had been deployed, with admiration and to some extent envy. However, it was not always good news from the front. Sometimes there were devasting incidents in which we lost and suffered a lot of casualties. The massacres in Matola and Maseru, the attacks and abductions in Gaborone and Harare, all perpetrated by the apartheid war machinery against the Frontline States resulted in the hundreds of innocent people. These attacks that killed comrades whom we knew and loved, refugees and nationals in the neighbouring states dampened the mood back in the camps in Angola.

The killings in Matola and Maseru followed a pattern. They were gruesome in that, instead of death by bullets, the bodies of our comrades were sliced and butchered beyond recognition. It was clear that the deliberate mutilation of the comrades was intended to send a message to those remaining behind. The attackers were making a statement meant to intimidate and create fear and uncertainty in all those who remained behind. The attacks also deliberately targeted citizens of those neighbouring countries to intimidate them and to ensure that they became reluctant to give refuge to ANC cadres in future.

The attacks of the regime on the Frontline States were meant to achieve some objectives and took the following format:

Utilizing parcel and car bombs targeting specifically members of the ANC and prominent figures opposing the Apartheid state.

Sending in commandos across borders: SADF sent groups of commandos to destroy infrastructure and kill political activists.

Lastly, the apartheid government abducted and kidnapped political activists who were then secretly transported back to South Africa for interrogation through torture. The captured activists could also be turned into an askari (A turncoat agent of the government. They were then effectively used to identify cadres that they knew and had trained with).

On the morning of 30 January 1981, SADF commandos drove 70 kms across the South African-Mozambican border to Matola, a suburb in Maputo. They attacked, destroyed three houses, and killed 16 South Africans and a Portuguese national, Mr. José Ramos, who bore a striking resemblance to Joe Slovo, the Secretary General of the South African Communist Party. For a brief period, the SADF celebrated the death of Slovo before news of the identity of the Portuguese national emerged. The commandos had painted themselves with black paint and caught those they killed off guard by pretending to be members of the Mozambican National Army.

Mbulelo Musi (Moss, one of my Comrades from the GDR unit), a survivor of the Matola raid, had this to say about the attack, "…the attack on Matola will forever remain as a reminder that freedom was not cheap, freedom came with a price, we dare not forget!"

There was yet another attack that left an ineradicable mark on our minds. The media account that reached us ran as follows:

"…in the early hours of December 9th, 1982, South African Defence Force commandos crossed the border into Lesotho. Their target was a cluster of houses on the outskirts of Maseru where members of the ANC were believed to be in hiding. Meeting no opposition from Lesotho's tiny 2 000-man paramilitary force, they blasted their way through numerous homes. By morning 42 people were dead, 30 of them believed to be members of the ANC. The remaining victims were Lesotho residents, including five women and two children."

President Oliver Tambo flew over South Africa to address a gathering of about 10 000 people that came to the funeral. We were all anxious because the South African rogue government was notorious for not respecting international norms, laws, and regulations. What was to stop the regime from bringing the plane carrying OR down to get at their number one enemy? At the funeral OR gave the following message:

"Pretoria murder squads have been deployed far around South Africa, to every conceivable country of laceration. They massacred in Kassinga, they butchered in Chimoio, they destroyed in Matola, they had destroyed within South Africa in SOWETO, they are killing everyday: The assassination of men and women, their massacres and murders by this regime, but, as history has shown, after Kassinga and Chimoio, the racists and their ally, Smith, were defeated and when they staged the Maseru Massacre and several others yet to come, at the end of the day history will repeat itself, they will be defeated."

CHAPTER 6

DEFIANCE WITHIN THE RANKS

"Positions are temporary. Ranks and titles are limited.
But the way you treat people, will always be remembered."
Unknown

The calm in the camp in Quibashe was suddenly broken when fourteen defiant comrades arrived from Nova Katenga. They were demanding to be sent home to fight and were refusing to take orders, completely disregarding senior ranking leadership of the army. I never understood why they were not disciplined in Katenga and why they were transported thousands of miles to the north of the country for their demands to be met. It became apparent that their attitude was disrupting established order in the camp, hence the decision to ship them away.

In Quibashe the group stuck to their demands and refused to do the daily chores. One of their leaders was a short, stocky and stubborn comrade called Dan Siwela. Siwela, a peasant from Kwa Zulu Natal, was firm and unmovable from the stance he had taken. He spoke in isiZulu and could not be reasoned with.

This new development created a buzz and divided the camp with one group sympathetic to the group and the other appalled by the level of indiscipline. Never had we witnessed such defiance and complete disregard for orders. We learned from 'Umgwenya' that back in the sixties the ANC had faced a similar incident when some cadres demanded to be sent back into the country.

The leadership, led by Parker, tried patiently to make the group see reason, but their efforts were in vain. Eventually the camp leadership decided that the continued defiance was undermining the established order in the camp and decided to put Dan, the leader of the group in detention, the disciplined unit from GDR was to execute the task. Those opposed to the authorities and loathed the involvement of the unit called the comrades who trained in the GDR fascist.

One particular evening Comrade Parker addressed the formation and gave the order for Dan to be arrested. Before that could be done, Dan hurled himself at the commander and the two started rolling in the sand.

A security guard intervened and hit Siwela on his back with the butt of a rifle. Siwela's supporters responded and joined in, at which point a scramble ensued, becoming a free for all. I was standing in the queue of instructors and was tempted to intervene with the intention of separating the comrades and help restore order. Mhlongo, standing right behind me, pulled me back pointing out that it is better to stand aside and observe. In the free for all, he reasoned, those who consider one an enemy might seize the opportunity to inflict harm.

Eventually, the defying comrades were subdued, but overall, the morale in the camp was very low. A very angry Commander of the army, Comrade Joe Modise, came to address us. This was followed by a visit from Mzwai Piliso. Both men made it clear that that kind of behavior would not be tolerated in the army. Modise announced that there would be a tribunal and that the comrades would be charged for their misconduct.

The tribunal consisted of senior comrades in the camp. I was appointed to serve and so were comrades Faro, Dire (Archie Whitehead), and Max Moabi (who was at the time the Deputy Chief Representative of the ANC in Angola).

The task of the tribunal was to determine whether the demand, by the comrades, to be sent home was genuine and made in sincerity, or whether it was a provocative move motivated by the enemy's desire to break up the organization and cause confusion. There was no question that they were already guilty of defying orders.

Due to the incessant and disruptive activities of the regime through its agent provocateurs it was always going to be difficult to distinguish genuine grievances from deliberate acts of provocation.

The South African Apartheid Regime had thrown in hundreds of its agents, with the intention of weakening the organization, cause dissent and demoralize the troops. The modus operandi of the infiltration by the regime was to send as many agents as possible, clearly with the knowledge that some will be exposed thus sacrificing many, but also with the hope that a few would remain undetected and penetrate higher echelons of the organization.

It became difficult to differentiate the agents provocateurs whose purpose was to create confusion, from genuine comrades. As it turned out, in the case of the dissenting cadres in Quibashe, many had a genuine desire to go home and fight. We were informed much later that many of them, given the opportunity, proved themselves in battle inside the country and executed operations exceptionally well. This fact alone does not, however, preclude the possibility that there could have been one or two of them that were motivated completely by a different agenda.

The entire group appeared one after the other before the tribunal. We read their charges and explained to them fully the implication of their conduct. All of them cooperated fully, the change in them was remarkable, with none of them displaying the arrogance that characterized the defiance they had shown when they arrived. In fact, many were trembling, genuinely believing that they could be sent to the firing squad if found guilty.

Several witnesses were summoned to give evidence, some of whom came all the way from Nova Katenga in the South. This included comrade Thami Zulu (Musi Ngwenya), then a respected leader in the army and chief of staff in the camp in Nova Katenga at the time.

Eventually on the recommendation of the Tribunal the comrades received light sentences, with Dan Siwela receiving the highest, a three-month detention for his attack on Parker. The others had their sentences varying from one to two months detention. In addition to the detention, the comrades were also expected to do chores in the camp during the day.

The incident in Quibashe was the first open defiance of leadership that I, as a member of the June 16 detachment experienced. It was unprecedented but heralded several other similar incidents that were disturbing. In various camps, a toxic environment emerged based on the feeling that the leadership was not doing enough to get cadres inside the country so that the enemy could be engaged. The case of the fourteen aforementioned heralded a difficult period in the army that was to be known as 'Mkatashinga'.

Mkatashinga describes a period of defiance within the ranks of Umkhonto We Sizwe in the camps' particularly during the 1984 period where some MK cadres protested being drafted to fight alongside Angolan troops in the battle against UNITA rebels. The comrades wanted to go home and fight rather than engage the enemy so far away from home. Some comrades could not understand why they had to fight Angolans and believed that the struggle in that country had nothing to do with their quest to liberate South Africa.

This was an unfortunate and difficult period in which mistakes were also committed. The defiance caused a debate with regard to two contradictory interpretations. One interpretation painted it as the work of apartheid. Others viewed it as an instance where patriotic comrades took a stance and in turn, had their views suppressed.

On the one hand, the massive infiltration of agents working for the enemy was creating insecurity and an environment of mistrust and paranoia. On the other hand, the determination by the leadership to root out these embedded provocateurs was always going to result in mistakes being committed and innocent comrades getting caught in the crossfire. The one big mistake was the excessive use of power by comrades investigating in the security department.

Some of the security operatives became infamous because of the way they extracted information from suspects. A cloud of fear and insecurity enveloped in ANC communities in the camps as it was never clear who would be next to face the interrogating team. In the morning we would wake up to whispers of who was taken away into custody by ANC security the night before. The arrests would be followed by reports of how some of these individuals have long been doing undercover work for the enemy.

> *"While there was no way of absolutely ruling out enemy interference, all narratives pointed to the presence of genuine challenges that could have been handled better.."* *
> Luvuyo Zantsi – Narrative of Mutiny in ANC Camps in Angola (1983/84).

Comrades already in the front-line states were sent back to the camps if they were suspects, or if they committed offenses and were deemed to be indiscipline. The administration of the camps ensured that for those sent back, life was far from comfortable. Those unfortunate to be sent back would be constantly reminded that they had wasted an opportunity that could have benefited deserving candidates. It was always everyone's wish to be released from the camps and be assigned to missions inside the country or in the front-line states.

These occurrences during this period in the ANC are well documented and were a subject of scrutiny by the Truth and Reconciliation Committee (TRC) that was led by the respected elder, the late Bishop Desmond Tutu. The judgment on what was the correct thing to do depended on where one stood in the debate of what was right or wrong. It is true that the ANC was able to uncover a huge number of infiltrating agents, but it would have to also acknowledge that this was done at a cost and that mistakes were also committed,

These mistakes have made it impossible for those affected to recover, especially many of those who were wrongly labelled as agents provocateurs acting on behalf of the enemy.

The TRC concluded its findings on the Organization by stating the following:

> *"On the basis of evidence available to it, the Commission finds that the ANC, particularly its military structure responsible for treatment and welfare of those in the camps, were guilty of gross violation of Human Rights in certain circumstances and against two categories of individuals namely, suspected enemy agents and or mutineers."*

Francis Tladi (Thlomedi Ephriam Mfalapitsa)

MK produced gallant fighters. As in all battles there are heroes such as Barney Molokoane, Solomon Mahlangu, Vuyhisile Mini to whom we remain forever indebted.

There have been traitors also, who voluntarily switched sides, betrayed their comrades and became Askaris (MK fighters who became turn coats). One such person I knew personally is called Francis Tladi (Real Name Ephriam Mfalapitsa)

I trained with Mfalapitsa, who later became an Askari. We were in the unit that I commanded in the GDR. I knew him as a pleasant comrade who was always smiling. Mfalapitsa did not have an opportunity to get formal education and he was therefore slow to understand the theories and concepts. Comrades in the group were always happy and patient to explain to him so that he could keep up with the rest of the group. Mfalapitsa was a simple man who demonstrated commitment to the ANC and the struggle. His unsolicited switch over to the enemy when he had the opportunity to be nearer South Africa therefore came as a big surprise.

In a statement he gave before TRC in South Africa, he claimed that after the regime's agents and their planes had bombed our military camp in Nova Katenge, Angola, the ANC became wary of infiltrators. He was appointed to join the security department of the ANC and became party to the torture of suspects and thereby witnessed the killing of a suspected operative by members of his unit. He claims that after the incident he became disillusioned with the ANC. When he was sent to operate in Botswana, he made his own arrangements to go back to South Africa and hand himself voluntarily to the authorities. Giving an account Mfalapitsa stated:

> *"I told the South African Police that I was not interested in joining either side of the conflict. I wanted them to debrief me and set me free because there was nowhere to go, and I had to come back because this is my country"*

On the one hand, considering Mfalapitsa's IQ and level of education it is not difficult to envisage that he could have been so naïve as to believe that even though he had risen to become a high-ranking commander of MK, the security apparatus would simply grant him his wish to be left alone and not see in him a pawn that could be utilized effectively to combat the ANC and MK.

On the other hand, it is also possible that despite his lack of education, Mfalapitsa was smart enough to deliberately make a statement like the one quoted with the hope that he could earn some sympathy to cover up his dastardly activities. His whole story is most likely a fabrication to cover up his voluntary collaboration with the enemy and an attempt to resist accepting accountability for the innocent lives that he cost.

As an Askari, Mfalapitsa was used as a pawn to lure four of our members to an explosive booby-trapped pump house at a mine in Krugersdorp. This was done under the guise that Mfalapitsa was going to train them militarily. Initially the four students, Eustice "Bimbo" Madikela, Nthsingo Mataboge, Fanyana Nhlapo and Zandisile Musi had requested Francis to assist them in leaving the country. They had approached Francis, aware that he had returned from exile and that he knew the two brothers of Zandisile Musi who had trained with him in the ANC camps. The four students were not aware that Mfalapitsa had become a turncoat.

When Francis reported the students' intention to leave the country to a Captain Johan Coetzee who was supervising the Vlaakplas camp where he and other Askaris were training, he was advised to dissuade the students from going out of the country with a promise that he would train them internally.

Arrangements were made for Mfalapitsa to transport the four students to the pump house which the agents had bobby-trapped with explosives. He would then leave them under the pretext that he was going to fetch more training materials. Once he was at a safe distance, he would notify Coetzee who would give instructions to have the explosives detonated.

Mfalapitsa was assisted by another notorious Askari called Joe Mamasela who posed as a taxi driver and picked up the students.

The explosives were detonated and killed three of the four students. Zandisile was the only survivor albeit with serious injuries. Mfalapitsa, who at the time of writing this book was facing judicial trial for this heinous crime, defended himself by saying that he was compelled to report the students when they contacted him as he was not sure that they were deliberately sent to him to trap him and thereby test his loyalty to his new masters. Zandisile Musi, who later died, was the younger brother of Mbulelo Musi (Moss Thema), the comrade I trained with in the GDR and who was also my Commissar when I was a Camp Commander at the Engineering Camp.

There were also comrades who did not end up in the enemy camp voluntarily. These were either kidnapped from the neighbouring states or captured inside the country and were forced, through torture, to work for the enemy.

A friend of mine, Mosses Moloele, was curious to know whether I habour any resentment for people who, after torture, collaborated with the enemy. I responded by explaining to Moss that it is difficult to have a blanket approach; each case would have to be considered according to its merit. I told Moss that personally I was never tortured by the regime and was therefore not able to condemn those who were turned around by torture.

The information we have is that the extent of the torture was such that many of those who underwent such conditions found it impossible to resist. The torture was perfected to ensure success. To break down the resistance of those who refuse to give in. It was indeed a choice between breaking down or death.

It was difficult therefore, on the one hand, to be disdainful of those who could not persevere the torture, while on other hand, I have the greatest respect for those whose conviction prepared them and enabled them to withstand such excessive torture. I was never tested to that extent. I am therefore unable to determine how I would have coped had I been faced with such a situation.

CHAPTER 7

DAR ES SALAAM
MY FIRST DIPLOMATIC MISSION

*"The art of diplomacy is to take an opportunity
and turn it into something."*
Brent Scowcroft

Early in 1978, I was informed by Comrade Mzwai that a decision had been taken by the National Executive Committee of the ANC to deploy me to our Mission in Lagos, Nigeria. I was to deputize comrade Mark Shope, the ANC Chief Representative at the time. I was excited. I knew comrade Mark Shope, a respected trade unionist who had been in the camps teaching politics. I welcomed the opportunity because I knew that I would learn a lot working under his tutelage.

After a period of not hearing from Mzwai, it appeared that for some reason the decision was changed. The next information I received was that due to some difficulty and technicalities I was no longer going to Nigeria but would now be deputizing Reddy Mazimba (Petrous Mampane) in Dar es Salaam, Tanzania. At the young age of twenty-three, I headed to Tanzania, with no clue what being Deputy Chief Representative entailed. I understood that the ANC was blending the youth of 1976 and creating an environment where they could learn from the experienced Mgwenya cadres. I was therefore expected to assist, but also to learn from Reddy who turned out to be a great teacher and mentor. Later I deputized him again in Zimbabwe. I am honoured to have had half my entire life in exile working together with Reddy in service to the ANC.

I remember it as vividly as if it was yesterday, descending the staircase of the flight from Angola. It was the summer of 1978. As I stepped onto the ground at Dar es Salaam International Airport which was later renamed Mwalimu Julius Nyerere International Airport, I was enveloped by the humidity and heat of the coastal town of Dar es Salaam.

Bra Rocky, a member of the Mgwenya generation, came to fetch me from the airport. At twenty-three years old and totally inexperienced, I wondered what Rocky thought of his new boss. I was to be the second in command and to oversee a large ANC community that included veterans, many of whom had proven their worth in the great peaceful demonstrations of the fifties in apartheid South Africa. I was young enough to be a son and even maybe a grandson to some of them. I had a great deal to learn, but I was ready.

Our community of South Africans was joined in their thousands by the June 16 generation (referred to as 'Xineselani' by the Umgwenya).

The difference between the ANC communities in Angola and Tanzania was that the first was military and the latter was civilian. In Tanzania, I was not going to bark orders as I was dealing with experienced and intelligent people who expected rational leadership. I was grappling with having to understand how the leadership of the ANC expected me to oversee people who were so experienced. "Would I even be taken seriously?" I wondered.

I learned later that many of the Mgwenya were also pondering this very new reality, and in the absence of a coherent and logical explanation, many theories were banded around. In exile, my nom de guerre was Kingsley Xuma, a name given to me by Lennox Lagu when we were in Mozambique. I was therefore sharing the same surname with the late ANC President of the nineteen forties, Dr. Alfred Bathini Xuma.

Comrade Problem, a Mgwenya comrade suggested to others, with a 'level of certainty', that I was Dr AB Xuma's grandson, hence the

ANC's decision to appoint me. Problem also had a different take on this puzzle and according to him, the ANC had made a sensible decision; Reddy being of the older generation would be the leader of Mgwenya and as his deputy, he expected me to lead and give guidance to the Xiniselane (The new arrivals of the June 16 generation). This was, according to him, a perfect division of labour.

One day I had a serious fallout with comrade 'Jimmy Mabuwafela' who wanted to let me know, in one heated argument, that when they were kicked about by the Boers in the fifties, I was still wearing nappies and enjoying the comfort of a cradle. Fortunately for me, there was a case of corruption pending against 'Mabuwafela'. He was accused of having diverted the second-hand clothing (referred to as mphando) that we received from Europe and other friendly countries, and allegedly sold the goods for his personal gain.

With the zeal and lack of maturity of a 23-year-old, I retorted that despite my age, the ANC leadership must have seen it fit to wait until I came along to hold the position he had eyed all along because he could not be trusted. Mabuwafela was not at all impressed with my retort, and we almost ended in a scuffle had it not been for Problem's intervention.

A senior comrade, Maruping Seperepere observed the confrontation and informed me that he 'is not sure that it is a good idea to appoint one so young into such a responsible position. In his opinion the ANC leadership was robbing me of my youth. "Kingsley, he stated, "these are positions for older men and women, you should be given a chance to grow within the structures of the youth such as the Youth League". I was humbled and in retrospect, he might have had a point. However, despite my age, the struggle had matured most of us way beyond our years.

In Tanzania with the large community of exiles, we were like one huge family and had each other's back. It was fascinating how effortless it was for comrades to be nicknamed after their habits or what they were accustomed to doing or saying. For instance, we had a comrade called George 'sharp fede, hoezit?'(George 'fine thanks and, how are you?') He earned his name because of his habit of instinctively responding in like manner whenever his name was called. If one called out "George" his response immediately, always based on an assumption that he is being greeted, would be "sharp fede, hoezit?" Comrade Elliot, on the other hand, was known as 'mabamba'(touching), a name he earned from patting the behinds of women passing by him.

There was a comrade we called Ben 'Shonas', who with his beautiful tenor voice, would give the best rendition of the revolutionary song 'Shona Malanga' (the sun sets). And then we had Jimmy 'Mabuwafela' (speaks whatever comes to mind emanating from the kind of unexpected issues he would raise.

The ANC households in Tanzania and Lusaka (ANC Headquarters) were littered with ANC heavy weights, real giants that were known back home for their contribution to the struggle. There were comrades such as Kate Dinkwetsi Molale, a veteran of women's emancipation.

She was also involved in the drawing up of the 1955 freedom charter and a veteran of various other campaigns such as the Alexander bus boycott of 1957.

She and her family moved and settled in Moletsane, the last township she resided before going into exile. Although she left the country much earlier and I never got to know her personally in South Africa, I was proud of the fact that her family and mine were from the same area and that my siblings and I were close to her daughter and two sons. In exile, she was settled in Morogoro, Tanzania, where she died from injuries sustained in a car accident.

We also had Comrade Mittah Seperepere, who was born in the Northern Cape. She was an anti-apartheid activist and a freedom fighter, a political activist and community builder. She was harassed and ultimately imprisoned by the regime. Upon her release she and her husband, comrade Maruping Seperepere, skipped the country and were eventually settled in Morogoro, Tanzania.

Eli and Violate Weinberg lived with us in Dar es Salaam. He was a renowned photographer and trade unionist. He was also a member of the Central Committee of the Communist Party of South Africa and had made immense contribution in the struggle.

Staying at the campus of the University of Dar es Salaam was the renowned writer and poet, Willy Kgositsile and his wife, Baleka Mbete-Kgositsile. Baleka was to become the Speaker of the National Assembly in the Democratic South Africa.

We interacted, belonged to units of the ANC, and regularly held discussions at the level of the Regional Political Committee (RPC). The veterans were an inspiration. However, even amongst them, like in any other community, there were occasions when they disagreed and had conflicts amongst the individuals.

When that happened, particularly if those involved were highly respected, it had a demoralizing effect on the entire community. For a protracted period, Kate Molale's and Mittah Seperere households were at loggerheads. This slipped through into the structures in Tanzania as members either took sides or attempted to mediate.

We held RPC meetings during which we had serious, often animated political discussions relating to the situation in South Africa, the state of the ANC in general, as well as giving our endorsement or expressing our misgivings on the direction the leadership was taking the organization. Not surprisingly, the nation building prospects for a post-apartheid South Africa was often the topic of discussion.

In one meeting the region received a report that a media outlet was given permission to video-record MK cadres in the camps. Apparently, this was comrade Thabo Mbeki's initiative. This generated a heated debate that divided the house with some applauding the initiative and others vehemently opposed. I had not met Mbeki then, but it was known that he was one of the leaders that were beginning to make a huge impact on the direction and way forward for the ANC. Later I had the honour of working closely with him in various situations, in exile and in the democratic Government of South Africa. I was then able to appreciate his ability to look deep into issues far beyond what appears on the surface. He is truly a strategic thinker, and, in his presence, one always learns.

Tanzania was going through a painful period of socio- economic development. The President of the country, the renowned and popular Mwalimu (Teacher in Kiswahili) Julius Kambarage Nyerere, and his party 'Chama Cha Mapinduzi' (CCM) were pursuing a policy of what they referred to as African Socialism and in Kiswahili, was called 'Ujamaa'.

"Ujamaa, the Swahili word for extended family, was a social and economic policy developed and implemented in Tanzania by President Julius Kambarage Nyerere (1922–1999) between 1964 and 1985. Based on the idea of collective farming and the "villagization" of the countryside. Ujamaa also called for the nationalization of banks and industry and an increased level of self-reliance at both the individual and national level.

"Nyerere argued that urbanization, which had been brought about by European Colonialism and was economically driven by wage labour, had disrupted the traditional pre-colonial rural African society. He believed that it was possible for his government to recreate precolonial traditions in Tanzania and, in turn, re- establish a traditional level of mutual respect and return the people to a settled, moral way of life. The way to do that, he said, was to move people out of the urban cities like the capital Dar es Salaam, and into newly created villages dotting the rural countryside".

Nyerere envisaged a villagization policy or rural socialism intended to create collective rural agriculture as a way of countering rapid urbanization sweeping throughout Africa. The villages that were created would then receive equipment along with fertilizer and seeds. Services such as health care and education would also be provided. To kickstart the project required 250 households to qualify for an ujamaa village.

Ujamaa produced mixed results. Many applauded Nyerere and

were hopeful that his policies would lead to a unified and prosperous nation. On the other hand, there were those who, based on their understanding felt that socialism kills personal initiative, opposed the said policies. Nevertheless, the disapproval of his policies by some notwithstanding, Nyerere was endearingly referred to as 'Mwalimu' ('Teacher") or 'Baba wa taifa ("Father of the nation").

Ujamaa had its pros, creating high literacy rate, uniting Tanzanians across ethnic lines and thus ensuring that Tanzania remained peaceful and untouched by the "tribal" and political tensions that affected the rest of Africa.

There were some challenges as well, resulting in some serious shortfalls that led to Tanzania abandoning this well- intended policy when Julius Nyerere stepped down in 1985.

When the project began, it was popular and received a good response from Tanzanians with many volunteering to be in the villages. However, with the passage of time and failure by authorities to live up to expectations, there were fewer people willing to be part of the project. The government, becoming impatient and being determined to meet the target of ensuring the completion of Ujamaa villages throughout Tanzania within a certain period, took harsh measures in forcing families to relocate, including destroying peoples' homes. An added problem was that the finances to support the project were also inadequate and success was limited. Transport networks declined drastically through neglect, while industry and banking were crippled.

Food shortages became the norm, characterized by long queues for essential products and food. Another critical mistake by Nyerere that compounded the situation was his belief that the banning of opposition parties would unify the country and thus Tanzania became a one-party state.

Crime was on the increase as conditions worsened, and people became increasingly desperate. There were brazen crime incidents that we witnessed and talked about, with some of them exhibiting creative thinking at its best. The common one would have two thieves approach a parked car where an unsuspecting driver, his arm wearing a wristwatch resting on an open window. One thief then rips the watch from the unsuspecting driver and makes a dash for it, whilst the other thief who is much more confident of his ability to run fast, holds the door firmly making sure that his partner running away with the watch is out of reach before releasing the door and bolting. For the driver to pursue the thief, he would have to either get out through the passenger door, a process that would be time consuming, or force his or her way through the blocked door.

One morning, our comrades from the more populated residence in Kinondoni suburb reported an amazing story of theft. They had noticed for some time, that every day they woke up to find missing items in their residence. They could not tell who the thief was with the result that they began suspecting some of the comrades at the residence. On this particular morning, a comrade went to the toilet and came across a non-resident in the passage. The comrade raised an alarm, and all the residents gave chase.

The invader was illusive and difficult to catch; they clasped him with both hands as he ran passed, but he slipped through their fingers. The thief was not wearing clothes and had smeared a lot of Vaseline to make himself slippery. Eventually one smart thinking comrade threw his body at the feet of the thief who was darting to all corners wherever there was room to squeeze through. The thief fell down, which ultimately brought the chase to an end and he was easily picked up.

In another incident, a comrade was listening to his radio that was on the veranda, but out of his sight. A thief grabbed the radio and moved away slowly and at the same time increasing the volume thus giving the impression that the radio was still where it was left, in the meantime the thief was increasing the distance until it was too late for the comrade to realize what was happening.

I was personally robbed of my pair of trousers. One night we slept late after indulging in a bottle of whiskey that comrade Musa Nkosi of the Radio Freedom Unit had brought from a visit he undertook abroad. I got to my room and undressed and neatly hung my trouser next to my bed, I forgot to switch off the lights and fell asleep. I was woken by a cool breeze coming through the window at around 3am. I had forgotten to close the window and of course, waking up in a lit room then trying to focus on the darkness beyond the curtains on my window was a challenge. When ultimately my eyes became accustomed to the darkness, I realized that there was a person lurking in the dark behind the curtain and the window who was patiently waiting in the hope that I would fall asleep again. I jumped out of bed, tried to get my trouser with the intention of giving chase. The trouser was gone, the thief had used a long wire, hooked my trouser from the chair and pulled it out of through the burglar proofs on the window.

With the increasing crime rate, many people took matters into their own hands, and vigilante groups emerged everywhere. It did not take much for people to beat up and sometimes kill perpetrators. In some instances, the police would not even respond to calls that a thief was being beaten by the crowd. There were stories making rounds that in some instances the police would, upon receiving a report that a crowd was beating a perpetrator, ask the question, "If the thief was still alive?"

Comrade Solly Kotane was chased down the streets and given a severe beating by a crowd that mistook him for a thief. He was running down the street in a hurry to be on time for an appointment when someone suddenly shouted in Kiswahili "Mwizi" ("thief") and pointed in his direction. Without much ado, people gave chase. The faster Solly ran to escape and save himself, the more the crowd gathered and gave chase. They ultimately cornered him and started beating him up. They would probably have killed him were it not for the intervention of some elderly man who recognized him and started shouting at the top of his voice. He managed to stop everyone by explaining that he knew Solly to be a "Mkimbizi" ("a refugee").

The difficult situation in the country was compounded by the Uganda– Tanzania War, known in Tanzania as the 'Kagera' War and in Uganda as the 1979 Liberation War. It was fought between the two nations from October 1978 until June 1979 and led to the overthrow of Ugandan dictator, Idi Amin, but not before subjecting the people of both countries to severe economic consequences and untold suffering.

The war pitted the Tanzanian government in support of the ousted Ugandan regime of Milton Obote and rebels led by Yoweri Museveni against Idi Amin's government supported by the Libyan leader Muammar Gaddafi.

Despite the poverty and their problems in general, Tanzanians were hospitable and accommodating of freedom fighters and refugees. Under the leadership of Nyerere, the country fully supported all those fighting liberations wars on the continent. Dar es Salaam became known as the home of almost all freedom fighting organizations in Africa. Ther were comrades from the MPLA of Angola, ZANU and ZAPU of Zimbabwe, SWAPO of Namibia, the PAC and ANC of South Africa and many others. Many of these liberation movements had their Headquarters based in Dar es Salaam.

Despite the numerous difficulties, Tanzania remained steadfast in its support for freedom. Nyerere was an outspoken critic of colonialism and apartheid. The OAU liberation committee, led by Colonel Hashim Mbita was also hosted by Tanzania. The whole country was energized; there were debates about various concepts of freedom and above all, the people were sympathetic to our cause. The University of Dar es Salaam became the Mecca of intellectual debates on colonialism, liberation, and socio-economic transformation where renowned speakers, such as Professor Ali Mazrui and others were invited regularly.

The ANC and the other liberation movements received humanitarian support from governments of the Scandinavian countries, non- governmental organizations in America and the western world and were therefore well provided for with food, transportation, and other necessities for the thousands of its members. We survived because organizations such as the Swedish International Development Assistance (SIDA), the Norwegian Agency for Development Cooperation (NORAD) and the Canadian International Development Agency (CIDA) and others all played their part in ensuring that we had bread on the table.

'Ntate' Thomas Nkobi the ANC Treasurer General at the time coordinated all this assistance and ensured that integrity and transparency was uppermost in dealings with all these agencies.

Given all the support we received and in the midst of all the hardship that confronted Tanzanians, the ANC members were, in fact, undoubtedly privileged. I recall that we were cautioned not to allow food wastage for it would not look good to be throwing away food when thousands of Tanzanians were struggling to make ends meet. In fact, there were some Tanzanians who did not understand how international solidarity worked, and they, therefore, believed that the government of Julius Nyerere was taking food and resources meant for them and diverting the same to support the liberation movements and refugees.

President Oliver Tambo and other ANC leaders were in and out of Tanzania either to consult with the leadership of the country, the liberation committee or to address the huge ANC community in Tanzania. It was always a pleasure and uplifting to interact with the leadership, and get a briefing on events in South Africa and internationally.

Oliver Tambo (OR), Moses Mabhida, Joe Slovo, Stephen Dlamini and many other leaders that were frequenting Dar es Salaam were national leaders, renowned for their role during the campaigns of the fifties. Their leadership and activities of the ANC gave hope to the people and the popularity of the leaders among Africans grew tremendously.

I had known most of these leaders only by their names, and by the fact that they were revered by the people in South Africa. Their names were only uttered in whispers because the mere mention of their names in the country during the apartheid days would have created complications with authorities.

My generation was born and grew up during this period where the viciousness with which the regime responded to the people's protest had brought some restrain and folks were much more cautious. It became evident as we grew up to become the rebellious youth ourselves, that the harsh repressive measures deployed by the regime had intimidated some of our parents. We were occasionally reminded that brave men and women who were much more intelligent than we could ever hope to be had, despite their courageous efforts, been unable to remove the illegitimate government from power.

"Where is Nelson Mandela and Oliver Tambo?" our parents would often ask us. This would be followed by an equally troubling question, "If they could not free this country, what makes you think your contribution will make any difference?"

There were fears of imprisonment and our militancy bothered our parents who were scared that we would meet the same fate as Nelson Mandela and Oliver Tambo. In retrospect, it must have been a terrifying time for parents who worried for their children even though they, too, wanted freedom to come to South Africa.

My first encounter with OR, as he was endearingly called, was at the Dar es Salaam airport. Reddy, my boss, had gone on a short course abroad and I was left in charge. The denim suit, a top and a matching trouser were in fashion then, so I had worn one of those to fetch OR at the airport. I greeted OR as he alighted the plane, and he then instructed that we go to the VIP lounge.

We had received news that Joshua Nkomo and Robert Mugabe, the Zimbabwean leaders of the two biggest national liberation movements were arriving aboard a later flight. OR was keen to meet and talk to the two leaders. Zimbabweans were holding talks in

Lancaster House in London and there was a lot at stake. It was vital that the Patriotic Front (PF) that was being forged out of the unity of both ZANU (Zimbabwean African National Union) led by Mugabe and ZAPU (Zimbabwean African People's Union) led by Nkomo be successful.

I took OR to the VIP section where he chose a comfortable seat facing the door, pulled out a paper and started reading. I sat on the seat opposite as we anticipated a long wait for the arrival of the two leaders. OR was engrossed in his reading and occasionally, without saying anything, lowered the paper and looked at me and went back to reading his newspaper. This happened several times and I was beginning to feel uncomfortable because I did not know why OR kept gazing at me every time he lowered his paper.

After a while OR lowered his paper, folded it, and look me in the eye, and the following discussion ensued:

"Kingsley, I am certain you know why we sent you here to this great country?" The emphasis of his words being on "This great country"

"Yes, Chief," I replied.

"That you are here as a proud representative of the people of South Africa?" he went on.

"Yes, Chief," I replied again, wondering quietly where the discussion was leading.

"And that as a true representative of the proud people of South Africa, you must demonstrate confidence and look the part?"

"Yes Chief," I responded. At this point I was beginning to feel quite uncomfortable and wishing that the earth could open up and swallow me because it was now apparent that he did not approve of my 'in -fashion' attire.

He followed what he was saying with a gaze at me, unflinching as he spoke, and gesturing slowly with his hand, moving it up and down to demonstrate that he was looking at both my trouser and the shirt:

"But look at you" he said, still moving his hand up and down.

"You could have been picking up stones," he stated derisively. I felt so embarrassed, apologized for the manner I was dressed and OR went on reading his paper. Later, Presidents Joshua Nkomo and Robert Mugabe arrived, and all the aides gave space for the three men to consult amongst themselves.

OR did not forget easily. On his next visit a few months later, he was leading a delegation to Madagascar with a stop-over in Dar es Salaam. Comrade Rebecca Matlou (Sankie Mthembi Mahanyele) was part of the delegation. Once again, I had opportunity to go and receive the delegation and recalling what transpired during the President's last visit, I made certain that I was dressed in the best suit I had available.

When I received the delegation, OR noticed my dressing immediately and commented to comrade Rebecca, but making sure that I heard him, "Wow! Rebecca, just look at how Kingsley is dressed! He looks like a perfect gentleman, doesn't he?" Rebecca responded, agreeing with the President that I was dressed impressively. She was, of course, not privy to the discussion of our first encounter, and probably took the comment as just a regular conversation.

In another encounter with OR, also in Dar es Salaam, I was privy to a discussion between Mshengu and the President. Mshengu was the President's aide and typed OR's speeches and statements. He was, therefore, always part of the delegation. He had a pleasant personality, committed and loyal to OR and was the fastest typist on those old typewriters that I had ever known.

On this occasion, OR was in Tanzania for a much needed break during which we were advised by the National Executive Committee (NEC) that he was not to be disturbed. Being the workaholic he was, we had to make sure that his presence is not known, and that he was not having any engagements.

A good Samaritan business family had offered their apartment in an affluent suburb nearer the sea as they were away abroad on extended holidays. Reddy had instructed that I should be attached and be nearer to OR so as to be the link with the office and to provide any assistance on the spot.

Mshengu was relating to OR his encounter with one of the Group of Eight. The Group of Eight were men who had parted ways with the ANC due to a disagreement on the role of the participation of the white community in the organization and the struggle.

Earlier Mshengu had taken a walk and met one of the men of the 'group of eight' and on his return he reported to OR, a discussion they held in Xhosa:

Mshengu: "Chief! I met u Mqxotha today" OR : "Mmmm! What did he say?"

Mshengu : "He said *"Hey! Mshengu, unjani?"* ("Mshengu, how are you?") and he went on to inquire further;

"Mshengu! nawe osathe ntsontsololo ko lo mbolo" ("Mshengu, are you still rooted in this rot (ANC)?"

OR "huh!"

Taken aback, OR inquired further, "And what was your response, Mshengu?"

Mshengu : "I told him," he responded, *"that O mbolo o nyoko"* ("The rotten stuff is your mom").

I was struggling to stifle my laughter upon hearing Mshengu's response. OR was such a gentleman and so dignified that I could not imagine such expletives being uttered in his presence.

CHAPTER 8

EDUCATION
THE ULTIMATE GIFT TOWARDS
FREEDOM

"Education is our passport to the future,
for tomorrow belongs only to the people who prepare for it today."
Malcolm X

Solomon Mahlangu Freedom College (SOMAFCO)
In 1977, the Tanzanian Government gave about 600 acres of land
to the ANC, and in 1978 construction of the Solomon Mahlangu
Freedom College began. The ANC entrusted this huge project to an
engineer that studied in the German Democratic Republic, Comrade
Oswald Dennis or Uncle Dennis as he was affectionately known.
He was later joined and supported by an architect by the name of
Comrade Spenser Hodgson.

The land situated in Mazimbu, in Morogoro consisted of some
farm buildings that the ANC used to accommodate students that
were in Tanzania prior to the completion of the college. The number
of students increased when a group of ANC students that had been
sent to Nigeria were withdrawn from there.

The ANC embarked on a campaign to recruit teachers and experts,
who were brought in to build the school and to teach. The recruited
teachers were mostly South Africans.

Our duty at the Mission in Dar Es Salaam was to ensure that

teachers and students who were arriving settled well in Mazimbu. It was an honour to work with Uncle Dennis who was committed and involved from the planning to the completion of the entire project.

The Tanzanians never regretted their decision to give land to the ANC. Just before returning to South Africa, the ANC gave back the land which has on it a highly developed technical college which the Tanzanians continue to utilize to date, as an extension to the University of Agriculture, to the benefit of the Tanzanian people.

Before the college was built there were some teething problems which included lots of infighting amongst the few students who were occupants of the old structures. At the time the school did not have a proper administrative machinery such as a Principal or Boarding Master to oversee students' affairs. The infighting became worse with the arrival of students that were withdrawn from Nigeria.

At some stage Ted Baholo, the ANC regional representative in Morogoro, had to go for medical treatment abroad for a period. Reddy Mazimba sent me to hold the fort in Morogoro. This gave me an opportunity to deal directly with the students. One early Saturday morning, literally at dawn, we were woken up by a report that two groups of students in Mazimbu, some fifteen kilometers from where we were staying, were fighting.

Mme Kate and I rushed to Mazimbu, assembled the students and addressed them. Around the same time there were reports that a member of the Pan African Congress had been killed in similar infighting in the organization's camp in Bagamoyo, Tanzania. We knew that we had to act fast if we were to avoid a similar situation happening in our camp. Mme Kate and I made it clear to the students that their fighting would not be tolerated, not in the ANC. Besides, we were guests in the country and our fighting amongst ourselves was a mark of disrespect to our hosts and a message that we could not govern ourselves and yet we were fighting for self- governance.

After these incidents we began to put proper authority in Mazimbu. Comrade Slim Zindela, became the first acting principal of the students even before the completion of the school. Upon completion of the school, Winston Njobe was officially appointed the first principal of SOMAFCO and Comrade Slim Zindela served as his deputy.

To its credit, the ANC created a school that provided an education that was superior to the inferior one that we received in the apartheid bantu education. SOMAFCO, therefore, provided quality education for the thousands who were denied the opportunity at home. The regime understood the ANC's intentions very well and strove to ensure that the project was still-born. It flooded the school with agent provocateurs whose mission was to sabotage and create chaos and confusion.

With each group of students that we received from the frontline states, we expected that there would be agents of the regime embedded amongst the arriving recruits. However, the enemy also made mistakes; it appeared that some of the recruits were handled by the same agents, given the same type of training and because they exhibited similar patterns of behaviour many of the infiltrated agent provocateurs were uncovered and exposed. Each time we received the students arriving from home at the airport, we would already be looking to see who amongst them was exhibiting the stereotype tendencies we had come to know from those arrested previously.

The students who were amongst the first occupants of SOMAFCO faced difficult conditions as we struggled to improve the situation. Despite the problems encountered, the students were an enterprising lot. They sang revolutionary songs, and regularly, through the entertaining artistic portrayal in drama and theater, renewed their commitment to a revolution in education. There was a comrade called Lemmy who was an incredible artist. He could perform a one-man show and be on stage switching performances from singing to a gun boot dance; he could also perform a one-man drama and do comedy. He had a great sense of humour and would keep the crowd in stitches as he performed his comedy.

Lemmy was an inspiration to many, and since he was always in a jolly mood, his presence and conduct inspired and raised morale. However, at some stage Lemmy's persona suddenly changed. We noticed that he appeared depressed and was no longer as sociable as he used to be.

This surprised many and no one could tell what the cause of his depression was. Soon after, we received information that Lemmy had attempted suicide; he had tried to hang himself. It was fortunate that a friend interrupted this and dissuaded Lemmy from going ahead. Tragically, Lemmy eventually succeeded. He threw himself in front of a fast-moving train that passed through Morogoro once a week on its way to Dar es Salaam.

The students were a close-knit community and Lemmy with his bubbly personality played a huge role in boosting morale. The college was some distance away from the city of Morogoro, and therefore was seemingly in the middle of nowhere. The students were a community of people who had left behind their loved ones and were uprooted from their country and natural surroundings. There was therefore a need to engage in activities that could boost morale and help them adjust to a completely new and from their perspective, a strange environment.

Lemmy's death was the first suicide at the school and it shocked everyone. It also dampened spirits of the students. Comrade Elliot Maroga, an elderly Mgwenya, also died in strange circumstances. He loved animals and was tragically killed by a hippopotamus. Elliot, who had considered himself a specialist on animals, captured and kept snakes and pets in his room. Word went around that one had to be careful not to cross Elliot because if angered, it was not beyond him to ensure that some of his friendly snakes paid a visit to his adversaries whilst they were taking a shower.

Elliot's death was a freak incident. One morning, a crowd of the local people had gathered on top of a bridge that was used to cross the stream that flowed not far from the college. They were shouting excitedly and pointing down to a lone hippo that had somehow strayed up the stream, but far from the main river that was way up north, far from Morogoro. There were no hippos anywhere close given the fact that hippos stay in the rivers and rarely wander in streams that have inadequate volumes of water. Inexplicably the hippo in the stream causing excitement had strayed from the river far away

The shouting and the noise were clearly confusing the animal that perceived the crowd to be attacking it. Elliot on receiving the information, rushed to the scene, climbed down to the stream bank presumably to calm down the agitated animal that was running in all directions, attempting to put some distance between itself and the maddening crowd.

When the hippo saw Elliot within reach, still confused and believing that it was defending itself, it charged, got hold of him and repeatedly slammed his body against the river wall that was holding the bridge. The screaming and noise from the crowd that looked on helplessly as Elliot was battered to his death forced the animal to let go of Elliot. It then slid back into the stream and moved on, attempting to distance itself from the troubled spot. It was already too late, comrade Elliot succumbed to multiple wounds.

The project of the ANC college took off amid lots of interest and activity. The road between Dar es Salaam and Morogoro became a hype of activity with cars driving to and from the college. International governments and supporters of the ANC demonstrated keen interest to be part of this promising project that was seen as a noble mission. In addition to teachers from South Africa, SOMAFCO ended up with volunteers from all corners of the world.

Unfortunately, the tarred Dar es Salaam-Morogoro Road also claimed a few lives. The death of Mme Kate Molale in May 1980 following an accident on that road was a huge blow to the ANC community and South Africa in general. Her death was closely followed by the death of the popular former Prime Minister of Tanzania, Mr. Edward Moringe Sokoine.

Sokoine was seen by many as a possible successor to Julius Nyerere and he was loved by all. His death was mourned by the entire nation. Sokoine's death also put the ANC in a difficult situation because his accident involved a comrade. According to reports received, comrade was travelling to Morogoro when his car rammed into the Prime Minister's car.

It was a freak accident that was bound to raise questions particularly to those with conspiracy theories. It appeared inconceivable to some that the comrade's car would, out of all the cars that were in the Prime Minister's convoy, collide with Sokoine's car that was in the centre. It appears that the motor bikes and security guard vehicles that usually flick blue lights and sound sirens to alert oncoming traffic were caught off guard. Some conspiracy theorists speculated that this was not an accident, but a plot by "political opponents "of the prime minister allegedly intended to eliminate him from the race to succeed President Nyerere.

It was the professionalism and maturity of the leadership of the 'Chama Cha Mapinduzi' party, including Julius Nyerere, that handled the matter calmly which diffused speculation. The matter was investigated diligently and the conclusion was that this was a genuine accident. The comrade explained that he was driving around a curve when he suddenly came across the convoy. The security elements, also taken by surprise by the appearance of a car, unexpectedly, sounded the sirens. This caused confusion, and the comrade was caught off guard. He tried to slow down when he realized that he was coming up to the Prime Minister's convoy. Braking suddenly forced his car, which was moving at high speed, to swerve and lose control and head straight into the prime minister's car.

Entrusted With More Responsibility
With the passage of time, Reddy Mazimba was beginning to have

confidence in my ability to be left in charge and would occasionally go abroad for short courses or medical treatment. During one
such occasion in early January 1980, I was in charge of the mission
coinciding with having to receive and welcome the Pretoria Three.
These were three comrades who had been political prisoners, men
serving long sentences under the 'Terrorism Act', that had escaped
from the notorious maximum prison in Pretoria. Their well-planned
escape made it possible for them to go past several steel doors before
reaching the outside wall.

The three men, Tim Jenkin, Alex Moumbaris and Stephen Lee
earned themselves great respect for their dramatic escape and were
hailed as heroes across the whole of Africa. No one could ever have
imagined that it was possible to escape from such a well-secured
prison, until they it pulled off. Their escape was a sweet victory
as they gained their freedom, but more importantly, they had also
punctured holes in the myth of the impregnability of the security at
the most secure prison in South Africa.

When they came to Tanzania, in what was no doubt a leap of
honour and an opportunity to meet people of the region, the news
of their escape was all over the media. They were able to link up with
the ANC just after they broke out of prison. They were then helped
to journey through Swaziland, Mozambique, Angola, and Zambia,
where they met President Oliver Tambo, the ANC leadership, and
also addressed members of the media.

They travelled to Tanzania in early January 1980. We received
them at the airport, and then took them to Eli and Violet Weinberg's
home where they were lived for the duration of their stay in Tanzania.

A few days after the arrival of the escapees in Dar es Salaam, I was
summoned to the offices of the Liberation Committee of the OAU
and confronted by an angry Colonel Hashim Mbita who demanded
to know why the ANC brought the comrades to Tanzania without
informing the Government. The escaped prisoners had, for their own
security, been given identity documents and passports under assumed

names. We had sent their new names to the Tanzanian authorities and requested clearance without taking them into confidence and letting them know the real names behind the assumed ones. And so when reports surfaced in the media that the three escapee were in Tanzania, the authorities genuinely denied their presence without realizing that the media reports were in fact correct. Mbita and the Tanzanian authorities were not at all impressed and made it abundantly clear that they had expected us to take them into our confidence and to trust them.

Our office reported to the Department of International Affairs (DIA) headed at the HQ by Comrade Josiah Jele. I am indebted to Jele for his mentoring and patience that gave me a firm foundation and thereby helped in my growth and understanding of international relations. Jele and the HQ office sent me to a number of international conferences organized by the UN and other organizations.

In one such meeting held in Rome under the auspices of the Food and Agricultural Organization (FAO), the SWAPO delegate and I were robbed by five men on our way to the hotel after we'd received our per diem. We offered very little resistance. I had read and heard a lot about the Mafia and immediately thought we were being attacked by the notorious gangsters known to have originated in Italy.

CHAPTER 9

THE AMERICANS
RATHER LATE COURTSHIP OF THE ANC

"The US government ... came to the realization...
that based on the support enjoyed by the ANC inside South Africa,
there was bound to be a change and that one day
the ANC would be in power."
Kingsley Mamabolo

At the height of the cold war, successive American administrations regarded the ANC and other liberation movements as surrogates of the Soviet Union and the socialist bloc. They therefore used the excuse of association with communist countries to justify their continued support for the Apartheid regime. American policy was influenced by the cold war resulting in the branding of the ANC and its leaders as terrorists. They denied the ANC, and by extension, the oppressed people of South Africa, any form of support whatsoever. This was the attitude of America and some European governments despite their vocalized 'criticism' of racial discrimination and Apartheid.

The Nixon Administration based its policy on the infamous National Security Study Memorandum (NSSM) 39 report that was requested by National Security Adviser, Mr. Henry Kissinger. The report concluded that "The whites in South Africa are here to stay and the only way that constructive change can come is through them".

Needless to say, it is difficult to see how the authors of that report came to the conclusion that the racist white minority regime was capable of bringing about any form of change to the racial discrimination that they'd so painstakingly structured and put in place in the first instance.

The ANC for its part maintained that apartheid and racial discrimination is an affront to humanity and violates human rights across board and was totally unacceptable. Human rights violations affect all and should be a concern of all of humanity, regardless of their political or religious affiliations. The ANC was itself a mass movement, a platform for all those fighting against the violation of people's rights, regardless of the inclination of their views towards a particular socio-economic system.

The bankruptcy of the policies of the approach of the US Administration and Western Governments towards the ANC and people of South Africa was perhaps demonstrated by the refusal of people in those countries to embrace these policies perpetuated by their Governments. The ANC and the people of South Africa enjoyed unqualified support from non- governmental organizations, personalities and communities in those countries.

The ANC did not expect preferential treatment from these governments because they were all friends of the Apartheid regime. We came to understand, however, that the US government made an analysis and came to the realization, quite early on, that based on the support enjoyed by the ANC inside South Africa, there was bound to be a change and that one day the ANC would be in power. Based on this analysis, the American government resolved to get close to the ANC and to understand it better. Suddenly our missions in different parts of the world were receiving visits from American missions.

In Dar es Salaam, while standing in for Reddy, I received a call from an official, a Mr. Pound, from the US mission. He expressed a wish to pay us a courtesy visit. We made an appointment, and he came over on a Monday and after our discussion that focused on the situation in South Africa, he extended an invitation to me for dinner at his house. Before accepting Mr. Pound's invitation, I made certain that my comrades knew and that everything was done transparently. At the time, the environment was such that one could not afford to be seen to be associating with the Americans without the knowledge of the comrades.

In an office meeting that was attended by, amongst others, Comrade Mendy Msimang, the most senior member of the office team, we resolved that I should go ahead and accept the invitation.

The objective was to find out what the interest of the Americans was, particularly with their renewed attempts to engage the ANC.

I agreed with Mr. Pound to meet at the Kilimanjaro Hotel, from where I would follow in my car, and he would lead as we drove to his residence. As I drove behind him, I began having doubts about dining with him. I was not sure that the decision we took at the office was the correct one. The comrades expected me to get information from Mr. Pound, but I did not trust that I was properly trained to accomplish such a task. I knew that Mr. Pound had very likely been trained by the Central Intelligence Agency (CIA). He would more than likely be better trained in eliciting information from me than I was from him.

We embarked on the long, winding road bordering the beautiful Palm Beach suburb and the sea on our way to his residence. The evening breeze was cool, ultimately bringing relief to the unrelenting heat that we experienced during the day. His residence was quite a distance and as we drove on the doubt increased and insecurity crept in. The fact that he seemed to be staying so far out of town did not help to calm my nerves.

"Where in the world was he taking me?" I wondered.

I was just about to make a U-turn and abandon the whole mission when suddenly on the side pavement I saw a board with huge, printed letters that read 'Mr. and Mrs. Pound' indicating the location of my host's residence.

He ushered me into his house, apologized that his wife and children were not around to welcome me as they had gone ahead of him to the US for their annual holidays and he was going to follow soon. My eyes were darting to all corners of the house, nervously taking in the surroundings. After settling down in one of his settees, he asked for my preference for a drink. "Scotch on the rocks" I said nonchalantly, giving an impression of sophistication, and a false appearance of calm and relaxation.

He excused himself, went to the backroom to mix the drinks.

As soon as he left the room, my mind was racing, "Why is he mixing the drinks in the other room?" My over- imaginative mind wondered whether there was something else he was adding to the drink, perhaps in the hope that I would loosen up and be off guard.

When he came back my eyes were focused on the drinks, particularly the glass he put in front of me. He had also poured himself some Scotch Whiskey. In my glass, he'd poured a double tot, which was enough to float a duck, and he had also added a couple of ice cubes. As I scrutinized the drink before me, I could have sworn that I noticed some powder lying in my drink at the bottom of my glass, but in my state of mind at the time I could not be certain.

It appeared that everything was done in the backroom. When the sweet melodious slow music meant to create a conducive atmosphere came to an end, he stood up abruptly to replace the cassette with a new one. I had not taken a sip of the whiskey, suspecting that something was lurking in there. I took advantage of his momentary departure to swap the glasses. I took care to place the glasses on the water rings that were created by the cold drinks on the surface of the small table mat and waited.

I observed him carefully as he returned to his seat, looking for any indication that he noticed the changes I made to the arrangement of the glasses. His face revealed nothing; he briefly glanced calmly at the glasses and looked straight at me with a smile. The man was well trained as I had suspected. If I had not scrutinized his face closely, I would have missed that fleeting look when his face expressed shock at the realization that I have changed the glasses. The expression of shock and anger came and disappeared in a split second, then he quickly relaxed and put on a smile.

I sat there momentarily, trying to figure out what might have made him realize that I swapped glasses? I had swapped the glasses flawlessly without leaving traces. What had I missed or done wrong?

I took some time to scrutinize the glasses again and soon realized how my host was able to notice that I swapped them. Looking carefully at the glasses, I noticed that he had put much more ice in my glass than he did in his. The ice had thus created more bubbles that were concentrated on the walls of my glass than in his. I figured that only a trained eye would pick such a difference because generally people would not pay attention to such minute details.

The atmosphere changed; there was an awkward moment of silence despite his quick recovery. I knew that on the inside, he had to be seething with anger, perhaps even struggling to come to terms with the fact that I could suspect that he could be capable of such an act. I was embarrassed. I thought that the man must be thinking very low of me, probably asking himself, "What an amateur? What diplomat would invite a guest only to poison them in one's house?"

I broke the silence and started, "Mr. Pound I..."

"Please call me Phillip" he retorted.

"Phillip, I must confess that, that I have not really felt comfortable so far, and you must have noticed that I eh!... I mean we've got to be honest with each other... you got to admit, this is awkward, it is not an ordinary visit. We, in the ANC, and the people of South Africa in general have always considered your country as a friend to our enemy. So you can well imagine, the question in my mind is, "What is the real motive for inviting me here this evening? What is it that has changed in the USA policy to now accept that it is appropriate to associate with those your government has always regarded as terrorists?"

The honest explanation of my odd behaviour must have melted his heart. He relaxed, gave a hearty smile, and mumbled something about his government's keenness to understand the ANC. The administration in power had recognized the overwhelmingly popular appeal the ANC had among the masses of South Africa.

After this discussion Phillip did his best to make me feel comfortable. With the whiskey flowing and the delicious food, I also began to relax and started chatting a little more freely. When it was time to leave after a pleasant visit in which we had the opportunity to get to know each other and by then we were on first name terms, Phillip commented, "Well Kingsley, I hope you enjoyed yourself. As you can see, I did not try to poison you or anything like that. I hope we can remain friends and hope to meet you again when I come back from my holidays".

It was, I believe, Phillip's way of letting me know that he was aware that I had swapped the glasses. I left his residence and assured him that I did enjoy my visit and his company. Later, I briefed Baba Mendi and other comrades of my dinner with Phillip.

CHAPTER 10

THE FIRST CONTACT
WITH FAMILY IN ELEVEN YEARS

"Family means no one gets left behind or forgotten."
David Ogden Stiers

A Call From Swaziland

One hot morning while I was in our Dar es Salaam office with the Personal Assistant, Comrade Doris, a phone call came through from Swaziland. I would have missed the call If I was not in the office. The phone reception was poor and not knowing my 'nom de guerre' the caller, who identified herself as Ivy, was using my real name.

"Who do you wish to speak to?" Doris asked the caller, clearly straining her ears to hear her. "Jeremiah", came the response from the voice from Swaziland. "Jeremiah who…? Doris asked again. "Mama…" came back the inaudible response. "Mama …what…?" Doris kept repeating as the bad reception prevented her from hearing the pronouncement clearly. Finally, after a long struggle Doris repeated the whole surname to make sure that she had gotten the pronouncement properly, "Is it Mamabolo…?"

Seated across from Doris in the hot room, I was dozing off, but at the mention of my last name, I became fully awake and sat up straight. Doris was about to indicate that she was not aware of a person with such a name, when I interjected, "Who is that?" I asked Doris. "A lady calling from Swaziland, she says her name is Ivy." I quickly grabbed the phone.

Ivy's call brought me such joy. Since I'd left the country eleven years before, there had been no contact with any member of my family.

Throughout the period, I could only visualize members of my family in my dreams and had almost given hope of ever seeing them again.

Despite the poor reception, we cried and talked excitedly on the phone. My sister, Ivy, informed me that the family never gave up hope of making contact. She and her husband, Zweli, having the financial means to do so, had resorted to visiting places such as Swaziland or Botswana regularly, with the hope of either finding me or meeting any of the students from our neighbourhood that left the country around the same time as I did.

In 1976, many students who left the country opted not to inform their families of their intentions. This was for security reasons to avoid risking the arrest of their family members who could have been accused of concealing information from the Apartheid regime. The downfall of this approach was that in most cases families had no idea of the whereabouts of their loved ones. There was no telling whether one was in prison or had, in fact, managed to cross the border into exile. There were rumours that some of the students whose intention had been to go into exile did not, in fact, manage to cross the border. The impression created was that they had been killed by security elements of the regime. This was a source of anxiety among those who were considering fleeing into exile. Their families would dissuade them in an attempt to discourage them from embarking on what they perceived to be a suicide Mission.

Initially we, the group of Tladi Club, had resolved that we would not leave the country. We were determined to stay and stand up to the apartheid regime and fight injustice. However, that position changed when I received a message from a friend, Stanley Thloale, alerting me to the fact that I was very likely to be arrested.

After a march that the students had organized in the Johannesburg

City Centre, Stanley, Michael Moipolayi and many others were arrested when the police broke up the march. They were taken to the Modderbee Correctional Services. A number of us escaped arrest from the prowling uniformed and plain clothes police that were scanning the city in their hundreds by a whisker.

I visited Stanley at the correctional services, but we could not speak freely for fear that the prison guards might be listening in on our conversation. However, Stanley still managed to convey a message that he and others that were being interrogated were shown a statement that was implicating and portraying me as one of the ring leaders of students protests. The statement would, presumably be used in court if and when they laid their hands on me. I knew, beyond the shadow of a doubt that the authorities would have ensured that there were enough coerced witnesses who would attest to my role.

I knew then that my life was in danger. I avoided sleeping at home for fear that they would come pick me up in the middle of the night as was their modus operandum. I stayed with friends and relatives and changed accommodation frequently to avoid routine that could lead to easy detection of my whereabouts. Essentially, I was virtually on the run even within South Africa. I had never been arrested and never tortured and I could not bring myself to imagine the magnitude of torture that was lying in wait for me in the event I got caught. Given the circumstances, a group of us who were pretty much in the same boat, decided to leave South Africa.

Faced with possible arrest, I decided to inform my mom of my intention to go into exile. The family convened a meeting to weigh the consequences of my leaving the country. At the time, with the rumours doing rounds relating to alleged killings of arrested students that were being tortured by the police, it became apparent that the best and safest option available was for me to leave the country.

In our telephone conversation, Ivy had a lot to tell me; the family was fine, mom never really recovered from the loss of one of her sons since my departure. I quietly grieved for my beloved mother. She had lost her husband in the very early years of their marriage and I had added to her grief by leaving the country.

Nonetheless, I was fascinated by what Ivy was relating and the changes she described. There was electricity installed in the township and the family had a telephone the number which she forwarded to me. I had never imagined that we could have electricity in the township. I had had to burn the midnight oil for my studies during my school days. This was a significant development indeed.

Ivy's excursions to the neighbouring states in search of my whereabouts had finally borne fruits. She got the address of our offices in Dar es Salaam from a comrade, and old schoolmate of mine, and had sent me a suitcase full of clothes that she and Zweli had bought and shipped from Swaziland. I was particularly grateful, not just for the clothes, but for the fact that they'd never given up on me. Knowing that they loved and cared for me so much made my fight for a better life even more worthwhile.

I told Ivy that I had been selected to go and study for a two-year course in Moscow and that I would contact the family when I got back. . Unfortunately for Ivy and I, the suitcase of clothes that she sent, was only going to arrive in Tanzania after my departure to Moscow and I was not going to see them for the next two years. I made arrangement for the clothes to be kept, after years I got what remained in the suitcase.

CHAPTER 11

MOSCOW 1980-1982

"May there always be sunshine."
Arkady Ostrovsky

In November 1979, I arrived in Moscow for the two- year course in social sciences. This was at the height of the cold war, and the arms race. Both the United States of America (USA) and the Union of Soviet Socialist Republic (USSR) were spending billions of dollars in a neck-to-neck race to outshine each other in the quest to lead in assembling the most lethal weapons in the world. The two countries had, between them, amassed deadly arsenals that could destroy the world several times over.

The USSR was a solid bloc of countries that were largely in the eastern part of Europe and had allies throughout the world. The USSR and China on the one hand, and the USA and the western countries on the other were sworn rivals competing with each for supremacy. At stake was the battle of the socio-economic systems, capitalism pitted against socialism and communism. It was a struggle to find a system that is fair, equitable and just, and at the service of society.

In Africa, the word socialism became a buzzword. Different countries, such as Tanzania, tried their own versions of the system. The one-party system became the preferred mode of political governance in most of the developing countries.

At international conferences, the developing world clubbed together calling for a new and just economic and social order. The group of developing countries referred to as the non- aligned movement grew in strength. The ANC remained true to the Non-Aligned movement by associating the struggling masses of South Africa with this movement. Within the ANC numerous discussions highlighting the importance of the movement were held. I recall seeing an article entitled "The spirit of Bandung" that appeared in Sechaba, the official magazine of the ANC, giving details of a meeting of Non- Aligned Countries that was convened to reconfirm the principles of Movement.

Globally the situation was tense; the devastation caused by the two world wars was still fresh in the minds of the citizens of the world. The cold war generated a lot of hysteria, paranoia and recrimination from those accused of enforcing a capitalist system responsible for the exploitation of the overwhelming majority of workers to benefit the privileged minority.

The hysteria in America was reflected through the communist witch- hunt of the Edgar Hoover era up to the McCarthyism of the 1950's.

The management of relations between the WARSAW pact and NATO military formations of the east and west was critical and delicate. The idea of a third world war could not even be remotely entertained as its impact would be too ghastly to contemplate. The USA and USSR avoided direct conflict, but engaged in different parts of the world through proxies.

Cuba became the flash point with the US attempt to overthrow the Castro regime through the Bay of Pigs invasion in 1962, resulting in the agreement between Soviet Premier Nikita Krushev and Fidel Castro Ruz to place nuclear weapons on Cuban soil as a deterrence. This precipitated a stand-off of humongous proportions between the Soviet Union and the United States. In fact, it was the closest the two came to a full-scale nuclear war.

Africa and the developing countries were not left unscathed. In the name of the fight against the spreading communist tendencies, America openly supported dictatorships such as Augusto José Ramón Pinochet of Chile. In Africa, Patrice Lumumba was killed with the connivance of Belgium and US secret intelligence agencies. Thomas Sankara of Burkina Faso and many African heroes suffered the same fate for having had the guts to believe in a vision different from that acceptable to imperialist countries.

With both the US and Soviet Union supporting opposing sides, the war in Angola raged for more than twenty-five years, bringing a potentially wealthy country to its knees in poverty. The American administrations were quick to embrace the racist monsters in South Africa and called them friends. It was thanks to the NGOs and the majority of ordinary citizens that brought sanity and a commitment to fight racism wherever it raised its ugly head, that ensured that we continued to enjoy support from that country.

Going to Moscow on the background of such an environment was most appropriate. The Soviet Union and the socialist bloc were leading the call for workers of the world to unite in the struggle against imperialism and colonialism that reverberated all across the globe.

In the midst of all the tension, each side told a different story and all were eager to not be seen as the aggressor. In Moscow, the Russians conveyed their propaganda through art and music and other means. I, personally fell in love with a popular 1961 anti-war Russian folk song written by Yevgeny Yevtushenko entitled; *"XOTRT LU PYCKU BOUNbi" "DO RUSSIANS WANT A WAR"*.

There was also the beautiful children's song written by Lev Oshanin and composed by Arkady Ostrovsky entitled *"May there always be sunshine"* whose lyrics sang in Russian are as follows:

"May there always be sunshine
May there always be blue sky
May there always be mummy
May there always be me…"

In Moscow essentially, I learned that a major contradiction exists in capitalist societies in the process of the creation of wealth. We were taught that the employers and labourers who are in the same space are united and engaged in creating wealth but are differentiated by their relation to the means of production. The employers are the owners of the means of production and therefore have the power to remunerate the workers whose labour is the huge source of the wealth created. Due to the skewed ownership of the means of production, there is consequently, an unfair and uneven distribution of the wealth created. This contradiction leads to a continued conflict between the forces involved in production. The unity and struggle of these opposing forces – the employers and labourers – will eventually lead to an eruption culminating in a new and different socio-economic system when, eventually, a change in the ownership of the means of production occurs.

Another interesting debate focussed on the so-called free market in capitalist societies. Our lecturer, Ms Ludmilla Tarasych reminded us from time to time that in the Marxist-Leninist school of thought, the concept of pure economics does not exist. Marxist-Leninists prefer the use of the term 'Political Economy' instead of Economy. They argue that free market economies operating independently as prescribed in capitalist societies are not feasible. According to this school of thought everything is influenced and has a political bias; the direction that the economy of the country takes depends on the intervention of governments and political parties.

These kinds of debate continue to this day and play out in everyday life in our societies. In South Africa, a perfect example that I can relate to came by way of a position of the Democratic Alliance (DA) presented by the party's prominent leader, Ms Helen Zille. Zille argues forcefully that Government must not regulate and pronounce on the need for a basic salary for workers (e.g. domestic workers). According to her these will be determined naturally by the market (that presumably operates freely, independently and regulates what direction the economy takes).

Logically this will be the position of the DA if it comes to power and when it will have the right to determine the direction that the economy of the country takes. It can also be expected that the ANC and its Tripartite Alliance, including trade unions, (whose political bias is toward alleviating the deplorable conditions of workers and ensuring that no one is left behind) would vehemently oppose Zille's and the DA's inclination.

During my time in Moscow I was honoured to lead a group of about ten disciplined and well-behaved comrades that included Comrade Tony Yengeni, who at the time of writing this book is a senior NEC member of the ANC. For the two years that we were there we held the South African flag high. There were other students from the USA, Canada, Latin America, Scandinavian countries, Asian and sister countries in Africa such as Angola, Senegal, and others.

The camaraderie amongst the students from all over the world at the Moscow School of Social Sciences was strong; we were aware that we had a common struggle and represented the same aspirations. On weekends as we sat leisurely over drinks, we narrated our personal experiences to each other and sang workers' songs such as the one written by Eugene Pottier and translated into English by Charles H. Kerr, that has the following lyrics:

"Arise you prisoners of starvation,
Arise you wretched of the earth...,
For justice thunders condemnation,

It's a better world in birth...
Then comrades come rally!
It is the best world we want
The Internationale unites the human race"

CHAPTER 12

BACK ON AFRICAN SOIL
ZAMBIA AND ZIMBABWE

"To be young, gifted and black".
Nina Simone

Zambia
From Moscow we were flown to Zambia, I joined the Department of Information and Publicity and worked with others for the publication the underground magazine of the ANC called 'Mayibuye'.

The Department of Information and Publicity (DIP) of the ANC, was headed at the time by Comrade Sizakele Sixase and the unit producing Mayibuye reported directly to Comrade Thabo Mbeki. Mayibuye was smuggled clandestinely inside South Africa and was the voice of the ANC giving guidance on events such as workers strikes, bus boycotts etc. I learned a lot from the comrades who were my immediate superiors such as Peter Mayibuye (Joel Nethitshentshe, Comrade Freddie and Mandla Langa – the renowned South Africa author).

With other members of the Department of Information, I stayed at a farm in Makeni. Comrade City (Don Ngubeni) head of Radio Freedom Zambia at the time, became my friend. City is an affable character, with an infectious laughter. He is also knowledgeable and communicates well, having a great ability to reach out to people. I had always thought that City would have made an effective diplomat.

We received no salaries for the work we did, the food and other commodities were rationed, and the cash that we received was just sufficient to buy cigarettes. In hind side I realize that apart from the fact that I genuinely admired City, part of the reason I was hanging around City was his wit and his ability to communicate. In the evenings when we went to the local bar, City's character always worked to our benefit. As soon as we arrived at the bar, many of the hospitable Zambians would call out for him to join their table and would buy beer in anticipation of the stories he would tell. The introvert that I was, it was difficult for me to communicate at the same level, consequently I benefited from being in his company.

City was also an ardent lover of Nina Simone's soulful music and on weekends early in the morning, we would be woken by the beautiful melody coming from his room. My favorite was Nina's version of the song, 'To be young, gifted and black'.

Zimbabwe

One day, Comrade Mbeki summoned me to his office in Lusaka and asked how I would feel if I was sent to Zimbabwe. A year before then, I had received a note from Comrade Sindiso Mfenyane, Administrative Secretary, informing me of the National Executive Committee of the ANC's decision to appoint me to replace Comrade Dan Cindi (Tebogo Mafole) at the Afro Asian Solidarity Conference Head Quarters based in Cairo, where the ANC had a permanent representation.

Mafole had been our representative and it was now time for his replacement. The transfer had been delayed several times because the head of the institution had written to Tambo requesting for the continuation of Mafole's services for a further period. I was frustrated as I had become bored with the routine in Lusaka and needed a change. When Mbeki suggested that I be deployed to Harare I accepted without hesitation.

My services we requested by a Mgwenya comrade, called Mfutshane (Shorty), head of an ANC unit operating in Zimbabwe. Mfutshane's unit was tasked with meeting operatives from South Africa, and preparing them for undercover activities inside the country, before these operatives return back home.

Mfutshane, had visited Zambia to give a report to HQ, and whilst resting in his hotel and watching television, he saw an interview I had with the Zambian Broadcasting Services. The ANC in Zambia had asked two other comrades and myself to go for a television interview on the commemoration of June 16. After listening to the broadcast and after making some inquiries, Mfutshane approached Comrade Thabo Mbeki, and requested that I be released to join in the work that was being done in Zimbabwe.

I was seconded to Zimbabwe in the official capacity as Head of Information and Publicity. I was clandestinely to focus on assisting the underground unit that was preparing people for work inside South Africa.

When I arrived in Zimbabwe, I was introduced to a vivacious lady called Geraldine Fraser who was always busy going somewhere and doing something. She and her husband Raphael (Jabu Moleketi), who joined us later from Zambia were to become family friends. Geraldine and Raphael belonged to Mfutshane's unit and we worked together as I would also meet the same operatives, but focusing on discussing the history of the ANC and other political issues with the operatives.

When I came to Zimbabwe, Geraldine was going through a difficult time. She had witnessed the assassination of Comrade Joe Qhabi, a prominent ANC leader who was killed in cold blood by agents of the Apartheid regime. As if the loss of comrade Joe was not enough, she was also stressed by the fact that Zimbabweans considered her a suspect. She had already been incarcerated and imprisoned for a period in Zimbabwe when the investigations were underway, and then later released without being charged.

Joe Qgabi was a veteran of the struggle, one of the first cadres of the 'Umkhonto We Sizwe' who were sent abroad for military training.

A communist and trade unionist that had selflessly committed his entire life to the liberation of the people of South Africa. Qgabi, who had spent several years in prison, including a ten-year stint at the notorious Robben Island, is also remembered for his influence on the leadership of the June 16 generation in 1976. He and other veterans such as Winnie Madikezela – Mandela were relied upon as points of reference that gave guidance to many a youth leader during the 1976 uprising.

My transfer to Zimbabwe in 1983 marked a huge, but welcome change in my life. Zambia, with the massive ANC community, had become stifling. There were so many of us that we appeared to imposing on the Zambian nation. Zimbabwe offered a few different things. For instance, there were a lot of South Africans resident in Zimbabwe, the majority of whom were not necessarily members of the ANC. Some of them were spouses and others were Zimbabweans of South African origin.

Unlike in Zambia, being a South African in Zimbabwe at that time was not necessarily interpreted as being a refugee or a member of the ANC or the PAC. I enjoyed the fact that I did not stick out like a sore thumb.

With Zimbabwe sharing a border with South Africa, coming to the newly independent country brought me closer home than I had ever been throughout my entire life in exile thus far. To all South African freedom fighters, revolutionary Zimbabwe was the vivid evidence of what prospect freedom held for a liberated country. Zimbabwe was the motivation for the intensification of our own struggle for freedom in South Africa.

Compared to many African countries further north, Zimbabwe and South Africa are much closer to each other and similar in many respects. For instance, both countries are former colonies of the United Kingdom and therefore share a similar history. They also share similarities in culture and languages. Compared to most countries on the continent, the two countries share between them a highly advanced infrastructural development.

Zimbabwe was always green and lush after the rainy season. The good rains augured well for agriculture and tobacco sales were doing well globally. At the time, the country had a thriving economy, posting a post- independence growth with GDP growth averaging 5.5%, with a population growth of about 3% - the highest GDP growth in the entire sub-Saharan Africa.

Zimbabwe was also obviously benefiting from the concerted mushrooming economic campaigns to boycott apartheid South Africa. These campaigns included economic sanctions against South Africa that, due to pressure, led to many companies closing shop in the country. Because of its proximity to South Africa and its relatively superior infrastructure compared to other countries in the region, Zimbabwe provided an alternative for investors. Meanwhile, South Africa and its policies were increasingly attracting the attention and the wrath of the international community.

Zimbabweans were friendly, hospitable and they had just emerged from a bitter-armed struggle to liberate their own country. As a result, they were very accommodating and understood the plight of freedom fighters fighting apartheid discrimination next door.

In 1983 Comrade Judson Diza Kuzwayo was appointed ANC Chief Representative in Zimbabwe. Kuzwayo was a veteran of the struggle. He was imprisoned for ten years at the notorious Robben Island where he served with the ANC leadership including Comrade Jacob Zuma. I was asked to deputize Kuzwayo and also continued as coordinator of the Publicity and Information.

Every revolution produces its best sons and daughters. We all Make our contribution to the best of our ability and according to our state of readiness. Each individual contribution we make adds to the whole, the totality of which determines the success of our revolution. Comrade Judson Diza Khuzwayo was one of those rare breeds in our struggle whose exceptional sacrifices, remarkable bravery and a probing intelligent mind provided critical leadership and guidance.

He made a huge contribution to our liberation and left behind a great legacy.

When Khuzwayo was appointed to become the ANC Chief Representative in Zimbabwe, the organisation was still reeling from a serious blow inflicted by the apartheid regime. Agents of the regime had succeeded in assassinating one of the organisation's renowned leaders and Khuzwayo's predecessor, Comrade Joe Gqabi, who was the ANC Chief Representative, appointed by the organisation to serve in the then newly independent Zimbabwe.

The regime had been relentless in its determination to pursue and kill Gqabi. There was an earlier attempt when in one incident, agents had placed a bomb in the engine of the car. Fortunately that attempt failed when the bomb was discovered before it exploded and caused harm. But unfortunately and eventually armed men waylaid Gqabi as he reversed his car and shot him point blank, killing him instantly.

In the prevailing environment all of us understood very well that just by accepting the appointment to succeed Gqabi, Comrade Khuzwayo demonstrated unimaginable courage. He was probably marked to be the next target and yet he was prepared to tread where cowards dared not.

Comrade Khuzwayo came to Zimbabwe at a point when the morale amongst ANC operatives in Zimbabwe was particularly low. The assassination of Gqabi had instilled fear. Many of us tended to go even more underground for fear of being the next target and so it became difficult to function and carry out the work of the organisation.

By appointing and assigning Khuzwayo to Zimbabwe, President Oliver Tambo and the National Executive were spot on; it was the right decision. Khuzwayo was energetic, full of life and with his incisive mind he made quick decisions on the go and provided insightful leadership. I do not remember that he, even once, referred to the possibility that he was targeted for assassination by the regime. He was about work, about continuing the struggle until the last gasp of his breath if needed.

Immediately after his arrival, He commenced on putting some structure together. Suddenly we had an office from which to operate. The PA at the time was Comrade Joyce Hadebe and other members included comrades June (Wisdom), Flint and I who had the privilege of serving as head of information and Publicity.

I realised that we were being impacted by his leadership when months after his arrival, Zimbabweans organised a rally in Harare to honour June 16 activists' and the ANC participated fully. We mobilised comrades and South Africans living in Zimbabwe to take part in the Rally with flags and a huge banner proudly adorned with the emblem of MK and the printing of 'ANC and Mkhonto we Sizwe' in big bold letters. The comrades holding the banner were competing with our brothers and sisters in the PAC formation, vying to position the banner in a conspicuous space to be captured by the cameras and the media.

The irony of this incident was that as opposed to our situation earlier, before Khuzwayo's arrival where these comrades would have been trying to go deeper into the underground, they were now vying for the attention of the media carrying a visible big banner of the ANC.

Kuzwayo came to Zimbabwe with his family, his beautiful wife Beauty and daughter Fezeka. Beauty, an activist in her own right was involved in promoting arts and culture to expose the atrocities of the apartheid regime: the arts and culture was an ANC form of struggle that featured prominently in the campaign to isolate apartheid.

Beauty and Judson's innocent daughter Fezeka was probably around five years old at the time. She was a pleasant little girl who was always the first to welcome anybody who visited the official residence in Mt. Pleasant where the Kuzwayos stayed. I knew every time I was summoned to the official residence that Fezeka would be the first to peep through the curtains once she heard the gate opening. And after recognising who the visitor was, would shout at the top of her voice, 'Uncle' or 'Aunt', accordingly, depending on who was entering the homestead. To her all the elders who were close associates of her family were referred to trustingly as Uncle or Aunt.

Personally, I am forever indebted to Comrade Judson Diza Kuazwayo for being a mentor. I know that the journey that I have traversed would not have been possible if I had not had the grounding his lessons gave me. He and others laid the foundation: his unwavering commitment to free the people and justice for all is a barometer for all of us remaining behind, to use as a compass to keep check on our activities as well as the social and moral value he projected and enshrined throughout his life.

Tragically, Kuzwayo died in a car accident in 1985 whilst driving to Lusaka, Zambia, for meetings at the headquarters. On the day he died, earlier before his departure, I was visiting Mkhulu and Joyce Hadebe when Kuzwayo came by and found us playing chess. He announced that he had been summoned by HQ and was on his way to Lusaka.

He instructed me to accompany him. Mkhulu interjected and pointed out that Kuzwayo couldn't take his deputy as someone had to hold fort. Both Mkhulu and I recommended that Kuzwayo should travel with comrade Marcus who was returning to Lusaka and who had intended to use public transport.

Midway to the Zambia/Zimbabwe border, tragically, the car rolled, killing Kuzwayo instantly. Unfortunately, he had not buckled up and when the car overturned and rolled, his body was hurled forward through the windscreen, resulting in his throat being sliced by the broken glass. Marcus was held back by the seatbelt and escaped with minor injuries.

At his funeral in Harare, some members of the family were not convinced that his death was an accident, and conspiracy theories abounded. A delegation of relatives and friends had travelled all the way from Kwa Zulu Natal. There were members of the National Executive Committee from the HQ in Lusaka. There were speeches made by, amongst others, Mr Kwenza Mlaba, a practising attorney from KZN, Father Micheal Lepsley an exiled priest who was with us in Zimbabwe and a representative of the NEC. I was asked to give account of how the accident happened.

Beauty Kuzwayo was huddled in the front chairs with a group of women from the women section of ANC, looking dazed. There were comrades on her left, right sides and behind her. A few of them stretching their arms to touch her and to give her a comforting and consoling grip. All the women were wearing black attires and had blankets wrapped around them. Beauty looked tired, she had been crying from the time news of the death of her husband reached her, it was as if she did not have the strength to cry any further. Little Fezeka appeared confused, she was trying hard to understand why everyone including her mom appeared so sad. She kept gazing back with the hope that her dear father would join soon.

Kuzwayo had been a trusted comrade of Jacob Zuma. Zuma himself, recalling the trust and confidence that he and Kuzwayo enjoyed between themselves, made assurances to become this dependable father figure to the family of his friend and comrade. In this context, the news received after South Africa became a democracy that Zuma was accused of raping Fezeka, was to the many who knew and loved the family, absolutely devastating.

Personally, I was saddened when, at the height of the accusations, I happened to run into Beauty, Kuzwayo's wife, and Fezeka at the Oliver Tambo International Airport. I was then South Africa's High Commissioner to the Federal Republic of Nigeria and on my way back to my Mission. Fezeka and her mom were on the run, fleeing the country with the help of sympathizers. They were going back into exile, according to them, because they were fearful of assassinations. She was to die young, at just 41 years old, in 2016.

After Kuzwayo's death, my old mentor that I served with in Tanzania, Reddy Mazimba (Jan Mampane), was appointed to take over as the Head of Mission in Zimbabwe. With me as his deputy, the old Tanzanian leadership was replicated in Zimbabwe. Our appointment as a team by the ANC was affirmation of the confidence the organization had in both of us.

If They Come In The Morning

On 14th June 1985, Mazimba phoned me. Apparently, he had been trying to locate me the whole afternoon and was now trying frantically for the umpteenth time. His call interrupted a dinner I was attending at the invitation of Geraldine and Raphael (Jabu Moleketi). The dinner was at Premi and Jaya Appellraju's residence and the guest was an activist from South Africa. What Reddy informed me over the phone took the wind out of my sails.

He had received secret information from the Zimbabwean Central Intelligence Agency (CIA) that a unit of South African Defense Force, the racist killer machinery that had already conducted numerous operations in the entire southern African Region - killing hundreds of innocent people, was in Zimbabwe and would be attacking ANC houses that night.

The instructions we received from the Zimbabwean security establishment were to avoid a confrontation with agents of the racist regime. We were to alert all our comrades wherever they lived - ANC residencies were spread out in the capital city of Harare - to vacate their residencies so that when the attack occurred the houses would be empty. The objective was to ensure that there were no casualties.

Reflecting on this decision later, I had difficulty in understanding the rationale. Here we were forearmed with information that placed us in a position to embarrass the racist bully. Together with Zimbabwean army units, given the privileged information we had, we were better placed to waylay the invaders, wipe them all out, and teach the regime to respect the territorial integrity of independent neighbouring states. Instead, we chose to allow the racist units to come in and out freely, damage property and retreat safely back to South Africa albeit without fatalities.

I, however understood and appreciated that there may have been many other considerations that the Zimbabwean Government had to make, amongst which was to risk retaliation by an enraged bully that, angered by the killing of its operatives, would have been capable of punishing Zimbabwe in many ways. There was always the possibility that South Africa could stifle Zimbabwe's growth and development through economic sanctions, a consequence that would have led to a crisis in that country and the suffering of innocent Zimbabweans.

Mazimba had instructed that I was to ensure that all comrades vacated the premises and that not a soul was in any of those houses. In retrospect, I have always wondered why we never thought of dividing the labour and ensuring that I had someone assisting. There were so many ANC houses and reaching all of them was not an easy task as not all the houses had telephones installed.

I started off by calling those that I could reach by phone and then together with Noreen, my fiancé, at the time and our daughter Yolanda (Poppy) drove to each house where there were no phones. In each house I gave the following instruction, "The racist forces are going to attack tonight please leave immediately, there is no time to pack or to take any of your belongings. Please ensure that no one remains in the house and leave without delay."

Some of the comrades pleaded with me to transport them to their next location of refuge, a request that I had to turn down; there was just no time to transport people if I was to reach all the ANC houses. Besides, I did not know the exact time of the attack.

I was overwhelmed by a feeling of guilt at Professor Kgositsile's house as I sat behind the steering wheel, watching Baleka Mbete-Kgositsile holding two of her little children by their small hands and carrying the third one on her back, disappear quickly into the darkness down the street. I waited patiently, taking just enough time to ensure that they had left the house before driving off to alert other comrades. I had no idea where they were going to find refuge at that time of the night, but I just could not transport them because there was no time.

With her husband, Professor Willy Kgositsile out of the country on a mission, Mbete-Kgositsile was alone with the children that night. Many years later, she became the speaker of the National Assembly.

As I drove from one house to the other, frantically banging at doors and waking up sleep-drugged comrades, shouting instructions – "Get out of here! go to the neighbours, friends or whoever, no one should sleep in this house tonight! I do not care what you do! Just leave"- it was fast approaching midnight; I was conscious that an attack was imminent and could happen anytime.

Eventually around thirty minutes past midnight and after criss-crossing the streets of Harare, Noreen, Poppy and I stopped at the gate of one of our houses in Santosa suburb of Harare. This was to be the last house that could be attacked and whose occupants had to be alerted of the possible danger. Until then, Noreen and I had been nervous and gripped by fear of the distinct possibilities that we could get caught in an attack as it happened. I kept assuring Noreen, not very convincingly, that we were still okay, "…experience drawn from previous attacks demonstrated that they never attack before 1.00am". Poppy who was eleven years old at the time slept peacefully at the back of the car, oblivious of the unfolding drama.

The house in Santosa stood in a big bushy yard that a whole platoon of soldiers could take refuge in without being conspicuous. At that time of the night, in complete darkness, there was no telling who was lurking in the bushes. I had some inexplicable feeling that they were there hiding in the bush.

Several comrades were staying at the house in Santosa, amongst them Vusi and Girlie Pikoli (Vusi was later to become South Africa's Head of the Prosecuting Authority). Approaching Santosa nervously, I got out of the car, opened the gate, got back into the car and drove into the yard, only to reverse out quickly without knocking on the door to alert the comrades. I repeated this exercise several times, until eventually, I summoned enough courage, drove the car, stopped right in front of the door banged loudly, alerted the comrades and as they were scuttling to find refuge, we left hurriedly.

After alerting all comrades in those ANC houses, at around 1.30am, Noreen and I, with Poppy sleeping soundly at the back seat, headed back to our flat. As we drove back, well after 1.30am, we heard the sound of explosions. There were two distinct explosions, both going off almost simultaneously. We learned the following day that our administrative office in the center of Harare, the capital city, and our residence at Ashdown Park had been bombed, both structures collapsed completely. The residence at Ashdown Park is where Joe Qhabi was assassinated, it was also one of the residences whose occupants I had just alerted of the imminent attack.

I was pleased that I had reached the comrades at Ashdown Park first before the Pretoria killers did. It transpired that when the killers arrived expecting to surprise the comrades, they were taken aback that the house was empty. In their frustration at not being able to claim victims, they resorted to placing explosions in the middle of the lounge of the residence, blowing the entire house to smithereens.

Later in the week, we also received information from Zimbabwe's intelligence that at the Santosa residence where I had, with a lot of hesitancy, alerted the comrades, armed men had taken position, waiting for the signal to attack. Apparently, there was to have been a simultaneous attack on three targets including Santosa. The Zimbabweans reported that the men aborted the attack after being disturbed. It transpired that my actions, driving the car into the yard and pulling out, served as an indication to the commandos that I was aware of the pending attack.

The assassins were startled; the ANC was to have been taken by surprise, so how then did information get to us. Fortunately for me, the yard occupied a huge area and I was not within grasp; If I was, I can only assume that they would have just figured out how to silence me quietly so that their operation was not disrupted. They could also not attack then as I made my appearance as that would not have been in keeping with their strategy and would have been a violation of the order that instructed that all attacks should occur simultaneously.

The onslaught in Harare was part of a coordinated, simultaneous attack the regime had launched in several frontline states. Together with Zimbabwe, Zambia and Botswana were also attacked on the same night. The regime chose the occasion of the visit in the region of the Commonwealth's Eminent Person Group. The Commonwealth was exploring prospects of peaceful resolution of the conflict and an end to apartheid. Staging the attack to coincide with the visit was literally the regime's manner of showing the middle finger to the International Community.

Mhlophe

On 11th May 1987, a bomb hidden in a television exploded killing Tsitsi Chiliza, born Marechera, a Zimbabwean national and wife of our comrade Mhlophe Chiliza (Vusumuzi Masondo).

Mhlophe had joined us in Zimbabwe just before the explosion occurred, having been transferred from our Mission in Mozambique. Mhlophe was married to Tsitsi and they had two beautiful little daughters. His transfer to Zimbabwe was a humane consideration, enabling him to be with his family.

Immediately after his transfer, our Mission received an invitation to send a delegate to represent the ANC Zimbabwe at a funeral of comrade Gibson Ncube who had died from poisoning by agents of the regime in Mozambique. We decided to delegate Mhlope Chiliza because he'd known the comrade personally and going back to Mozambique would afford him the opportunity to wind up, and complete his transfer to Zimbabwe.

In Mozambique, Mhlophe was gifted with a television by some one posing as the uncle of my friend Victor. They had apparently come from South Africa to attend the funeral.

Once we had received the necessary documents for the clearance, Mhlophe installed the TV in the bedroom of his flat. But it appeared

134

that due to some technical problems the TV could not function. Both Mhlophe and Tsitsi kept fiddling with it in the hope that it would function. Eventually they got some fuzzy sound with no pictures. According to Mhlophe, the situation of the TV was particularly frustrating to Tsitsi who had gotten into the habit of constantly fiddling with it every opportunity she had.

On the fateful afternoon, Tsitsi returned from work, went past the eastern half of the house, where her two children were in the sitting room with a family member, proceeded to, and locked herself in the bedroom to change her clothes. Once in the room she tried again to see if the TV would function. This time around the TV exploded, ripping off the roof and demolishing the western side of the house. The explosion ripped Tsitsi to pieces; she died instantly. Luckily, the explosion affected the one part of the flat and left intact the east wing where the children were playing games.

Noreen and I were at our flat that is about 10 km from Mhlophe's when we heard the explosion. "It's an explosion," I cried out. We rushed out into our car and started driving. We could not tell where the explosion occurred, but were determined to find out. Fortunately, as we edged out of the yard onto the street, there were already emergency cars with sirens moving at great speed in the direction of Mhlophe's Flat. We simply followed them and ended up at Mhlophe's place.

We found a dazed Mhlophe with his two girls by his side. The scene was a hype of activity with the emergency officials and detectives scanning the place. Sadly, in the little backyard, there were some men and women officials with black plastic bags picking up whatever remains of Tsitsi that were spread around; it was a gruesome death.

Experts explained that a bomb with a time delay mechanism was embedded in the TV. With each passing day and with the fiddling by Mhlophe and Tsitsi, the trigger mechanism was getting activated. We could only deduce that the purpose of the delay was meant to confuse and hide the identity of the perpetrator.

Having brought the TV into Zimbabwe, Mhlophe became the prime suspect, and was immediately arrested and held in jail. Mhlophe was not allowed any visits and after I persisted in my negotiations with the authorities, I was eventually allowed to visit him. I was shocked at the state in which I found him. He had not bathed in the one week since he was arrested. Fortunately, I had brought along soap, toothpaste, a toothbrush and a change of clothes. The ANC was furious with the treatment that Mhlophe was receiving from the Zimbabwean authorities. The trauma he and his children were subjected to was unimaginable.

The ANC was able to trace the origin of the bomb to the gentleman who brought the TV to Mozambique, Mr. Leslie Lesia, who later confessed to have been an agent of the regime, and was responsible for gifting the booby- trapped TV. When ANC operatives got in touch with him inside the country, he was not aware that people were linking him to the bomb. He was easily lured to leave South Africa after being told that the ANC leadership in Lusaka was ready to meet him.

He was excited and immediately agreed to leave the country via Mozambique. He'd been trying for a long time, without success, to get introduced to the high- ranking leadership in Lusaka. He was transported to Lusaka where he was arrested and eventually brought to Zimbabwe to face charges.

Joan and Jeremy Brickhill

On the 13 October 1987, a car bomb explosion nearly killed comrades Joan and Jeremy Brickhill. I was at the office that was 6km away when the bomb exploded at the Avondale shopping center. Joan and Jeremy were a young married couple. Jeremy, a Zimbabwean national and Joan, a South African were members of ZAPU and ANC respectively.

At the time, as a coordinator of the ANC publicity and information, I worked closely with Joan who was working at the Zimbabwean

Broadcasting Cooperation (ZBC). Through Joan we were able to have a lot of ANC leadership interviewed and to organize other programs.

We used the ZBC as a platform to promote anti-apartheid programs.

As a young couple, Joan and Jeremy got into a routine every morning. They would take their two children to school and then before going their separate ways for the day, they would take some time to have breakfast at the Avondale shopping center. Their movements were monitored and accordingly waylaid with a perfect plan that was meant to eliminate them.

On the day of the explosion, the couple followed routine and parked their car at the usual spot, then entered the restaurant to have their breakfast. After breakfast they returned to their car, entered and were about to drive away when a huge explosion ensued. It was not their car that exploded, but the one next to theirs. The car parked next to theirs was loaded with explosives that had a mix of shrapnel meant to cause maximum damage.

The explosive was remotely controlled, there was therefore someone at distance watching their every move and targeting their arrival. The killer had waited for them to get inside their car before exploding the bomb. Apparently, the intention was to explode the bomb in the car next to theirs with the hope that the shrapnel would kill them instantly, and if that did not happen, their car would catch fire due to the explosion and they would die trapped inside their car.

Our offices, the new ones we got after the demolition of our old ones at the city centre, were not far from the Avondale shopping Mall. With the sound of the huge explosion, I jumped into my car and rushed to the shopping centre. I arrived in time to see Joan and Jeremy being taken away by a good Samaritan who had offered to take them in his van (*bakkie* as they are known in South Africa). I rushed straight away to the hospital. There was a case of mistaken identity as they had been incorrectly identified as the perpetrators. It transpired that the agents of the regime had chosen a car exactly like the one they were attacking. When I saw the situation I explained it to the officers and resolved the misunderstanding. I really had thought that they had died and I was hugely relieved to find that, although unconscious, they were both still alive.

The scene that met my eyes will stay with me forever. Jeremy appeared to be the hardest hit. I took a glance at him and immediately concluded that he would not make it. It is truly a miracle, that many moons later I was to meet a Jeremy that is not only alive but appeared to be as strong as an ox, It defied all odds.

Joan was also badly hit; she was fortunate that a shrapnel missed slitting her throat by inches. When I arrived and saw them in the ambulance, Joan became conscious briefly and on seeing me there tried to say something, but she was inaudible, and fell back into unconsciousness. They were both really traumatized by this incident. to this day Joan does not feel comfortable in areas that are closed in, such as house-lifts.

Joan and Jeremy survived because the killers' plot did not go according to plan. The killers expected that both cars would catch fire, but Joan and Jeremy's car did not. What saved both of them, is that Jeremy had just filled the petrol tank to capacity. The car was filled to the brim and did not allow room for air to circulate. For a combustion (fire) to occur there has to be oxygen. Simply by filling up the tank with gas, Jeremy had unknowingly, saved both their lives.

*   *   *

Life in exile was a roller-coaster of emotions. Amidst the ongoing war with agents of the regime life appeared normal; comrades got married, children were born, we buried our dead (many of whom were killed by the regime) and so accordingly we had weddings and birthday parties and attended funerals. Comrades prayed in their churches on Sundays and others got together for a drink or a game of soccer, scrabble or chess.

However, the reality was different and life was not normal as it should have been. We lived in constant fear of assassinations, and our presence constituted a danger for the communities we lived in. Many of our neighbours were killed in Zimbabwe, Mozambique, Swaziland, Lesotho, and other countries in the region.

One Saturday afternoon, I got home to find that the tenants of a block of flats where I was residing in Harare had convened an emergency meeting. I learned later from one close friend that the meeting was convened at the instigation of one of the residents and that the discussion was about a possible petition to the owner complaining about the danger of living in the same space with me considering that I was targeted by the Apartheid regime.

They were rightfully pointing out that their lives were threatened by the very fact of my living amongst them.

The threat was real, the regime's executioners had been busy. After all, in Zimbabwe they killed comrade Mhlophe's wife with a bomb hidden in a television set, almost killed comrades Joan and Jeremy Brickhill by a remotely detonated bomb and launched a frontal coordinated attack on two of the ANC's properties – a residential house in Ashdown Park and the offices in the centre of Harare city.

In Maseru, Lesotho, and Matola in Mozambique, they massacred dozens of ANC refugees. These events and many others had driven fear into the hearts of local Zimbabweans, Mozambicans, Botswanans and citizens of all the frontline states.

Life for black people living in Apartheid South Africa was also unpalatable. Thousands died of hunger, disease and many more died in prisons. Many others were exiled and many were butchered by the apartheid's killing machinery for daring to stand up and speak out against the injustice.

The international community declared the apartheid system a crime against humanity. The regime and all the perpetrators of all these atrocities should have been liable for prosecution by the

International Criminal Court (ICC) for their violation of human rights. The negotiations for a democratic South Africa led by Mandela and De Klerk meant that space needed to be created. This essentially meant that the ICC should not rush to arrest the perpetrators, but allow the mechanisms established by South Africans to deal with the issue of the violation of human rights. South Africa opted to deal with the crimes that were perpetrated through the Truth and Reconciliation Commission.

*   *   *

In August of 1987, Noreen and I decided to take our relationship to a higher level and got married. She was pregnant, and we were expecting our son. Because we did not have enough funds we planned the wedding way ahead, collecting hard liquor bit by bit throughout the year. Our friends from the diplomatic corps and others also contributed whatever they could. The wedding date was set, but before we could go ahead, we had to ask for permission from the national security agency. An event of this nature was considered risky as it had the potential of attracting agents of the regime.

The big day arrived, the women's section of the ANC were most helpful. They cooked up a storm and some even brought food. Jabu Moleketi and Vusi Pikoli were the best men. My sister Ivy bought me a beautiful dark suit from South Africa and to my joy and delight, arranged for my Mom and Aunt Annah to come to Harare. With the money that we had banked for more than a year, we were able to buy a lovely lace wedding dress for Noreen so as a bride she looked absolutely beautiful.

The Zimbabwean Government not only gave permission for the event, they also sent two truckloads of police to guard the hall where we held the wedding reception. To ensure that no bomb found its way through, people were made to open the presents at the door before handing them over.

Unlike myself, Noreen was not an exiled member of the ANC. She was born in South Africa and in later years her family relocated to Zimbabwe. She knew that marrying me entailed risks and despite being cautioned by some of her family members, she stuck to the decision to get married to me. That kind of commitment made me love her even more. She has been my partner for more than 37 years at the time of writing this book and we have four wonderful children who have also shared in the journey that we have traversed.

Mozambique

Immediately after the birth of our son, Mahlatsi Sam, the ANC decided to send me to Mozambique to represent the organisation. I was excited as this was indeed a promotion. In both Tanzania and Zimbabwe I had deputized, but this was going to be the first time I was given the responsibility to head an ANC mission, as Chief Representative. All the mentoring and working under dynamic leaders had prepared me adequately so I knew I was up to the responsibility.

Being newlyweds, we decided to go to Mozambique as a family, so Noreen, Poppy and Hlatsi joined me. This proved to be a mistake since moving around with such a big family that included a baby of several months proved to be difficult and put us under a lot of pressure.

After our arrival in Maputo, we were nervous and did not feel safe in the allocated residence of the ANC. We saw the opening on the balcony of our fourth floor apartment as a weak link in the security and argued that this could be the entry point for agents of the regime. We did not feel safe to sleep at the official residence. We resorted to changing our accommodation every night, moving around the city to wherever we found accommodation. It became evident that it was not sustainable to move around with such a big family.

Ultimately security was reinforced, grilles for doors and windows including the open area of the balcony were installed. Armed security was provided to guard the apartment by our security team headed by comrade Iscor (Abbey Chikane).

I was also provided with a small hand pistol that I kept on the inside pocket of my jacket as I moved around. These measures gave us a little comfort and some assurance.

However these measures did not completely do away with our security concerns. When one day, Iscor informed me that HQ (Lusaka) had told them that they had, through their means, uncovered the regime's plot to kidnap and take me back to South Africa, our anxiety began all over again.

The torturous process entailed finding a parking place for the car that I drove, and this was not because of shortage of space, but having to ensure that the car was not accessible to those who would want to plant explosives under the cover of darkness in the night whilst we were sleeping.

In Maputo, most of the parking spaces are situated in the basement of the flats/apartments. Noreen and I would drive around every evening, checking in the rear-view mirror that we were not followed, in and out of these parking lots for an open space to leave our car for the night. In this manner, we managed to park the car at a different location every day. Sometimes I would park at somebody's allocated space and the following morning when I fetched the car, I would receive a note placed on my window by an angry tenant.

In 1984, Mozambique and South African racist regime signed what became known as the Nkomati Accord. South Africa had, through its murderous attacks on Mozambique and by supporting the rebel anti- Government terrorist group called RENAMO (Mozambique National Resistance Movement), managed to coerce the Mozambican government into toning down its support for the ANC. RENAMO, led by Alfonso Dhlakama, had imposed a reign of terror on the people of that country. The operational methods used by RENAMO included a campaign of slicing off people's limbs such as noses and ears, off their faces. The reign of terror, coupled with economic sanctions that starved

Mozambicans pushed the government of Samora Machel to sign an accord designed to restrict the activities of the ANC.

One the demands in the Nkomati Accord, was that Comrade Jacob Zuma should leave Mozambique. The regime's perception was that Zuma was providing leadership to underground activities inside South Africa using Mozambique as a base. The ANC was forced to find a replacement for Zuma, and so comrades Simon Chabalala (nicknamed FAPLA- Mkhonto) and Sidney Seate were appointed respectively before I was sent to take over. Both comrades served for brief periods until I took over in 1988.

The ANC was keen to portray those that came after Zuma as diplomats who had nothing to do with the military and underground activities. I was therefore expected to do diplomatic work and to attend public events, such as receptions and to address meetings on topical issues about the struggle in South Africa. This presented a problem because the visibility expected of a diplomat meant one could be an easy target as agents would not have problems in establishing one's whereabouts. I remember complaining to Mathews Phosa who was in the underground structures, that they probably had a better chance of survival than I had. They were operating underground and were therefore difficult to locate, whereas I was expected to be a public figure of the organization.

The Apartheid regime did not buy the story that I was just a diplomat and made this fact known. They had done their research and knew of my military training in Angola and the GDR. Three days after my arrival, Richmond Ramotse, a comrade I had worked with in the Department of Information and Publicity (DIP) in Lusaka showed me an article that appeared in a South African newspaper. The article reported that the ANC had appointed a new Chief Representative in Mozambique. It was stated that the new man was Kingsley Xuma and added that he was also known as Jeremiah Mamabolo, an indication that they had all the information they required.

Concerning the demand that the ANC Representative should have nothing to do with the underground, the reality was that it was difficult to separate the two completely. It was important for the Representative to be in the know of activities occurring in Mozambique including underground activities.

The ANC had learned from experience; a short while before my arrival, a group of youngsters destined for operations inside South Africa were arrested by

Mozambican authorities. Through an act of indiscipline, they had veered away from their hideout and were unfortunately accosted by Mozambican police.

The Mozambican authorities wanted to verify if indeed these youngsters were ANC members as they had claimed. They approached my predecessor, the Representative at the time, comrade FAPLA-Mkhonto. He was, unfortunately, not briefed by the underground structures and therefore did not know of the presence of these youngsters. He rejected their claim and consequently they were arrested and not treated well by authorities.

From this incident, it became imperative to ensure that an ANC Representative responsible for public and diplomatic affairs was adequately briefed whenever ANC operatives were passing through Mozambique.

The excitement I had about coming to Mozambique was short-lived. Maputo is about 505 miles from the South African border, one was literary within arm's reach of the vicious killer agents of the regime.

Within a short time of our getting there, it became clear that our stay in Mozambique was not going to be a comfortable one. The country was itself in the grip of a terrorizing insurgency led by the rebel movement, RENAMO. The Resistance Movement used horrifying methods to terrorize the ordinary folks, and many were caught in the middle of an onslaught that claimed thousands of lives. The people were traumatized; their government had for security reasons placed restrictions on movements of diplomats, international agencies and non- governmental organizations to operate within a restricted area that is within a certain radius around the city of Maputo.

Armed agents of the apartheid regime had also turned Maputo into their hunting ground where they were in and out killing innocent people. Shortly before my arrival, an attack was planned on our office. A truckload of agents of the regime arrived at the office in the early hours of the morning presumably to plant a bomb and destroy the building with its contents.

The ANC in Mozambique had taken a decision to guard the office and armed comrades took turns. On the day of the attack, comrade Richmond Ramotse, armed with a Russian made Kalashnikov (AK-47,) was guarding the premises. At around 2.30 am, with the office in darkness, he heard some clanking on the door as the agents tried to open the locked door.

Richmond grabbed the gun and without hesitation began firing, there was pandemonium as the agents retreated to safety, got into their car and drove off. It transpired that they had poor intelligence, and were not expecting anybody there. They were, therefore, taken completely by surprise when Richmond opened fire. Unfortunately, Richmond pointed his gun up. Bullets were found lodged on the upper side of the frame of the door and consequently there were no casualties. He was criticized by some comrades for this, because had he fired straight through the door, there would have been a lot of casualties in the passage. Richmond defended himself by saying that he did not know for certain that the intruders were agents of the regime.

*   *   *

We were welcomed to Maputo by Tom and Thandi Moyane, who became great friends of the family and have been ever since. We had a little community that looked after each other. There was Rob Davies and his family, Albie Sachs, Indris Naidoo, Alpheus and Nadja Mangezi, Mom Elma, Tom and Thandi and many others.

Albie Sachs

On the 7th April 1988, a Mozambican holiday to honour women, Albie Sachs was nearly killed by a car bomb. He had parked his car outside the block of flats where he lived. Albie's apartment was on the same street as the official residence of the Chief Representative.

On that day, as the lazy day unfolded, the jovial mood of the people increased as they went about their business. Many like Albie were headed for the beach, some were engaging in various sporting activities, chattering and laughing. The fishermen and women were returning from the sea with their catch and fresh fish was available for sale. The sun was becoming increasingly hot with each passing hour.

It was a bright sunny day and Albie woke up late and was preparing to go to the beach. Attired suitably for the beach, with a towel hanging over his shoulders he approached his parked car, and stretched his hand to open the door.

I had woken up, having slept in the early hours of the morning. Tom and Thandi had visited us the previous night and we stayed late after enjoying a bottle of wine and grilled chicken. That morning, after waking up at around 10 am, I tried to clear my head and therefore decided to go out to inhale the fresh morning air. I had just stood on the balcony, leaned on the rails, and turned nonchalantly to face the direction of Albie's apartment, when the bomb went off.

There was a shattering sound followed by a plume of smoke with flickering flames billowing into the sky. I also saw the tyre of a car shooting straight up in the air like a jet. Although we were on the same street, Albie's apartment was not quite visible from where I was standing. I knew a bomb had gone off even though I could not tell who the victim was. I quickly changed my clothes and rushed in the direction of the smoke and got there just in time to see Albie being whisked off to the hospital by an ambulance.

A time delayed bomb had been planted in his car the night before. The opening of the car triggered the bomb, set to explode a few minutes after the trigger, but allowing for sufficient time that was calculated to be the amount of time he would take to get into the car and be seated when it went off. Albie got to the car and opened the door, but just before he could enter, a friend passing by waved at him and Albie returned the greeting.

The greetings that ensued resulted in Albie taking a few more moments before entering his car. When the bomb exploded, Albie was not inside the car, but still outside with one hand holding the handle and the other waving, the explosion ripped off his whole arm. Had it not been for the time spent in exchanging greetings with his friend, Albie would have died. Instead, he escaped with only his arm ripped off.

Security was tight at the Maputo hospital where Albie was recovering because there was always a possibility that those who were trying to eliminate him could still pursue him. A comrade very close to Albie was the only one allowed to bring him food and no other visitors were allowed. Being the head of the Mission, I was eventually allowed to visit him. On my first visit, Albie had not yet regained consciousness. When I visited again, Albie was awake, I found him in high spirits, joking with those who attended to him.

As I sat on the chair next to his bed, I was at a loss, and had no words good enough to console a comrade who had experienced such trauma. Albie, who was in a jocular mood, was quick to make me relax. He informed me that when he regained consciousness and saw the nurses and the pure white sheets, he was of the impression that he had arrived in heaven. I chuckled.

I, however, burst into laughter when he described that when he realized that something had happened to him, he used his remaining hand, moved it slowly down his body to feel if his private parts were still intact. He was relieved to find everything in order. "…they can take away any other limb, but they were not going to deny me my manhood," he quipped.

I left the hospital in good spirits, since it was clear to me that Albie had accepted his fate and knew that this was not the time to give an impression of a dejected, demoralized and defeated cadre. He chose to portray an image of a true revolutionary who never gives in and consequently allow the enemy even an ounce of victory.

Albie Sachs became a prominent judge of the constitutional court in the democratic South Africa. He was part of a team put together by President Oliver Tambo, to draft what was later to be the basis of the democratic South African constitution. The South African constitution is today heralded as one of the best in the world.

Albie also had the opportunity to face one of the perpetrators of the crime committed against him at Truth Reconciliation Committee (TRC) that was set up to heal the wounds caused by Apartheid South Africa. Applying for amnesty in the TRC, Mr. Henri van Der Westhuizen claimed that Albie was not the intended target, and that comrade Indress Naidoo was. Responding to a question, van Der Westhuizen had this to say,

"There was a stage when each and every ANC member who moved in Mozambique was placed on the potential list, but with regard to this specific incident, according to my knowledge, Mr. Indress Naidoo was the target."

Indress Naidoo was an activist who committed his entire life to the fight against Apartheid. He served 10 years, between 1963 and 1973, in Robben Island for sabotage. He was exiled in 1977 and served the ANC in Mozambique, Lusaka, and the GDR. In 1994, after the ANC won the general election, Naidoo was appointed to the Senate and served in Parliament until 1999. In 2014, Naidoo was awarded the Order of Mendi in Silver for bravery.

After one nerve-racking year in Mozambique, I was informed by

HQ to prepare to go to Cuba where I was to represent the organization. I received the news with a lot of excitement as we were tired of having to constantly look over our shoulders. The threat of an assassination by agents of the regime was always lurking somewhere nearby.

Cuba, we imagined, would provide the much-needed rest and security. I was also excited about the prospect of succeeding legends of our struggle such as Alex Laguma and others who had been representatives of the ANC on the Island before me.

At the time, Cuba was in the throes of a dilapidating economic stranglehold imposed by the USA that had been put in place since February 1962. After the battle of the Bay of Pigs that resulted in the missile crisis of October 1962, the Americans were hell-bent on punishing Cuba by imposing severe economic sanctions. The intention was to bring the country to its knees. The effects of the sanctions brought about extreme poverty that was visible and palpable.

The dissolution of the Soviet Union exacerbated the difficult socio-economic conditions in Cuba. The country's key imports and exports that were heavily tied to the Soviet Union, collapsed. Cuba's trade with the eastern bloc that was the lifeline of economic growth in the country ground to a halt. As a consequence, there were shortages of everything ranging from food, clothes to oil and other essential commodities. The Cubans referred to this period as: 'periodo especial en tiempo de paz' ('Special period in peaceful times').

The resilience and perseverance of the people of the tiny island is amazing. They stood up to the pressure of a cruel and punishing economic blockade from the most powerful country in the world. They found ways of surviving through creative alternatives, and graciously shared the very little they had. In contrast to the rest of the world, they have made huge strides in gender equality, provision of free health care and free education.

After his release Nelson Mandela visited Cuba accompanied by his wife at the time, Winnie Mandela. There were throngs of peoples in the streets who came to welcome them. On 25th July 1991, Mandela and Fidel Castro addressed a huge crowd in the city of Matanzas. In honouring the Cuban support to Africa Mandela said the following,

> *"The Cuban people hold a special place in the hearts of the people of Africa. The Cuban Internationalists have contributed to African independence, freedom, and justice, unparalleled for its principled and selfless character. From its earliest day, the Cuban revolution has itself been a source of inspiration to all freedom loving peoples…"*

Being in Cuba representing the ANC, I was in a position to appreciate the extent of the support the ANC and the people of South Africa had received through the years. The Cubans trained our people in various areas. For instance, many South African students were educated at the *"Isla de la Juventud" (Island of Youth)* and other centres of excellence throughout the country. My own family benefited when my second daughter, Maloyela Dinah Mamabolo, was born there. We were introduced to the exemplary medical facilities provided by the Cuban government.

In Cuba, staying healthy is considered a national responsibility. Despite the serious economic shortfall, health resources are made available to the community and are free. Primary care is local and comprehensive in that a physician and a nurse live and work in each community and care for about 1800 families. With the scarcest of resources, the Cuban Government has been able to build a health culture that benefits its people and to extend international support to those who need it most.

Whilst in Cuba, we renewed contacts with Tom and Thandi, our friends in Maputo and learnt that they had been invaded by the agents of the regime. According to Tom, armed men scaled onto their balcony, using ropes, and descended from the top of the roof of their building. Their apartment was on the 17th floor and there were five more apartments to the top of the roof.

Alerted by strange noises, Tom quickly grabbed his AK47 and waited ready to surprise the intruders. On the first sighting of an individual on the passageway leading to their door, he opened fire. Taken by surprise the men scuttled back and retreated, abandoning their colleague who had already landed on the balcony. The intruder was caught by Tom's fire which pushed him back and threw him down to land with a thud on the floor. The man was pronounced dead by Mozambican authorities who rushed to the scene after being alerted.

CHAPTER 13

HOME BITTERSWEET HOME

"With the power in people's hands good
and sometimes bad things happened."
Kingsley Mamabolo

In 1991 when negotiations for a democratic South Africa ensued inside the country, I returned home from Cuba.

South Africa had been through a vicious mass struggle of the eighties that had pushed the country to the negotiating table. During this period, the people had taken matters into their own hands, the country had been rendered ungovernable and the regime had lost control. The communities were governed by the street committees that were created and mushroomed during the struggle. With the power in people's hands good and sometimes bad things happened. On the one hand the people used the power they had to weed out collaborators of the regime embedded in the communities, on the other, mistakes were committed. The story of my cousin, David Nhlapo, is illustrative.

On the Sunday of the week I arrived, I was reading a Sunday Newspaper, The City Press, when I came across a full length story of what befell David who I had not seen since I left the country in 1976. Two youngsters of a family that lived on the same street where David and his wife lived disappeared and were missing. A wide ranging search was conducted as fear gripped the community that increasingly was beginning to anticipate the worst.

A neighbour dragged the teary family to a local witchdoctor for consultations. After throwing his bones the doctor gave a prognosis of the whereabouts of the children and according him, 'The children were kidnapped by a man with a big stomach who lives in the south of where the family resided'. No one bothered to interrogate the vagueness of this prognosis; there was no measurement of the distance given to guide the search and logic would dictate that if one cast eyes to the south without limit, inevitably one will come across 'a man with a big stomach', particularly in South Africa that is facing serious obesity challenges.

Poor David, who was running a successful butcher shop in the community, was not only unfortunate to have his residence on the South of the home of the missing children, but also happened to have a big tummy. The comrades of the Street Committee fetched David and his wife and interrogated them, then put the tyres of a car around each one of them, brought petrol in a container and threatened to burn them. They took both of them to their butcher as they rummaged his meat storage, pushing aside carcasses and throwing some on the floor with the hope of finding the children there.

Their lives were saved by a regional leader with ANC connections who suggested that David and his wife must not be killed as the whereabouts of the children will not be known. David told me much later that they were paraded down the streets, moving from one house to the next. In one of those houses, the owner took pity and put a bottle of whiskey in front of David to calm his nerves. He finished the entire bottle, got so drunk that nothing mattered any longer. In his drunken stupor he feared no one and resorted to bravely hurling insults at his captors. Eventually after much ado, the missing children turned up. They had just forgotten to inform their parents that they would be visiting family outside their area. On realizing how close they were to committing a serious injustice, the community was so enraged that the family of the children who were missing was forced to flee and relocate elsewhere.

The Mamabolos
On 13 August 2005, my wife, Noreen, and I decided that my 50th birthday party should be a small family affair to which outsiders were not invited. The birthday party was going to be the first event we held to bring the family together since returning to South Africa. Our house in Pretoria East was big and could easily have accommodated a bigger crowd, but I knew that Noreen, being a very private person, would not be too comfortable with a large crowd and a lot of noise.

This was also to be an opportunity for our children, Yolanda (Popi), Mahlatsi, Maloyela (Loyi) and Tawanda (Tawi) to mingle with their cousins who would accompany their parents to the event. My siblings, Buti (Isaac), Ivy (Dineo) and Ashley, were amongst the invitees, and they came with their immediate families. Ivy came to the party intending to narrate the history of the family. It began with the interesting account of how, as a newly wedded couple, my mom and dad worked together to ensure the survival of the family

Incidentally, our parents had reached an agreement immediately after their marriage. They had decided to invest in their future. Their agreement was that Dad would complete his studies as a lawyer and Mom would in the meantime be the sole breadwinner of the family.

Unfortunately for Mom and the family, we did not benefit much from this investment because my dad died early at the age of forty-five, leaving behind a family struggling to cope with the new realities of having to live without the cushion of the income he'd provided. My widowed mother found herself with the responsibility of looking after a family of four children. We were blessed that notwithstanding her hardships, she lived up to the age of seventy-two years.

Buti and Ivy who were old enough to understand what was happening, narrate always the story of the vicissitudes of life endured by the family, particularly during the period when Dad was out studying at Wits University in Johannesburg.

As the sole breadwinner, our Mom worked and looked after the family. Every morning before going to her place of employment, she left us in the care of friends and family members. Ivy, barely a teenager herself, was heaped with the responsibility of assuming the role of a mother to look after me, the baby of the family at the time.

Some of the friends and family members meant to take care of us were not very nice people and did not treat us well at all. Ivy relates this story with emotion, her narration is interspersed with comments like, "Ooh! How I wish Ma and Dad were still alive, Stranger (that is what everybody calls me back in South Africa), so that they could witness what a man you have become.

I was born on the 13th day of August 1955; in Vanderbijlpark, Vereeniging. I am the third born child of Percy Mamabolo and his wife, Dinah Maloyela Mamabolo. We lived in a South Africa where from birth the colour of the skin defined one's place in society. As Africans we constituted the downtrodden majority, victims of a crude and ruthless white minority rule that discriminated and treated us as third-class citizens. When I was one year old, our family moved to Sophia Town for a brief period and ultimately settled in Soweto.

I was born into what could be considered an African middle-class family, by township standards. My father was a lawyer so his income was therefore relatively better than most black people around who did not have the privilege of getting a sound education like he did. Due to this, our lifestyle was marginally better than most of our neighbours. Our family at least owned a family car, a maroon Zephyr, as they were in fashion then.

As a black lawyer, my father was restricted to defending only Africans, as it was not permissible for blacks to prosecute or defend whites just as we were prohibited from sitting on park benches designated 'whites only' in places of rest or entertainment.

My father was a short and humorous man, who also possessed an explosive temper if provoked, and he was known to brook no nonsense. All of us in the house knew very well that it was not advisable to upset him. He would rarely punish us though punishment was always a corporal one and on the rare occasion that he did, it was usually very severe.

For any wrongdoing and when mom failed to control us, she would just simply resort to threatening that she was going to report our behavior to Dad. That strategy worked all the time, and mom would immediately get a positive response from us. We would suddenly be eager to demonstrate our readiness to comply and to follow her instructions, whilst at the same time pleading desperately that she should not report our indiscretion to dad.

His temper notwithstanding, my father strove to give his kids a good upbringing. The Mamabolo kids were known in the vicinity for their discipline, education, and good manners. My dad was indeed a strict disciplinarian. The result was that our family earned respect and its place in the community; the family was highly regarded and the neighbours would, on seeing my siblings and I, often make comments like:

"Look at them, these are the Mamabolo kids, can't you see, with their big heads, just like their father's, those big heads are carrying big intelligent brains."

The author, with his wife, Noreen.

The author, with his wife Noreen and their two sons, Mahlatsi and Tawanda, at the a Graduation of Tawanda, their last born, in New York.

The author with his elder brother Isaac, his sister Ivy and his younger brother, Ashely.

The author's wife, Noreen, with their second daughter Maloyela (Loyi).

Yolanda (Popi), the author's eldest daughter, getting married to James Mazhandu, with Loyi as the flower girl.

Omry Makgoale (Mhlongo), a childhood friend *(above left)*. The author with his assistant Mr. Cage Banseka, in the desert city of Nouakchot, Mauritania *(above right)*.

Childhood friends of the author, members of the Tladi Youth Club, *(below, left to right)* Stanley, Moses, Paul, Molebatsi, Kingsley and Jappie.

At the United Nations, as Chairperson of the G77 plus China, speaking on behalf of the group *(above)*.

With President Thabo Mbeki in a mediation session between the Government of Sudan and the fighting armed forces *(right)*.

With President Jacob Zuma *(right)*.

With the President of South Sudan, Mr. Salvar Kirr Mayadirt *(right)*.

With the President of the
Republic of Zimbabwe,
Robert Mugabe, at the
Bulawayo Trade Fair 1995.

Signing a joint declaration
of cessation of hostilities
between the FNL armed
group and the Government
of Burundi - 2008.

With Prime Minister
of Sudan, Abdalla
Hamdok, an old friend.

The author and his wife, Noreen, being awarded Honorary Chieftainship in East Nigeria *(above)*.

Representing UNAMID, briefing Dr Nkosazana Dlamini Zuma, Chairperson of the AU *(right)*.

Victims of apartheid, Michael Lepsley, Albie Sachs, with George Monyamengena (rearground) and the author *(below right)*.

With Nelson Mandela and Alfred Nzo in Harare, Zimbabwe *(above)*.

In Berlin, celebrating the Berlin Agreement, with fighting armed group of Darfur and the Government of Sudan *(left)*.

At a bazaar organized by women in the UNAMID Camp in El Fashir (Darfur) - 2018 *(left)*.

As High Commissioner to the Court of St. James, welcoming President Ramaphosa and Ministers - November 2022 *(above)*.

With Pope Benedict XVI *(right)*.

With the Deputy Secretary General of the UN, Ms. Amina Mohammed, and the Secretary General's advisor and compatriot Mr. Fink Hayson, in El Fashir, Darfur - 2019 *(below right)*.

The author presents his credentials to King Charles, who confirms him as High Commissioner Kingsley Mamabolo - November 2022.

In November 2024, following in the footsteps of his compatriot Nelson Mandela thirty years earlier as he is awarded the Freedom of the City of London and granted privileges in recognition of his contributions to business and society.

When in a good mood dad had a loud and hearty laughter; he would tell jokes and then join in on the laughter until tears rolled down his cheeks. He and his friend, our neighbour Mr. Makgoka, Philly's dad, called each other 'Hommie' (homeboy) as they both came from Pietersburg (renamed Polokwane in the new democratic South Africa). They would stay up until very late hours on weekends talking loudly and laughing at jokes they cracked between themselves.

We were not allowed to sit in on their conversation most of the times, and when we were fortunate enough to do so and got to hear some of the jokes, we were enthralled. The discussions of the two men left an indelible imprint on our minds. Long after, we would cherish and talk about what we overheard and repeat the jokes amongst ourselves.

I recall this one story dad told Mr. Makgoka. He narrated how he caught a pick-pocketer on a crowded SOWETO - City Center-bound commuter train. My father explained that the train was packed to capacity, and the passengers were shoving and almost crushing each other and there was hardly any room to move. Dad suddenly felt a hand in his pocket. He looked around at the faces of all the people hard-pressed against him, but he still could not tell whose hand it was from the faces staring blankly at him.

His only resort was to clutch his pocket and squeeze very hard almost crushing the foreign hand in his pocket. It soon became evident who the culprit was. Dad looked back and saw a young man grimacing in pain not far away from where he was standing.

My father was a good narrator and told many humorous stories, so I did everything then, just to be able to gain a seat at the conversation table, listen attentively whilst pretending not to pay attention. Some of the exciting narrations I remember were the blow-by-blow account of the boxing matches that Dad, an ardent boxing fan, would give Mr. Makgoka after watching a match. We had great boxers then; there were legends such the great Joe "Axe Killer" Ngidi, Enoch "the School boy" Nhlapo,

Levy "the Golden boy" Madi, Anthony "Blue Jaguar" Morodi, Norman "Pangaman" Sekgapane, Elijah "Tap Tap" Makhatini and others.

We grew up calling Dad 'Maide'. I literally thought that was his real name, and it was not until I was in my teens that I got to understand how the name came about. Apparently, this version of my dad's name was Buti and Ivy's interpretation of my mom's loving reference to our father as 'My dear.'

Despite his occasional temper, 'Maide' was a loving father who dreamed of a bright future for his family. He strove in many ways to augment the family's income. He clearly did not have an entrepreneur's business acumen, and therefore, some of the projects he contemplated demonstrated some impulsiveness, irrationality and lacked proper research and planning.

One hot summer holiday, 'Maide' bought a Mercedes Benz van, stacked it with watermelons and chose a strategic spot near the railway station for my Mom and the family to sell the watermelons. This gave the appearance of a good plan; it was, however, not well conceived.

There was no provision made for the melons that could not sell immediately, no refrigerators or cool storage. As result a lot of melons went to waste due to the heat and had to be thrown away.

In the early seventies, our next door neighbour of many years moved to some other location. Many families could not hold on to the houses due to lack of finances and the inability to pay rent.

The new neighbours who arrived happened to have the same surname, Mamabolo, as well. Maide was very excited and sought more information relating to the background of the newly-arrived family. Which clan of the Mamabolo were they and which part of Pietersburg did the family come from, etc. After gathering enough information and establishing the links, the newcomers were immediately declared part of our family.

"This is family," my mom was told. The one consequence of this newfound relation was that the men in the families decided that the middle-wired fence that separated the two household was no longer required. We were henceforth going to live together as one big happy Mamabolo family.

Tearing down the fence was also prompted by business interest. The two families quickly resolved to plough the land surrounding the houses, now increased a little by the removal of the middle wire, to make a field and grow peanuts. The heads of the household naturally reached this kind of decision; the women and the rest of us had very little input or were not consulted at all. We were just simply informed of this apparent ground- breaking decision that, it was anticipated, would change our lives for the better.

The decision had two unintended consequences; firstly, the same surname did not necessarily imply that the families got on well. The chemistry between the ladies of the household was not very good and the fact that there was no middle separating fence made it worse. The families were too much into each other's space with little room to manoeuvre. As can be expected in the difficult struggle to survive against poverty, sharing the meagre sources was bound to create some conflict. Removing the middle fence also infringed on the privacy of both families.

The houses in SOWETO are almost on top of each other, so rather than tearing down the boundaries most families tend to be protective of the little space allocated for their privacy. Many families – those a little better off than their neighbours – would often be heard boasting that they were able to nip the menace of the pestering neighbours in the bud and this they did by building huge separating walls – which they referred to as 'stop nonsense'. It came as no surprise, therefore, that after my father's death and burial, my mother immediately moved quickly to restore the wired fence delimiting the boundary.

Despite these little irritants, we got on very well with the other Mamabolo family and I became great friends with the two sons, Mmemeti and Bethuel.

157

The second unintended consequence was that Maide bought bags full of nuts that were to be planted as arranged. These bags were put just outside the door leading to our house. I learned later that nuts are a delicacy for mice, and indeed, before the groundnuts could be planted, a host of mice from the neighbourhood came daily to feast. Considering that there were a lot of hiding places in our own house, so in own wisdom the mice saw it fit to set up residence in our home to be nearer the source of the abundant food supply. The mice were a menace; my phobia for rats did not help my state of mind as we battled frantically to get rid of the new threat.

*   *   *

My childhood was, despite the prevailing circumstances, a relatively happy one.

In the sixties, crime in South Africa was not rampant and people did not live in as much fear as they do today. The children played 'hide and seek' until very late hours on summer evenings with our parents relaxing and chatting with the neighbours, sipping tea or the traditional homemade sorghum beer, doors wide open in the cool breeze.

It is in those 'hide and seek' games that young boys and girls approaching puberty discovered changes in themselves that began to differentiate them from boys to men and girls to women.

We giggled childishly and excitedly amongst ourselves as we conspired and made deliberate choices of which girls to partner with in the hiding places. Naturally, the girl partner chosen would have evoked 'this deep, confusing feelings'. In most cases, the girls chosen would go along and pretend that they were not aware of the conspiracy, secretly wishing and cherishing that moment alone with the boy partner of their choice, to steal a passing kiss in the darkness of the hiding places. Sometimes partnering would be a perfect match, when the boy and the girl desired to be together in the hiding places;

although there were times when the matching was not according to the desire of the one partner, in most cases, the girl.

Nothing serious ever happened beyond the shy stolen pecks on the cheeks. It was mostly just puppy love and the excitement we experienced was but just a figment of our imagination. While giggling and gibbering afterwards we would describe, with a great measure of exaggeration, our perception of what really happened in the hiding places. It is uncanny that even at such a tender age, the characters of individuals began to come to the fore. In relating their exploits in the hiding places some would tell blatant lies and boast about their non-existent achievements. The liars were mostly exposed and denounced by the girls. The stakes were high; those who could charm the girls were envied by all.

In our teenage years, we became conscious of how we dressed, the type of clothes we wore and where they were bought as that made a statement.

American brand names such as John Craig, Stetson, Crocket and Jones became household names. Having a girlfriend was like winning some trophy, somehow it distinguished the men from the boys. Those boys who were hesitant, those not yet hooked up and perhaps fearful of declaring their love to the opposite sex were frowned upon, mocked, made fun of, and called 'Izishumane' (Zulu for scared of girls).

The 14th April proved to be a bad omen for the family as for two consecutive years bad luck befell us. On the 14th April 1967, my family was attacked by a group of marauding thugs, wielding sticks, and other dangerous weapons. These men who attacked us were migrants from neighbouring Lesotho, notoriously nicknamed the Russians. On the same date the following year in 1968 my father died.

These events were taking place at the height of the cold war between the east and western countries. The fact that the notorious migrants from Lesotho were known as 'Russians' spoke volumes of the mindset of people and the effect of the western propaganda machinery against socialism and the rising new order of the Soviets that was in fierce competition with western capitalist social order.

South Africa was not absolved from the global contest, and was forced to choose sides. The regime did so by spinning pro-western propaganda against communism worldwide to include justification of its continued unjust racial policies. Its own propaganda machinery spread scary messages of the hellish consequences that would be the fate of all if the struggle against the Soviet Union and China were lost. The Russians and communist China were used as a scarecrow. Ordinary folks who protested against racist laws were branded and labelled agents of communism.

The blanket-clad 'Russians' from neighbouring Lesotho did their bit to traumatize and terrorize the community in SOWETO. Clad in winter blankets wrapped around their bodies in their traditional manner, they constituted themselves into various groupings that served different purposes. They were vigilante groups, during daytime some administered a form of discipline in the community and oversaw traditional courts that meted out 'justice' and punished 'defaulters'. The punishment constituted many lashes on those unfortunate enough to be convicted.

Like the Mafia in olden days America, these men, with their dubious methods ran a parallel justice system in the community and were presumably in partnership with the authorities in ensuring the rule of law. They were in fact a reign of terror, terrorizing and traumatizing the community. These men were giving the proud Basotho nation that is found in both South Africa and neighbouring Lesotho a very bad name.

It was a known fact that some of these men who administered justice during the day would at night move in groups to join the hordes of criminals who robbed and killed innocent men and women for their possessions. These are the same men who robbed my family on the night of the 14th of April 1967.

Cases of domestic violence were mostly reported to the 'Kangaroo' courts hastily set up by the 'Russians.' Invariably the judgment favoured those who came forward first to make a complain. In most cases the accused would be presumed guilty even before they were charged, and would then be faced with the difficult task of having to prove their innocence.

When our family fell victim to an attack by the 'Russians' it appeared that they had inside information and knew that Maide would come home with a lot of money. Pursuing his business interest that hopefully would bring extra needed income for the family, Maide had on him huge amounts of money with the intention of buying a new truck. They were waiting and waylaid him where he usually parked the family car.

He had just hired a driver, another Lesotho national. Maide's cases were spread throughout the country, particularly in the then Orange Free State. He needed a driver to enable him to rest as he travelled from one town to the next. He was always preparing for his next case and would be up studying and writing notes into the early hours of the morning.

On the 14th of April, arriving home after his long trip, Maide and the driver pulled the car to park at our usual spot when the mob attacked.

The 'Russians' emerged from their hiding places, they grabbed Maide by his shirt; the driver made a bolt for it, but was pursued by two of the men who struck him with a stick several times on his head. There was blood all over his shirt, but somehow, he still managed to outrun them and disappeared into the dark. They came across the money in my father's possession, but were still not satisfied – they wanted more.

Maide directed them to the house where Mom, who was already awoken by the commotion outside, was forced to open the door. Pushing and shoving, a group of about twenty-five to thirty men entered the house. They were not orderly, and it appeared as if they all wanted to come through the narrow door all at the same time.

Buti and I shared the same bed in the one bedroom and were fast asleep and oblivious of the commotion until these marauding vandals crashed into our bedroom. We had just enough time to half-lift our upper bodies from the bed as the men entered the room. We froze in the same position- almost half sitting up, supported by our elbows - and did not even twitch for the entire period of their presence in our room. We both lay still, we dared not move, scared even to make the slightest of sound, I was holding my breath, as if just the sound of our breathing would annoy these evil people into causing us bodily harm.

At some point, one of the men sauntered in our direction, stared at Buti and myself with the curiosity of an agile cat toying with the hapless body of its captive rat just before devouring it. I could hardly breathe as he stood by the edge of our bed contemplating what to do next. I even stopped praying, thinking the end had come.

I knew that it will only take a couple of blows to our heads with his big, rounded knob-stick to snuff the life out of each one of us.

He stood there for a while staring at us, then apparently, he made a decision and quickly collected all the newspapers that he could lay his hands on. He formed them into a little mountain just below the edges of the hanging blanket and set them alight. The intention was clear, he was going to burn us alive.

Scared even to twitch a muscle, we remained in the same position even as the fire began picking momentum. We were fortunate that one of the men saw what his colleague was doing and being sensible enough, stepped towards the bed, reprimanded his friend, scattered the accumulated papers, and put out the fire. Buti and I breathed a sigh of relief.

After this incident, the men ignored us and went about their work as if we did not exist, they operated fast, grabbing clothes from the rails, collecting items such as the sewing machine and whatever they could carry. We noticed that they did not even have time to bend and pick up any item that fell to the ground. As such, most of our possessions were gathered on the trail they left behind as they left in a hurry. They left with the same kind of commotion that saw them invade our house, exiting the door as if afraid that the last to leave would be captured and be held accountable for the heinous acts of the rest of them. The men left hastily; they were never apprehended even though the story of the robbery was published by the local media.

*   *   *

The long hours of preparation that my father always put in before a case paid off; he was clearly a brilliant lawyer who won most of his cases. During our school holidays, Maide took my brother Buti and I along to accompany him as he travelled to defend cases in various places. As a girl, Ivy was always left behind to help mom with chores at home and Ashley was then still a baby.

I was about seven, eight years and Buti was a teenager when we undertook these journeys with dad. By then I did not have an appreciation of the impact of my dad's successes of the cases he won, but slowly this grew on us as communities where the cases were won would throw a party where speeches and praises of my father were made. Most his cases were considered then in apartheid South Africa to be of a political nature. It was mostly cases of white farmers accusing black workers of theft of cattle or sheep or other things and so such cases appeared to be addressing some form of injustice.

In one event vivid in my memory, a group of boys mostly about Buti's age and a few of them much older, passed the car and one of them shouted "Kaffir" (A derogative swear word the racist whites used to insult blacks in South Africa. It has the same impact as the N word in the USA, literally it means non-believer). Buti opened the window of the car a little and retorted "Rooi tomatie" (similarly, a derogative word blacks would use to insult whites, it is Afrikaans for red tomato)

163

My Mother, Dinah Maloyela Mamabolo

My father, Percy Mamabolo

The boys turned back towards us, we had to quickly ensure that all the doors were locked, and windows closed. They were fuming, with some of them in their anger with visible red and green veins in their bulging eyes. They looked like they were going to rip the car apart to get to us and moved around the car as if looking for a loophole that would allow them entry into the car.

One of them was shouting on top of his voice "Die blicksem se kaffir" (Another expletive). They were angry, they were full of hate and there was no doubt what their intention was, if they could pull the car apart, they were going to rip us apart limb by limb given the chance.

At the tender age that I was, all this was too much for me, I had never been so rattled before in my life, my 'bilirubin' shot up and was very high. There were only the windows of the car separating us from this enraged mob. Finding myself in the prevailing situation, I did the only thing left for me to do in the circumstance and that was to cry.

I was barely fourteen years old when the situation took yet another unfortunate turn. On the 14th of April 1968, my father died of a stroke. The day before he died, a good Samaritan who recognized him immediately found him in his parked car on the side of the road, paralyzed on one side and unable to move. He had lost his speech and was unable to communicate.

As he was driven into our yard, we all came out to receive him; he could only stare at us unable to utter a word. Maide was later admitted at the Intensive Care Unit at the Baragwaneth Hospital near SOWETO where he remained unconscious until he passed on.

At his funeral, Ivy and I cried uncontrollably. Buti, already a teenager was much stronger and better emotionally controlled than all of us. He had pulled Ashley by his side and got him to promise not to cry in public. Ashley was only eight years at the time and tried very hard to keep his promise to his older brother.

The death of my father robbed us, at a very early age, of a father figure that would have undoubtedly played an inspiring role in our upbringing. He was strict, a disciplinarian, but his employment of tough love would have, I believe, contributed to moulding and preparing us to face the rigours of a complex and difficult life.

There's no telling if there was a connection between my father's stroke of the 14th of April 1968 and the robbery of the 14th of April 1967.

After his death, the family status in the community dropped from middle-income African class citizens to lower income earning citizens. After some effort, my Mom secured a job as a typist at the school board whose offices were situated in the compound of the Tau-Pedi High school. The meagre salary she received condemned the family to an uphill struggle of trying to make ends meet. Nonetheless, even though the situation was tough, my mother was determined to educate all her children.

Our lifestyle changed so much that on some days it was difficult to put food on the table. Nonetheless, Mom improvised a lot just so that we could go to sleep on a full stomach. Sometimes when we lacked supplies, she would take a stroll into the bush and come back with some foliage which she would cook after persuading us that it was 'wild bush spinach'. In my view, she became an icon of culinary creativity and ingenuity.

My Mom, a very pretty lady, particularly from her youthful years, judging from her pictures when she was a teenager, bore the brunt of the hardship of single- handedly raising the family with dignity. Her husband died at early age, and as I later learnt from Buti and Ivy there were always men at different stages, some with lots of cash, who fancied themselves as possible suitors that could fill the gap. She turned them down and chose to struggle in raising her children and focusing on our getting an education.

Just before he was incapacitated, sometime before he died, my father wrote a letter addressed to my mom, where he made a plea "please ensure that my children are educated". She had to navigate the fortunes of the family through trying times by herself, while worrying at all times where the next meal was going to come from.

My siblings and I are truly indebted to her; the selfless contributions and sacrifice she made speak volumes of her character, of the type of person she was. We are all agreed that if God had sent some of his angels to this earth, to assimilate and be amongst people on earth, then our Mom was definitely one of them. She was elegant, a soft-spoken lady, very considerate and extremely kind. The eloquence she had was amazing considering that she had received little education. But then again, I realized that whatever education she received those yesteryears, perceived to be lower - she belonged to the generation of what was called 'Royal English Education'- was comparatively way superior to the 'Bantu Education' that we were receiving.

I was always taken aback at the quality of books she read and recommended for me to read. One of the books I am grateful that she recommended is a book written by Baroness Orczy entitled 'The Scarlet Pimpernel'. Years later I also read the sequel to the book, 'The Elusive Pimpernel'.

The books were made even sweeter to read because our hero of the struggle, Nelson Mandela, was often likened to Sir Percy Blakeney, the main character of Orczy's book. Just like Sir Blakeney, Mandela, at the height of his exploits, used disguises to evade arrest. Consequently, Mandela was nicknamed 'The Black Pimpernel'.

My mom was a religious, woman of faith. Consequently our family went through the normal routine required for acceptance in any Christian community. We had to be baptized at a certain stage, receive holy communion, and go through the religious rituals that puts a Christian family in good standing. For instance, the custom in any Christian community is that babies are baptized, but I was not. Nonetheless, I got baptized when I was a teenager. It was never explained why I missed out on being baptized earlier. According to rules of our church, a teenager can only be baptized only if they are grounded in religious and Christian teachings. I was, therefore, required to attend scripture lessons.

For a whole year from 2pm to 5pm on Sundays we attended classes. This coincided with my football matches, and I was hard-pressed to forgive my Mom for that. At the time, I was the captain of the street team that plied its skills on the dusty streets of SOWETO, but later on we graduated to playing for the local team, Wings United. And therefore missing matches to attend scripture lessons cost me a great deal.

My Mom never forgot the trouble she had every Sunday; she would recall how I disappeared when it was time to go for the scripture lessons and reappeared, dusty from rolling in the sand, in the afternoon just when it was about time for those who went for lessons to come back, innocently asking a question; "Mom, is it time to go for classes?"

This situation was worsened by the fact that after baptism I was also obliged to attend another whole year of classes, this time to qualify to receive communion.

I have fond memories of my Mom during my childhood. I recall how she made time for all of us, my siblings and I. My bonding time with her was particularly special at the end of every month. One of my duties was to accompany her to the grocery store.

Every month, when going to the store and back, we had time to discuss life. She would ask questions like, "Stranger, what would you want to be when you grow up?"

We are a close-knit family and our parents taught us to love one another. Long after they passed on, we continue, to this day, the close bond and looking out for each other, becoming one another's keeper, caring for each other and providing a protective shield in difficult times.

Buti

My brother Buti initiated me into politics, despite himself being apolitical at the time. When Buti was gainfully employed, one of the first things he bought was a battery-operated radio; there was no electricity then. Buti was very strict such that no one could touch the radio in his absence. We would all wait patiently for his return to be tuned in.

One day, as Buti was tuning in aimlessly and scouting the band waves, he came across the Zimbabwe African National Union Patriotic Front (ZANU PF) broadcasting station which was broadcasting from Mozambique. The program was preceded by a sign-tune with the sound of heavy guns being fired in the background. An announcer with a heavy voice, introduced the program with the following words "People of Zimbabwe, your commitment, your fight, your struggle will break the chains of slavery". Although the radio station talked to the situation in Zimbabwe, the similarities with our own was so strong, I could immediately identify and knew that this is what I wanted to pursue, the fight for my own freedom in South Africa.

Every night when Buti came back from work, at around 9pm when we could get the signal from Mozambique, we would listen quietly and comment in hush tones as the propaganda from the Zimbabwean revolutionary organization came through. The broadcast was mostly about reports of attacks carried out by the Zimbabwe National Liberation Army (ZANLA) on outposts of the Rhodesian army.

The broadcast was of great inspiration and made me realise that there were people ready to stand up and fight white oppression. The powerful sign-tune and the rich baritone voice meant to entice Zimbabweans to join the struggle for freedom won my heart as well.

Many years later when I was stationed in Zimbabwe, I was to know and got on very well with the announcer of the ZANU PF broadcasting services. His name is Webster Shamu, who became a prominent politician in independent Zimbabwe.

Shamu's voice and the message got my attention immediately, and I knew I wanted to hear more so every night I would wait patiently for Buti to come back from work and to tune in.

I also remember Buti's fervent belief that he would one day win the jackpot and become an instant millionaire. The Sunday Times jackpot was of the type that asked for a solution, and then provided several possible responses that were very similar to choose from. One had to fill all the slots pairing the words to match the solution provided by the newspaper the following weekend. It appeared simple at face value, particularly when one or two million was dangled as a price for matching the answers provided by the newspaper.

Every Sunday Buti would give us money and we ran around buying Sunday Times from all the media outlets in the vicinity, sometimes collecting as many as a fifty. The Sunday newspaper was quite bulky, incorporating a lot of adverts, and so the result was that we would be literally swamped in newsprint. Our task was to cut out the piece of paper where the jackpot is printed, fill in the choice words provided and reconfigure each jackpot differently from the others. However, no matter how hard we tried, we just could not get it right, the big prize was elusive. Despite the disappointment, every week we would somehow get motivation to try again.

Buti and I also liked music and very often we would be huddled in his brown car that had a radio, listening to our favorite songs. New Year's Eve was very special, and each year leading to midnight, there was a program on the radio called Top Forty that played all the favourite songs of the year. We would sit the whole evening debating which song would get the revered spot as the best of the year.

Ivy

Ivy, the queen of the family and the only girl among my siblings, was very pretty, considerate, and greatly concerned with taking care of all of us. At some stage, Mom was selling ladies hats to try and augment the income of the family. Some of her friends would take the hats on credit and refuse to pay in the time they committed to make the payment. Ivy took it upon herself to go and embarrass these defaulters, shout at them and demand that they pay the money they owed.

Bra Pule, the ruthless township bully, showed interest in Ivy. This news had the family in panic mode. I had never felt so helpless in my life, the mere mention of Pule sent shivers down the spine of many. We all knew that the worst thing that could happen to any girl was for Pule to force an affair. That girl was going to be enslaved because thugs like Pule were abusive to women as a way of getting what they wanted. I was much younger than Pule and besides, he was renowned for his ruthlessness. There was therefore not much I could do to protect my sister if Pule went ahead with his ambitions. We were lucky that fate intervened; Pule committed some crime and was jailed for a long time saving us the trouble of having to deal with him.

Ashley

Ashley is the last born of the family, and he relied on me as his big brother to defend him from bullies much older than him. Mosanku, a boy in our neighbourhood who was older than Ashley, had been bullying him. I took it upon myself to go beat up Mosanku, and he, in turn, reported me to his sister, Nnuku. This set up a scene for a confrontation with Nnuku

Nnuku was fierce and always stood up for her younger brother. She was not like an ordinary girl; she had a reputation for fighting and winning against boys. Her secret was simple, in a fight she would withstand all the blows and just dive to grab the private parts and not let go until the opponent was screaming with pain on top of his voice.

One afternoon, Nnuku challenged me to a fight for beating her brother. I accepted because my ego would not allow me to chicken out. I was not going to let a girl get the impression that I was scared. We went to the nearest bush, with our supporters and were just squaring up, when an elder came running with a belt, scattered the fight and reported us to our parents. After the beating we both got from our respective parents, Nnuku and I never challenged each other again. I have no idea who would have emerged victorious had we gone ahead and fought.

CHAPTER 14

OLIBAME LINGASHONE

"Let Not The Sun Set On You!"
~ Zulu Proverb

In the sixties, SOWETO (the South Western Township) did not have flushing toilets; we used the bucket system instead. The essential services of collecting the smelly sludge for little salaries and benefits were provided by men recruited from the rural areas of South Africa, the majority of whom were from Kwa-Zulu Natal (KZN) and the Eastern cape. The new arrivals were also recruited from the neighbouring states such as Botswana, Eswatini, Lesotho, Mozambique, Zimbabwe, some as far as Malawi.

The men whose energy defied all logic, would, jut in-and- out of our tiny yards in the townships, collect the waste that was lodged at the make-shift toilets in our backyards and with the buckets balanced precariously on the shoulders, ran out of the yards, to catch up with the constantly slow-moving trucks and deposit the contents.

They executed their job with great exuberance and perfection, displaying remarkable strength and energy. They worked every day, missing only when they fell ill or were somehow incapacitated. Their task was heavy, backbreaking, and they were always inhaling the toxic fumes. The task at hand required them to be fit and to have lots of stamina, and they did not fail. Despite all this, they went about their duties every day, seemingly happy, laughing and singing.

Given the opportunity, many of these men would have undoubtedly made good award-winning athletes at the Olympics.

Naturally expectations would have been that the residents of SOWETO would have embraced these men, been proud of them and grateful too, considering that they were making life easier by removing the unpleasant foul- smelling waste. This was not the case. In fact, we looked down upon these men, and made them the subject of crude township jokes. We feared and hated them, called them derogatorily, in the township language, 'abo tshotsha ama bakete' (shit collectors). We considered them as 'outsiders' and didn't reach out to accommodate them.

The men were accommodated in the 'men-only' hostels that were located within the shantytowns we lived in, whilst within the townships the hostels were secluded somehow ensuring that the residents were not integrated in the community. These hostels were set up by the regime to accommodate hundreds of these single men that were pouring in from the rural areas, looking for employment.

The hostel dwellers were lured by the prospect of making a quick buck in the fast-paced city of gold, (Johannesburg). They were young men in their thousands that had left behind their families and the serene village life in the rural areas, hoping to make a fortune in the far- flung city. All they did though was eke a living that barely sustained them.

Since the discovery of gold there had been a steady stream of new recruits arriving in from other parts of the country and the neighbouring states. The booming gold industry required and depended on the cheap labour that was provided by the recruits. For decades, the mine bosses and the government of the day guaranteed an uninterrupted flow of labour.

A coordinated strategy was deployed that, on the one hand, ensured that the black farm owners in the rural areas were stripped and forcefully dispossessed of their land and made to be desperately in need of a source of income. And on the other hand, the mine bosses were at hand to recruit these 'previously land owning and now landless' individuals and to provide them with transportation and facilities to work in the cities where gold was mined. From land owners they we forcefully transformed to become wage earners for their survival

The ANC Aptly described what was happening in many of its official documentation as a situation where Africans were being turned into "hewers of wood and drawers of water" in their own land.

A recruiting agency whose job was to recruit young black men in South Africa and in the neighbouring countries, was established. The Witwatersrand Native Labour Association (WNLA) was then popularly called WENELA by the recruits. This agency was set up to recruit young men to work in the mines in the city of Gold. In these strange places where they were ultimately settled, the men lived on their own and were always suspicious and distrustful of anybody that was not part of them, while the surrounding community equally held them in disdain.

The system encouraged and exploited the differences between the men and the communities that were suddenly forced to host them, deliberately cemented hostilities and used the divide and rule strategy to its benefit. The hostilities between the communities were considered a safeguard measure that was always available to the regime to use whenever it wanted to destabilize the community. Instigating one group against the other created some respite for the authorities as focus shifted from genuine grievances against apartheid rule when fighting flared up within the community.

The hostel dwellers, particularly the newly arrived, found it difficult to settle in the strange and hostile environment. Their fear of the city folks, that in any case, considered them inferior and backward was very often justified. The sleek, nefarious, and notorious characters within the community, such as the hardened criminals and gang members, were quick to take advantage of the confusion overwhelming the hostel dweller. The fanciful, fast pace of life in the cities made it difficult to cope with. Their awkward adjustment in the cities made them vulnerable to the 'vultures.'

Year after year, the hostel dwellers, and the community coexisted, but lived fearful and distrustful of each other. There was always the silent, undeclared and never-ending war between the two. The children of the township copying from their parents, teased hostelers and called them names at every given opportunity. The poisoned environment often led to violent clashes that sometimes resulted in dire consequences.

For their own safety and security, the men were accustomed to moving through the township in large groups. They would be armed with what people called 'cultural weapons', these were sticks with knobs at one end that they used for protection.

It was always a spectacle when they moved from one point to the other. It was colourful when they 'strutted- their stuff' through the streets of SOWETO, their traditional gear which consisted of a combination of animal skins, feathers, seashells and beads was mystical to say the least. They would sing traditional songs and move in unison down the streets. They were something to behold if truth be told.

As part of the Nguni culture, from childhood, men and women pierce their ears to create small round holes. A cork/stopper is then inserted in each hole forcing a gradual expansion over the years. Proportional to the increasing size of the hole, an even bigger cork then replaces the smaller one over time, thus extending the hole and making it bigger. Eventually an adult male or female will be able to display a hole that is covered by a big round stopper that occupies a place in the middle, surrounded by a thin layer of the skin of the ear. Sometimes the big cork in the middle of the hole gives the impression of a clock or a miniature wheel of a car with a rim. The children of the township found this profoundly interesting and teased the hostel dwellers over this traditional ritual.

One day during the month of April 1966, when I was ten years old, I stood in our family's tiny yard in SOWETO. I saw an old

Zulu man pass by on the street just outside our gate riding his bike. I yelled out, mischievously teasing the old man.

'Sithini isikhathe endlebeni baba?' ('What is the time on your ears, old man?')

In his anger the old man replied, *"Oli bambe lingashone mfana wame!"* ('Pray, Let Not The Sun Set On You my boy'.)

With that sentence alone, the enraged old man conveyed a clear response to my tease, and anybody who cared to listen was in no doubt of the old man's intent. His message was a curse akin to the ayatollah's *'fatwa'* on Salman Rushdie. The old man had sentenced me to death and according to his curse I was destined to die after sunset.

The was no time nor any need to seek further clarifications on the details of the execution; I was already wondering whether death would come peacefully in my sleep or was I going to be a victim of some mythical disaster? None of that mattered, the biggest concern to my friends and I, was that I was 'going to die'.

To say that we were frightened would be an understatement. We were traumatized, the superstition in us kicked in and we believed genuinely that the old man had some mystical powers to terminate the lives of those who crossed his path. I was shaking like a leaf because after all, I was the intended target.

In the ensuing confusion, my friends, Philly (Phillip Makgoka), Kono (Ishmael Lerutle), Memethi and Bethuel Mamabolo (the brothers), were all talking and gesturing at the same time and in the process giving incoherent advice. Panicking and in desperation, they urged me to beg for forgiveness, to plead with the old man to reverse the curse.

I followed the old man at a safe distance and begged for mercy. With tears in my eyes I pleaded for the reversal of the curse. Philly, Kono, Mmemethi and Bethuel followed some distance behind me.

Ignoring my plea for mercy the old man, who was pushing his bicycle up a steep hill angrily marched on, increasing his pace with each step he took. My eyes were red from crying. I cut a pathetic and remorseful figure that was lingering behind, just a few paces beyond his reach. The old man moved on, mumbling obscenities, not for anyone to hear, but more to vent his anger. Occasionally he looked back and whenever his eyes set sight on me, he became even more agitated, increasing his voice and yelling boisterously. It was as if the sight of my figure was a rude reminder of the source of his rage.

"Msunu kanyoko" ("your mom's ass") he screamed menacingly. *'U zu gunya namhlanje'* ('you going to shit today') followed another expletive. Seething with rage, he ignored my petitions completely, and so I followed meekly. With his increasing anger, I became even more determined to reverse the curse. I was not about to give up and walk away.

After what appeared to be an eternity, by which time I had become really desperate, agitated, and remorseful and yet the old man had not shown any mercy towards my incessant pleas, He suddenly stopped his bicycle and waited for me to approach. On seeing me hesitate to come any nearer, he barked orders in a voice that brooked no nonsense.

"buya la mfana" "come nearer boy" he ordered.

Knowing what to expect, I hesitated. The old man was fuming, his anger visible from the furrow of wrinkles on his forehead, while my eyes bulged and the hair on my body stood on end like the quills of a fretful porcupine.

Ironically, by asking me to come nearer the old man was now addressing my concern. He was offering an opening, giving me an opportunity to redeem myself, precisely the reason I had pursued him for a considerable distance, begging for forgiveness. The time had come for me to own up and be a man.

I stepped forward, edged a little closer to him, bracing for the anticipated pain. It was then or never, the big price for the reversal of the curse. The old man could have his 'pound of flesh', I thought.

He appeared to have finally reached a decision and appeared

determined rid himself of the revolting tail behind him and to end the drama once and for all.

"Sondela" (come closer) he shouted with a raised voice. *"msunu ka nyoko!"* he barked, I moved forward slowly, crouched and timidly, praying and hoping that the punishment would be quick and painless.

In a swift movement unexpected from a man his age, the man slapped me hard across my face. For a moment I stood right in front of him, dazed, while my teary eyes picked up small, coloured, moving figures.

I retreated after the attack and the old man turned his back on me and continued his journey, he had got his 'pound of flesh.'

Later, assessing the encounter, I considered myself lucky because things could have been worse. It was a stroke of luck that the old man was not carrying one of those cultural weapons like a knobkierie (a stick with a knob at the top), that would have certainly caused a lot of damage.

The good Lord in his infinite mercy had also ensured that it was not a much younger and stronger man I had encountered. The old man was probably in his late seventies, and I suppose the strain and hard life he had endured had begun talking its toll on him; he was no longer the athletic strong youngster he must have been in his youth. An attack from a younger man would have been devastating.

Also, the impact of the blow was absorbed more by my forehead and not the soft delicate parts such as my nose that could have easily broken had that been the case.

Eventually after recovering slightly, I ran away back home crying, but elated that the curse was reversed and that I could revert to living without any threat hanging over my life. I am certain that similar incidents of hostilities between the hostel dwellers and the community were the order of the day throughout SOWETO.

SOWETO

Barely twenty-four kilometres outside the huge modern city of Johannesburg lies the Southwestern Townships, popularly called by its acronym, 'SOWETO'

After 1948, South Africa's former all white government built tens of thousands of small, cheap houses to accommodate the large black population in a segregated neighbourhood. SOWETO is simply a sprawling conglomeration of households in townships, shantytowns, and squatter camps that were developed since the late 1940s, with the intention of housing black workers that were to provide the required cheap labour. At the time South Africa was booming after the discovery of gold and diamond, and therefore, lots of cheap labour was required.

The houses built to accommodate the labourers were all similar in shape. They were set up in rows, and their appearance gave a picture akin to a maize field when observed from an aerial position. The unending rows of identical single-story houses produced a monotonous urban landscape with few trees, gardens, parks or playgrounds. Opponents and critics of the regime often referred to the houses as matchboxes.

The authorities painted our house, together with the rest of the houses in that section, sky blue. Tenants were never consulted and therefore had no choice in deciding their preferred colour. The colours used were varied; some houses were blue, light-blue, red, brown, green etc. It was always by sheer luck that a colour agreeable to the eye was chosen.

All the houses were provided with a fenced little yard that was big enough for a small vegetable garden. The houses were then sub-divided into zones and sections intended to give identity and to differentiate one section from the other. Some zones would be referred to by numbers, zone 1 or 2, or 3, etc.

In any modern urban setting such zoning and sub- division would be considered normal, and would be intended for the provision of efficient administration, communication, and the evolution of the socio -politico and economic development of the community. Under apartheid rule, however, the zoning of the townships produced a discernible pattern, with a clear and calculated design that was characteristic of the white regime's intention to foster, not only just white and black segregation, but also, wherever possible, to further subdivide the Africans into tribal categories such as Zulus, Sothos, Tswanas, Xhosas, Shangaans, Pedis, Vendas, etcetera.

The houses of SOWETO had the basic minimum; they constituted cement floors and four small square shaped rooms with no ceiling. Each room was fitted with a small window to allow the sun and fresh air to enter.

The asbestos roofs were not flat, they created undulating rows and were placed on wooden rafters which allowed for small holes that were the size of a tennis ball. In the cold South African winter, if not sealed, a cold breeze entered through these gaps, turning the house into a semi freezer. The cement floors were also bitterly cold and very few of the families could afford cushy warm carpets to keep the houses warm.

Each house was also fitted with a small chimney in the kitchen that channelled the smoke from the coal-heated stoves. For the poor majority who could not afford a ceiling, the chimney was yet another inlet for the cold breeze.

Some five or six meters from the house was an outside toilet and a tap for clean, running water. We did not have the luxury of en suite bedrooms, and so the outside toilets served as showers as well. Those with large families would take turns queuing for an opportunity to take a bath, one person after the other, since the small toilets had room for only one person at a time.

The shower consisted of a small water bowl filled with warm water that one scooped and splashed over the body.

Considering the usual rush in the mornings, kids going to school and parents getting ready to catch the early commuters' trains and buses, taking a bath was, for many families, a source of tension and stress as people vied to be the first in the queue.

Africans are mostly supportive of their extended families. It is not inconceivable that some families would consist of ten or more people per unit. In such families, sleeping places would be anywhere where space was available, with some sleeping in rows under the tables. For such big families taking turns to have a 'shower' was a nightmare.

Almost two million blacks lived in conditions of abject poverty in these unique structures. Over the years the population of SOWETO continued to grow, spurred on by the forced relocation of Africans from other areas of metropolitan Johannesburg that the government had unilaterally declared as white areas.

Forced relocation from the slum areas west of Johannesburg began in the early 1950s, when the government moved over 58,000 blacks to the Meadowlands and Diep Kloof areas of SOWETO. Blacks were moved from areas such as Sophia Town and several other western suburbs to make way for the new white neighbourhoods. Sophia Town initially occupied by black South Africans gave way and was converted and renamed 'Troimf (Afrikaans for triumph), an exclusively white suburb.

The regime sought various methods to foster divisions within the black community, hence the division of townships into tribal sections. There were the Zulu, and the Sotho sections, while the Shangans and Vendas also had their separate areas. Sometimes the barrier between the sections divided according to tribes would only be a street.

The strategy of divide and rule was not successful largely because despite the fictitious divisions, people from the different tribes worked together in their places of employment in the city centre and were able to mix. In the townships, the barriers separating the tribes were not insurmountable. People interacted, played sports together and there were also intermarriages that created families across the tribal divisions. Also, the schools at a higher level, particularly at secondary, high or university, were very few. Consequently, the one institution in the region would cater for a wider community that included all the tribes, which invariably created bonds between them.

With the false barriers and categorization of the Africans into tribal zones, the regime's desired outcome was to fragment the black community, to ensure that instead of consolidating the unity of the black people, they would become consumed with and become increasingly more conscious and prouder of our tribal origins. Certainly, people should be encouraged to be proud of their culture and tradition. It should, however, not be used as a divisive tool or used in a way that will denigrate other tribes.

On Sundays, the townships were a melting pot of cultural and traditional displays. From the Ba-Pedi, Ba-Tswana and Ba-Sotho to the Ama-Zulu, Ama-Xhosa, Ama- Shangani and Ama-Venda with beer flowing, men and women used Sunday afternoons to relax and entertain themselves and each other.

Among all the tribes, the songs and dance conveyed a certain message. They were for every occasion; there were songs and poetic recitals to honour and praise their chiefs or brave warriors and heroes, some were to inspire, to energize the men and women and urge them on in their performance and execution of herculean tasks.

We were accustomed to these scenes of groups of about twenty men or so singing in unison as they dug and pulled, maybe in the construction of a railway or some tasks. On occasion, the content of the recitals and song would be making a mockery of the very white man sitting in the shade and watching over them with a grin on his face, obviously enjoying the entertainment and not realizing that the songs were referring to him. The one typical song I have heard on many occasions:

> 'Abelugu! wo dam! wo dam' - (Damn the whites! damn the whites)
> 'Abelungu wo dam! wo dam' – (Damn the whites! damn the whites)

CHAPTER 15

NARRATIVES FROM SOWETO

*"In many ways, winter exposed and exacerbated the
poor conditions of the overwhelming majority."*
Kingsley Mamabolo

Gogo (Granny) Nomvundla'

South African winters are very cold with temperatures sometimes
reaching below 10 degrees Celsius. In many ways, winter exposed
and exacerbated the poor conditions of the overwhelming majority.
The sad story of the old lady 'Gogo' Nomvundla, and her grandchildren is very instructive.

'Gogo' Nomvundla lived with her three grandchildren whose
fathers were unknown. Her two daughters, Thembeka and
Nomasonto would give birth, dump their newborn babies in the old
lady's care and disappear in pursuance of greener pastures. The old
lady had no option but to look after her grandchildren. Her two
daughters occasionally made home visits after prolonged absences,
sometimes of up to six months.

In their wild adventures Thembeka and Nomasonto hooked
up with unsavory characters, lived a life of drugs and moved from
one place to wherever there was promise of excitement. One could
say they lived a life of nomads. Their promiscuity guaranteed the
possibility of an increase in the number of grandchildren that would
be in the care of Gogo.

With each visit home after a long absence, Thembeka or
Nomasonto would be accompanied by a new partner that Gogo

would proudly parade as the future son in law. Gogo would boast of the "high qualifications of her sons in law" who were either teachers, doctors, or lawyers. And if their shabby appearance betrayed their lack of qualification then their parents were cited as the qualified ones. The focus was always on the newly arrived partners, but there was never a reference to the previous partners who accompanied the daughters and were introduced with the same pomp as the new ones. Cautious not to embarrass 'Gogo' and out of respect for her, the community never probed or asked awkward questions.

Taking care of the grandchildren was almost an impossible task for 'Gogo'. She was old and needed to be looked after herself, and she did not have financial resources or any means whatsoever. Thembeka and Nomasonto did not send much money after their escapades. They lived an exciting 'la vida loco' away from home and forgot that they had a family to look after while Gogo just had to make do with the scarce resources she had.

Every day in freezing winter mornings and as soon as it became light, 'Gogo' Nomvundla and her grandchildren, carrying containers, would trail the horse-pulled carts delivering coal in the neighbourhood. They'd collect the coal that fell inadvertently out of the carts and onto the ground in the process of delivery. 'Gogo' and her grandchildren would follow the horse carts until they accumulated enough coal to enable them make fire at home, warm the house and to cook breakfast. Sometimes they would be lucky when out of pity the coalman would scoop the lose coal on the cart and fill their containers.

The community we lived in was poor, but also materialistic and competitive. There was some differentiation amongst the poor and those who managed to have slightly better means than the rest, and who then occupied a special place in society. Those who were more prosperous made themselves conspicuous by dangling the expensive labels of their clothes, furniture, or cars.

Collecting coal in the manner that 'Gogo' and her grandchildren did was frowned upon if committed by anyone else. There appeared, however, to be a tacit understanding that 'Gogo' Nomvundla and many others in similar conditions were in such a hopeless and desperate situation that their actions could be excused and did not warrant any criticism.

After making the fire to warm the house, Gogo would then prepare breakfast or lunch. One good meal was enough to sustain them until the next day, occasionally they were able to have dinner if they were lucky. To prepare the fire, the old lady would have to ask one of her neighbours for a stick of matches to light the fire, while another neighbour would be expected to provide wood. The same procedure was followed in the preparation of breakfast; a neighbour would be asked to provide maize meal flour to cook porridge, and someone else would be asked for the tea leaves, the sugar to put in the tea, cooking oil, salt, tomatoes, onions and so on. The exercise would be repeated at different mealtimes or whenever there was a need.

None in the community dared to refuse Gogo's requests, we always understood whenever Thembela, Mbali or Vusi (Gogo's grandchildren) showed up on our doorsteps that we were called upon to be of service to humanity. We were now familiar with the nature of the request that came with the accustomed lines:

"Gogo requests that you please provide a spoon of cooking oil/ a teaspoon of salt" followed by an assurance never fulfilled; "she will return it as soon as mom (Thembeka or Nomasonto) brings home our monthly supply of groceries."

Gogo and her grandchildren were not the only ones caught in the web of poverty under very harsh economic conditions. There were millions of others in similar conditions such as the street kids whose blankets in the open winter breeze were sheets of plastic and those whose meals were prepared with remnants rescued from the garbage dumps.

In recent years, the cold South African winters and hunger are not the only threats to the African child. Many are out of school;

there are thousands of aids-orphaned families where nine- and eleven-year-olds are forced into early parenthood looking after their younger siblings.

In most parts of Africa, the most tragic instance of waste as it concerns the African child is being trafficked as an economic slave. This does not imply the outlawed model of slavery prominent in the nineteenth century, but a contemporary model where a young child is lured away from their communities and sold into child prostitution or labour. In my travels all over Africa, it is common to see young children hawking freely on the streets at a time they should be at school.

As a teenager, I was obsessed with Dolly Parton's song entitled "Coat of Many Colours". I now believe that my fascination with the song was because it had resonance and depicted similar deplorable surroundings that defined my very daily existence. In this song Parton relates a story of how, way back, in the season of her youth, somebody had given her mother a box full of many coloured rags. And because Dolly had no coat, her mother had stitched the rags, every small piece together, to make her a coat of many colours which she was very proud of.

Parton relates that she proudly tried to convince her peers that her coat was beautiful, but in turn her friends laughed and made fun of her. She sings; -

"Although we had no money, I was rich as I could be in my coat of many colours. My coat of many colours that mama made for me was worth more than all the clothes."

"They did not understand, and I tried to make them see 'one is only poor if they choose to be," she concludes.

Dolly Parton's song although describing a situation in faraway America could be supplanted to describe a similar situation confronting a young, poor South African girl.

Violence In The Township

Lincoln 's death
They stabbed him several times, his body was found riddled with multiple wounds. Word doing rounds indicated that it was his best friends that had ganged up on him at the local bar and killed him. The neighbours describing the last moments of his death, related how he had apparently run from one corner of the yard to the other, furtively. Like a cornered rabbit he moved from one side to the other, looking for a loophole, occasionally turning to face the gang pursuing him and putting up a desperate bid to free himself from the encirclement. He was pleading for his life, calling his assailants by name evidently shocked that they were attacking, stabbing, and out to kill him.

Fighting for his life he let out shrieking howls of pain that pierced the stillness of the night. The screams were a desperate cry for help, he was hoping, however remotely, for some intervention that could stop his persecutors. His desperation grew increasingly with the passing of time and no help in sight. The neighbours could discern from his screams that he was gripped by fear, the realization dawning on him that he was all alone, nobody was coming to his rescue and that eventually on that cold South African winter night, he was destined to die at the hands of his friends who had become his killers.

Like a pack of wolves, with their knives drawn out they pursued him, and ignoring his pleas, they stabbed him repeatedly. They were merciless, sadistic, and relentless in their attack as he retreated, their motive was clear – it was their sheer determination to end his life once and for all.

We never really got to know what could have made them so angry and heartless; what on earth could have forced those youngsters collectively to turn against one of their own in such a brutal a manner. As family and friends searched for an explanation, we believed that his killers were more than likely motivated by jealousy. Lincoln was handsome, fashionable, classy and drew the attention of many pretty young women in the neighbourhood.

The following day, the police and observers witnessed traces of blood from one corner to the other, confirming the neighbours assertion that he was heard darting all over in a desperate bid to escape.

I was hardly a teenager then, and I am positive that some of the details about Lincoln's death were not meant for my ears, but I got to listen anyway. The death of a loved one in the community, killed in such a gruesome manner sent shivers down my spine. Psychologically it left a scar, a lifelong impact of vulnerability, a feeling of insecurity and fear. I grew up convinced that South Africa, the community I lived in, and the world were not secure places to live in.

'Bra Pule'

Bra pule was the township bully. Occasionally he would demonstrate his prowess by beating up an unfortunate victim on the streets and in most cases, he picked a fight with anyone for no reason. Some of the brawls would start at the nearest local drinking place called the shebeen (drinking place – usually a house whose owner converts it to sell liquor under license from the authorities). The fighting would then spill over into the street and the victorious Bra Pule, having knocked his opponent unconscious, would take time to demonstrate, to a traumatized public, his kicking prowess.

In one such demonstration, Bra Pule got hold of a wheelbarrow from a nearby house and pushed the unconscious victim up and down the streets, parading his conquest. At intervals, the victim was offloaded, and Bra Pule demonstrated his kicking abilities. After a demonstration lasting for long periods, Bra Pule flipped the man's unconscious and lifeless body across his legs with the victim's face facing down to the ground and his backside exposed, just like a mom or dad would position their son for a good spanking. He then stabbed the man repeatedly and relentlessly on his bums until the victim died of the multiple stab wounds.

Bra Pule was arrested, but released shortly thereafter. Sadly, the pattern of this kind of behaviour was common. It came as no surprise that Bra Pule was released soon after he had butchered that victim in public view. Other murderers and criminals were arrested for a couple of months, released, and immediately sent back to the communities they'd been traumatizing.

The regime's intentions reflected the attitude of the racist authorities, many of whom were preoccupied with what they perceived to be a population explosion and a huge increase in the numbers of black South Africans. They lived in perpetual fear of what they perceived to be the beginning of the extinction of the white race.

Indeed, if there were thousands of characters such as Bra pule in the black community that were prepared to lend a hand in the reduction or possibly the extermination of the black population, these racist authorities were ready to afford them the opportunity to do just that.

Ntate Mampuru
Violence was common in our communities. A fierce looking elderly man, Mr. Don Mampuru lived with his family across our street. Mampuru was a short-tempered middle-aged man, who was always ready to do battle with anyone who dared to cross his path. He lived with a constant belief that everyone bore ill intentions against him. He was always making claims that people were bewitching him or were jealous of his achievements.

He was superstitious, believing strongly in the power and mysticism of witchcraft, and was suspicious of all, neighbours, friends, relatives, and even strangers. Mampuru instilled such fear that most people opted to take the long way around rather than pass next to his house. If one braved passing by his house, a quick glance at his window revealed his watchful eye scrutinizing carefully and following each step of whoever was passing by. He, like a sentry, spent most of his time seated behind the curtain, anticipating an "imminent attack".

One summer day, Mampuru woke up to find a dead black cat in his yard. No one could tell how the cat came to be there though there were a few possibilities. It is possible that, considering his penchant for superstition, his foes could have deliberately thrown the cat in the yard to make him uncomfortable and perpetuate his fear of his own conspiracy theories. It may well be that someone, with the same inclinations as Mampuru, was putting into practice their power of witchcraft.

Mampuru was angry as he could not tell which direction the cat came from. So, he decided that his most hated neighbour was the culprit. The neighbour did not cow- tow to Mampuru's intimidating antics and was the only one brave enough to occasionally stand firm on a toe-to- toe shouting match across the separating wire.

Mampuru carefully wrapped a newspaper around the tail of the cat, swung it over his head and flung it across the separating fence. The dead cat landed with a thud in his neighbour's yard. When the neighbour woke up and found the cat in his yard, he knew immediately who was responsible. He threw the cat back where it had come from and retreated to his house. For a whole day, both men went about their duties and also, depending on whose yard the cat was in, threw it back into the enemy camp.

From the safety of our houses we watched in disbelief, enthralled by their calmness as they went about this exercise. Throughout the day, routinely and without uttering a word they went about throwing the cat to and fro. As it became dark, we could not keep track and were never able to tell who finally gave in, or rather who had the maturity to end this senseless and unwinnable competition by simply throwing the cat into the garbage bin.

Mampuru's three boys bore the brunt of his outrages, and he often molested them physically. 18-year-old David who was the first born received the most severe punishment. At times, Mampuru would set his vicious dogs on him in full view of the neighbours as he screamed and pleaded for mercy. David's punishment was always intended to serve as a lesson not only to the two other brothers, Bob and Paul but also to all around the neighbourhood that Don Mampuru stood for 'no nonsense'.

Bob, the second born and Paul the baby of the house at 13 and 11 years respectively were perhaps too young to receive the vicious dog attack treatment, but they were never saved the trauma of watching their brother writhing in pain as he tried to fend off the dogs. I never got to know Ntate Mampuru's wife. My mom informed us that she fled the household many years ago, taking David's sisters along with her.

When such domestic violence was perpetrated, the elders did not intervene for fear that Mampuru in his anger would turn on them. As the boy's screams grew louder, the elderly would only hiss and mutter obscenities quietly. The police were never called, perhaps because reporting any case was cumbersome as there were no phones at the time. There was also the probability that they would not have bothered to come anyway.

There was also the danger that Mampuru would come to know who the whistle-blower was. Very few, if any in the community, would have dared to cross Mampuru's path and risk the possibility of being added to his short list of those publicly known as his enemies.

I never understood why David, at the age of seventeen or eighteen, did not just pack and leave. He probably realized that life as a young, homeless teenager would have been a living hell. Even though David had a lot of sympathizers, very few would have risked taking him in. It is also possible that for the love of his brothers and a sense of responsibility towards them, David chose to stay and endure this inhumane treatment.

Mampuru's house was dark and very quiet when he was not physically or violently punishing any of the boys. David and his siblings were not allowed to talk loudly or make noise. They walked quietly in and out of the house, took their designated places when it was time to eat and hardly moved unless instructed by their father. They took turns praying for the food to be blessed, ate quietly, then took turns collecting the dishes on the table to wash and pack away.

This routine was repeated at every meal, breakfast, lunch, and dinner. Every day, quietly and eerily, as if programmed, they went about their routine, without uttering a word except for the occasional "can you please pass the salt". They had no maid and David the oldest son, did most of the chores. It was the responsibility of the boys to keep the house clean.

There was no laughter emanating from that house. It was like a morgue, exuding a chilly discomfort associated with the departed.

School Days

The authorities did not admit children under seven years of age, the assumption being that at that age the child was not mature enough to attend school. This rule was strictly applied with teachers demanding birth certificates before registration. In cases where certificates could not be made available, the children would be subjected to a variety of physical and mental tests to ascertain that they had reached the requisite maturity.

Lerechabetse Lower Primary School was at that time the only lower primary school in our vicinity. The teachers did their best with the little they had, to educate, manage and discipline a rowdy group of children. The classes were overcrowded, and the desks were never sufficient to accommodate us all. There were so many children that the school had to allocate sessions so that the pupils in the lower level would attend the morning classes while those in the upper classes were taught in the afternoon. Some of the lower classes were held outside under the trees, in the open air.

The winters were cold and so the coal stove in the centre provided warmth for the entire classroom. There was always a pot on the one plate stove cooking hot soup or some delicacies for the class teacher.

Some teachers created an environment of competition amongst the students.

Those whose parents could afford it, brought delicacies such as cakes, curry etc. and would in turn receive enthusiastic praise from the teacher.

*   *   *

We used to fight a lot and challenges to a contest were very common, akin to the duels of the fastest guns we saw in cinemas. These would be declared with the mere mention of the words 'after school is after school'

Throughout the day word would go around and excitement would build up. In hushed tones in the school corridors, the message would be passed on, boys and girls would be calling out "Paul and David are fighting after school". During break, friends of the contenders would be seen gathering in some corners, with the contender in the center, devising a strategy to win.

Self-appointed coaches would be giving advice:

"When he makes his move, just duck, and aim for his testicles, grab, and hold tight and do not let go, it does not matter how hard he hits you, just hold tight; eventually the pain will overwhelm him, and he will start begging for mercy."

This would be the typical advice given, despite the well- known rule of fair fighting usually understood in such contests which is 'Hai bambe hai lume' (Zulu for fair fighting, literally meaning no holding and no biting). In later years, when I was now training in boxing professionally, I was to receive similar advice meant to encourage one to strive for persistence and endurance.

The coach would stress: "Just focus on punching his stomach, eventually the head will roll."

Let The Sun Not Set On You

There was never a winner in these kinds of fights, even if one subdued his competitor, one still faced punishment from their parents. Rolling in the dust and torn clothes always incurred the wrath of parents. Sometimes the fights would go on for days, with neither of the fighters giving in, with each determined to revenge the beating they received the day before. Eventually such a contest would warrant the intervention of parents. Experience taught that those tempered in the "never retreat, no surrender fights", eventually became the best of friends with great respect for each other.

Disciplinary Committee (DC)
My excitement of a promotion to Tau Pedi Higher primary School dissipated as soon as I realized what was in store for me.

"Spare the rod and spoil the child 'Nkgonne'" (Setswana for my brother)! In a loud booming voice reverberating through the corridors, Job Kgoro, a teacher at the Tau Pedi Higher Primary School would often be heard calling out as he waddled in between the classroom blocks. Corporal punishment was the order at the school. The whole school would be eerily quiet, an environment of fear hanging in the air like a thick cloud.

The classrooms were small, and the walls in between had thin layers and each time we were punished the repeated thudding sound of the stick as it landed on the soft- rounded buttocks of a teenager would be heard through the empty corridors. Each thump would instil absolute fear in those who could hear it.

A couple of teachers who were known and feared for their severity in meting out punishment grouped themselves into what they called Disciplinary Committee (DC) and were called in frequently to discipline unruly students. Tau Pedi Higher Primary school distinguished itself from others for its disciplinary conduct and teachers that were fierce.

The standard punishment was multiple castigation from two to three teachers that would stand in a row as the victim was passed from one to the other. The teachers would be holding different sticks and punishment tools, some made of animal hide. A boy or an offender would bend his torso, head down and touch his toes with his fingers and thus receive several lashes on his buttocks.

When the DC was operating, there would be complete silence. None of us dared to raise our heads from the textbooks that we pretended to be reading lest we attracted unwarranted attention.

Somehow in that stillness induced by the fear of punishment, with the silence broken only by the rhythmic sounds of the strokes meted out and as we were vaguely gazing at our reading material, we would at the same time be reaching out in sympathy and solidarity to the victims, understanding fully the pain that was being inflicted. The fear was so real, one could almost taste it.

The spirit of solidarity was at times broken when the victim receiving punishment bolted, jumped out through the open window, and ran for dear life. A member of the DC, would scream an order; "After him, boys!" All the boys present would then scramble through the door to give chase with the obligation to catch the fleeing colleague weighing heavily on those who gave chase because the consequence of failure resulted in severe punishment for the entire group.

Wednesdays were traumatic, they were set aside for handiwork inspection and all the senior schoolboys would gather in one classroom with their artwork. The DC would oversee the inspection with one teacher acting as a judge and deciding what form of punishment was appropriate for defaulters.

There were a few items of the work of art we were expected to make, we made woodwork that included postboxes, benches etc. On the other hand, grass work included place mats, and hats, while for horn work we made flower pots, and various other decorations using the horn.

Each item was inspected separately and depending on one's performance, punishment was meted out. For the sloppy ones like me whose performance on each item was ridiculed and laughed at by the inspecting teacher, Wednesdays were a nightmare.

The horn work involved a lot of effort; one had to boil and clean the horn, remove the innards, and scrub the horn until the white surface was replaced by the shiny black underneath. If this were not done properly one of the teachers, Mr. Tau, who did the inspections, would laughingly ridicule:

"'Broer' come and see what this lazy Mamabolo has done, look at his horn work". So many times, I was told "Hey Mamabolo! Moswi kgomo e tla go re bolaya ga tsoga fa, a be a fithlela re tshameka ka lenaka lagagwe" ("Hey Mamabolo! The dead cow will kill us when it wakes up and find us playing with its horn") - implication being that one did not scrub enough to disguise and differentiate the horn from its original state. When the punishment was meted out and as one writhed in pain, the teachers would laugh and pass jokes at one's misery.

There were two students, Gilbert Moilwa and Jim Phokela who were extremely good at their work, producing professional work. Tau and the DC members were always full of praises. For both Jim, and Gilbert's artwork, woodwork, and grass work, everything was perfect. To their shock and disbelief, the two students would occasionally receive one or two lashes and be told, "Rea go kgothatsa" meaning, "we are just encouraging you".

Psychologically this had a devastating effect for if Jim or Gilbert could be punished despite their excellent work, what were the implications for me and all those whose work was obviously shoddy.

There has always been a debate on whether corporal punishment is a good form of disciplining children during their upbringing in South Africa. Those that are pro-corporal punishment point to the difference between the disciplined older generation and the youth of today that is characterised by indiscipline.

There is a need to ensure a conducive environment that includes discipline, however, the kind of punishment we received from the DC was torture and depressing and it left a lingering bitter taste in our mouths regarding school. Personally, I dreaded going to school and many of my contemporaries who could not endure the pain did not complete their schooling.

We were taught to cram and to know by heart all the poems, biblical verses, and psalms, that we learned. We recited these poems before the white inspectors that occasionally visited our schools on a mission for the Department of Bantu Education. To prepare for these visits, our teachers put us through rigorous paces to ensure that our performances on the day of inspection would meet the expectations of the inspectors, who would, in turn give a positive assessment of the school.

The history we were taught was distorted, intended to ensure that we did not honour our heroes nor feel proud of our origin. Our forebearers were portrayed as brutal; they were said to be uncultured and uncivilized. The implication of these characterization was to create an impression that we were all invariably saved by the "civilization" of the white colonizers.

As the saying goes:

"To colonize people's minds, you must first demonize their cultures, then their traditions."

A poem by A.G. Visser that we learned by heart entitled Amakeia conveyed a poignant message well intended.

Through poetry, A.G Visser brilliantly relates an event that occurred in 1834, during the 6th Xhosa wars. This is the story of Amakeia, a brave Xhosa maid who was employed by a Boer family that was part of the settler community camping just outside the settlement of the natives.

He describes the way the Xhosa warriors, after they had killed the invading white soldiers, went on a rampage to annihilate the women and children that were left in a camp at the border. When she saw the approaching *impi* (Army), one Boer madam realized that her baby stood a better chance of survival if Amakeia, the maid took him under her wing. Facing the prospect of death bravely, she handed the child to Amakeia who in turn was to protect the baby by whatever means. Amakeia with the baby on her back made a dash for the mountains to hide.

Unfortunately, some black scouts saw her and the baby heading to the mountains. The scouts were later able to point out her hiding place to the warriors. Both Amakeia and the baby were killed mercilessly. Visser's poem relates this encounter beginning with Amakeia's escape to the mountains whilst calming the crying baby. Her story is captured in the following verse translated into English by Nikita:

> *"Hush now, hush now, pikanini*
> *Over the mountains the moon rises*
> *No one will see us here*
> *Tomorrow we'll go home."*

The warriors discovered Amakeia's hiding place and showed no mercy as Amakeia begged with her hands stretched:

> *"Save him, he is so little*
> *"Ragingly snarled the wild gang*
> *Die or give the white child here!*
> *Over my lifeless body, replied Amakeia vivaciously. "*
> *My promise to my madam,*
> *The best I could ask for:*
> *Where he goes, Amakeia goes, to care for him. "Unite in death, if*
> *in life you cannot be parted.*
> *Quick death with her maxhosas,*
> *Let the glinting spears rain down!*
> *In the Amatola valleys*
> *Howls only the winter wind*

Through the reeds in the moonlight:
"Thula-thula (hush-hush) - sleep my child."

Long after Amekeia and the baby were killed, the hissing of the wind through the reeds, gave a howling sound that mimicked the voice of Amakeia when she and the baby were hiding in the cave, "thula-thula (hush-hush) -sleep my child".

The emotional story of the demise of Amakeia and the baby at the hands of the 'beast-like' Xhosa impi had a huge effect on the minds of teenagers. In a subtle manner, it was intended to convey the message that our forebears were barbaric and beastly. Our acknowledgement and acceptance of the "barbarism" of the forebears would lead to the appreciation of their so called "white civilization". Through beautiful poetic expression the narrative is conveyed in a manner that exploits and conjures emotions, and by omission or commission of facts the stories only give a one-sided message.

Scratching a little below the surface, certain facts emerge: the narrator is a partisan source who is telling his people's version of the story. Visser's story is one-sided and very selective; he does not say anything about the atrocities that had been committed by the invading white settlers who descended on these peaceful communities throughout the Eastern Cape and later in Natal. There is no mention of the crime and killings they committed as they ploughed through with their superior and dangerous weapons with the express intent of conquering the ancestral land that the Africans had been occupying for centuries.

Before descending on Amakeia's people, the notoriety of the white intruders preceded them. They had already conquered other territories. The cruelty of their enslavement of the people they had already colonized was no secret and had spread by word of mouth by the few that escaped and sought refuge in territories not yet captured.

Visser does not describe the mood, fear, and anxiety of the warriors when they encountered the invaders thus explaining why they chose war and to eliminate the enemy rather than welcome the new arrivals. The killing of a defenceless woman and innocent children cannot be condoned, however, history also records that the Xhosa tribes that were peaceful were forced into a war they did not initiate. For a hundred years, the Xhosas in the Eastern Cape fought desperately to hold on to their ancestorial land. They suffered a lot of casualties fighting against the white settlers who were equipped with superior and sophisticated weaponry. Hundreds of innocent women, men, and children lost their lives in the onslaught by the white settlers.

It is obvious that the warriors of the Amatola region had been preparing long before the arrival of the cruel visitors. They were psyched and determined to resist the white menace. Considering their fear of the power and ability of the invaders to cause mayhem and to harm their community, Amakeia's brave refusal to comply, seen from their point of view, was probably construed as a treasonable act.

The history we were taught was selective. For example, we learned and correctly so, of the genocide that Germany, under Hitler, committed by killing millions of Jews. However, inexplicably, we were not taught of a similar history where King Leopold and the government of Belgium committed genocide, killing millions of

Africans in the Congo, whilst greedily in pursuit of mineral wealth, animal skins and elephant tusks.

The Tladi Youth Club
Not everything about the system was bad. There were a few things that produced some positive results. One of those was the creation of social clubs for the youth throughout Soweto. I belonged to one, the Tladi Youth Club.

Hundreds of young women and men benefited from these social clubs which were spread out in the entire SOWETO. Here we were taught and exposed to events that are critical in socializing such as dancing, gun-boot dance, acting, performing drama, table tennis, soft ball, chess, and many others.

At the Tladi Youth Club we were blessed to have a mother- figure, Mrs. Phaladi, who we endearingly called 'Mizah.' (From Miss). She guided us, moulded us, smoothening the rough edges to produce the fine young men and women most in the group turned out to be.

Mizah may not have been our biological mother, however, in the spirit of ubuntu she became one to all of us. She gave us the tools we needed that were necessary to build confidence in our interaction in the complex society that we lived in at the time, and eventually found ourselves in around the world. Most importantly she taught us respect and how to hold our heads high with dignity in an apartheid society that was depressing and dehumanizing.

It is an enigma, to me, that such social programs are not continued in today's democratic South Africa. I believe that the Ministry of Social Affairs must be more creative in engaging the youth. The programs such as the ones we were exposed to may have been created under the apartheid regime, but many can attest to the good they have done in contributing towards the nation.

We did have our fights with Mizah, but she did her best to discipline and contain a group of teenagers that were becoming increasingly adventurous. One misadventure was organizing a trip to Lesotho, using the resources of the club, without informing her.

We elected an organizing committee; I was elected Chairperson, Benedict Diphoko became my Deputy, while Stanley Thloale was elected the Secretary and Isaac Losaba the treasury. We made members pay a token amount for the trip and then used the cash to invest and increase to enable us to cover the entire trip. This included hiring transportation and having sufficient means to survive in Maseru for the duration of our stay.

However, I believe the greatest show of defiance towards Mizah was when we hired a film, used the clubhouse, and made people pay and used the profits to augment the funds needed for the trip to Lesotho. We hired the film, "The Taking of Pelham 123" starring Walter Matthau, Robert Shaw, Martin Balsam and Hector Elizondo.

In hindsight, I realize the seriousness of the offence. Mizah could have expelled all of us from the club. Although we were of the impression that she never got to know, I have a feeling that she was told, and that she went along and pretended that she did not know, perhaps intrigued by our creativeness and wanting to see if we would be successful. What we undertook was a huge responsibility for teenagers that age. I also believe that much as she let the incident pass, she was invariably hurt that we would do things like that behind her back.

The journey to Lesotho was a huge success. We had enough funds to pay for accommodation and entertainment and to buy a sheep for celebration at the end of our stay. Ntate Phalatsi, a social worker from South Africa who had migrated to Maseru, welcomed, and took care of us at the youth compound he'd built. The Lesotho excursion was the first that we arranged on our own without Mizah's guidance and assistance. It was the defining moment between men/women and boys/girls. It gave us confidence that we were now ready to face the world as mature adults.

CHAPTER 16

REPRESSIVE MINORITY WHITE RULE AND AFRICAN RESISTANCE

*"The Africans were left with no
other option but to fight for their very survival."*
Kingsley Mamabolo

The student generation of the late sixties and seventies were an angry lot. We learned of and witnessed the brutal repression of peaceful appeals and resistance of generations before us. Generations whose crime was to seek to redress the historical injustices that resulted in a white settler community colonizing and usurping our ancestral land.

White racism, anxious to preserve its domination over the overwhelming black majority had over centuries evolved a legal system based on entrenching racial discrimination and minority domination. The system was perfected to guarantee the accumulation of wealth and to ensure prosperity for the white community.

The overwhelming black majority, living side by side and in the same country with their white oppressors, watched as their land was taken, they were robbed of their wealth and witnessed the gradual erosion of their culture, customs and traditions. The Africans were left with no other option but to fight for their very survival.

The colonization of South Africa created these inherently manifest contradictions of two groups of people, the oppressor and the oppressed, living and coexisting in one country, but pursuing completely different objectives and interests. Marxists describe this in what they call dialectal laws of development as the "unity and struggle of opposites".

The situation impacted generations of people as colour defined and determined for South Africans their place in society, as either, part of the oppressor race or destined to join the struggle of the oppressed for equality and justice. My generation was no exception.

Resistance to white domination dates to the days when Africans fought back the technologically advanced armies of the British and Boer colonizers. Armed only with spears in their hands, from 1652 when white settlers came from Holland to 1912 when the ANC was formed, many bitter struggles were fought, initially over land and cattle. The Xhosa tribes of the eastern cape became the first line of defence and fought bravely against occupation. Despite their inferior weapons they sustained resistance for more than a hundred years.

The youth of the sixties and seventies, to which I belonged, were motivated and inspired by this proud history of struggle and resistance. We drew strength from the heroic feats of our heroes such as Makhanda, Hintsa, Nonqgause, Shaka, Dingaan, Cetshwayo, Moshoeshoe, Sekhukhune, Modjadji and others. The true history of the African people was passed on to us largely by word of mouth from our parents as apparently most African history was not recorded.

The young people learned and were captivated by the growing militancy of the ANC which was enthused by the courageous leadership of the youth league of the 1940's. We admired the courage of leaders such as Albert Luthuli, Yusuf Dadoo, Moses Kotane, Govan Mbeki, Walter Sisulu and the militant youth then such as Nelson Mandela, Oliver Tambo, Anton Lembede, Robert Rhesha, Duma Nokwe and many others.

The ANC gave hope to the people and the popularity of the leaders among the Africans grew tremendously. Their influence became a major threat to the state. The regime resorted to drastic measures to curb the rising tide against its oppressive system. The ANC, the communist party of South Africa (CPSA), the Pan African Congress of Azania were banned and declared prohibited organizations. Nelson Mandela, Robert Sobukwe, and many other leaders were put in prison, while Oliver Tambo was exiled and for a time it seemed that the state had contained the militancy of the people.

The ban imposed on the ANC and its ally the CPSA made it illegal to read literature relating to these organizations. However, the banned material was always available underground and passed on secretly to those keen to read it. My friend, Molebatsi, somehow managed to get hold of Nelson Mandela's speeches in court: the first one in the Treason trial where he was asking the court officials to recuse themselves, arguing that as a "black man in a white man's court" he would not be afforded a fair trial, and the second one, where faced with the possibility that he and his comrades could be sentenced to death, he declared, "I am prepared to die".

These leaders were true Pan Africanist. All of them, men of peace and many were devout Christians, who later on, after exhausting all available avenues of struggle were forced to consider armed struggle as a viable option in the face of a violent and brutal repression from an insecure and illegitimate racist regime.

From when it was founded, the vision of the leadership of the ANC was of a united Africa. The founders of the ANC, then called the Native National Congress, were drawn from South Africa and beyond the borders of the country. The vision of a united Africa is also clearly captured in Enoch Sontonga's classical song, 'Nkosi Sikelele i Afrika' (God bless Africa), adopted in 1925 by the ANC as its anthem.

In time, it became evident that with the refusal to listen to grievances, peaceful and legitimate demands, the ANC, and its supporters would run out of patience. The formation of 'Umkhonto we Sizwe' (the spear of the nation), the armed wing, was inevitable. Expressing the frustration of the leadership and the people, particularly the youth of that time Nelson Mandela declared thus,

"It would be wrong and unrealistic for African leaders to continue preaching peace and non- violence at a time when the government met our peaceful demands with force. It was only when all else had failed, when all channels of peaceful protest had been barred to us, that the decision to embark on violent forms of political struggle was considered."

A calm before the storm existed, feeling more insecure the regime meted out stringent draconian and repressive measures intended to subdue the people. Over the years, the agitation led to spiralling protests that activists referred to as 'rolling mass action'. Even from exile and the prison walls, leaders of the ANC continued to inspire mass action against the state.

Discriminatory practices became the norm in the daily lives of black women and men in South Africa. In most cases whenever such incidents were related, we laughed off the escapades and quickly forgot the unfortunate incidents and readied ourselves to face many new ones.

In my teens, I recall a story I read in the local newspapers whose narration was as follows:

"After delivery, an unknown desperate teenager dumped her unwanted baby and left it to die. The ethnicity of the baby was not clear. It was difficult to tell whether the baby was white or so-called 'coloured' as some 'coloured' folks are white- skinned and could be mistaken for whites."

According to the newspaper, authorities were in a dilemma, it was not clear what decision to take. There was indecision as to which ambulance to send, should it be the one designated for whites or one intended for use by blacks only. A debate also ensued on whether the baby should be sent to a black or white hospital. Eventually the baby was given the benefit of doubt and was accommodated in a white only hospital. The baby could have died while these debates were raging on.

I remember feeling sick in my stomach when I read this story. What kind of animals were we dealing with where even the health and well-being of a child had to be subjected to racial prejudices? It was well understood that if the child was deemed to be from black parentage, its chances of survival would have been reduced drastically.

There was another intriguing discriminatory practice that did not follow logic. I could never apprehend the wisdom nor the rationale and economic sense of rejecting millions of 'rands' (South African currency) by making it illegal for Africans, who constitute about seventy-five per cent of the population, to buy hard liquor, such as whiskies, brandies and wines then considered to be for the consumption of whites only. The foolhardiness of the system and its policies was incomprehensible. The white policymakers could not imagine blacks enjoying the same drinks as they did. Their hatred for the black race was so entrenched that it superseded their sense of logic in making economic decisions.

Africans were only permitted to drink and enjoy what they termed 'Bantu beer,' the fermented liquor made from sorghum. Our parents who also enjoyed whiskey or wine had to endure the humiliation of having to wait outside the bottle stores where these drinks were sold, for a chance appearance of young 'coloured' boys (descendants of mixed African and white blood), young enough to be their children, but who, in the eyes of the system were fortunate enough to be recognized for the flow of white blood in their veins and therefore deemed to be qualifying and entitled to a little more privilege than Africans.

The 'Coloureds' were permitted by law to enter the stores and buy the 'white man's liquor'. Some of the little boys would hang outside the stores and at a fee, go in and out buying liquor for the Africans who had to wait just outside the entrance.

The only sorghum beer officially recognized was produced by multinationals and transported by huge trucks to designated township bars. The beer produced traditionally by many African households was not recognized and was deemed illegal, and those found producing it were convicted of criminal offenses.

Hundreds of women, who brewed and sold the so-called 'Bantu beer' in their houses were constantly on the lookout for police raids. If they were unfortunate not to conceal the 'illicit' brew in time, it would be emptied in the yard and they would face charges of illicit brewing.

To avoid surprises, the women would position young boys in strategic locations in a similar way the army posts sentries. These would sound-off alarm bells in the event of a possible raid, thus allowing sufficient time for the women to conceal the 'illicit brew.'

Miriam Makeba, the popularly known South African singer and a political activist in her own right, captures this scenario aptly in her Xhosa song which depicts a desperate child alerting her mother of the arrival of the police. She sang:

Khauleza mama, khauleza, khauleza mama khauleza!
(please hurry mama, hurry, hurry mama. hurry!)
Naka ama polisa asongena endlini mama, khauleza, khauleza!
(the police are here and they are about to enter the house mama, hurry, hurry!)

In apartheid South Africa, Africans could lay claim to only 13% of the land that was carefully designated, most of it in dry areas that were not suitable for large-scale agricultural production. The 13% was further subdivided to create specific areas for the Zulus, Sothos, Xhosas, etcetera. In the 87% of mostly rich and arable land that included the urban cities, the blacks were considered sojourners.

To ensure the lines were well drawn, the blacks were made to carry passbooks that were also a way of controlling the movement

210

of blacks from one place to another. The passbook contained the individual's name, tribe and homeland. The pass also indicated if an individual was working or not. Each black person was required to be in possession of a passbook at all times. In fact, it was an offense not to have it on your person and no excuses were entertained at checks points. Further,

Blacks required special permission to enter and remain within urban areas.

As a teenager, I observed on countless occasions how blacks, sixteen years and older, that were not in possession of the passbook or whose documents were not in order were constantly on the lookout for black policemen nicknamed 'blackjacks' (so nicknamed because of the uniform they wore). The unfortunate ones who could not escape the net deployed by the 'blackjacks' would face the humiliation of being handcuffed to complete strangers and together with a group of others, young and old and in full view of residents forced to march in rows, in some sort of parade through the township, while awaiting police vans on the other side of the location.

Sometimes the transportation would take almost the whole day to arrive and only leave when there was a truckload of defaulters. Arrested suspects would have been waiting the whole day in the hot summer. Those who were deemed illegal and not entitled to be in the cities would eventually be transported to their so called 'bantu stands' and dumped there. For their nourishment on the way they were given brown bread and a pint of milk to help sustain them on the long journey. Many of those forced back into those territories, were born in SOWETO, and had no connection to those places whatsoever. Many would be left stranded in these foreign and strange faraway places.

From birth we were constantly reminded that we were not the same. It was always a situation of us and them, blacks versus whites and vice- versa, an environment of division in which hatred existed and was fostered. Discrimination existed in every aspect of our social life; the hospitals, restaurants, schools, public transportation, parks or malls, and even places of worship, were not spared the discrimination. There was a white and a black section of everything. Anyone caught violating these laws risked physical abuse, imprisonment or even death.

There were marked signs written in big bold letters that read "whites or non-whites only" everywhere. We were never referred to as blacks, but always as non-whites. These signs that littered everywhere indicated where blacks were or were not allowed to stand, sit or eat, and even toilets were segregated. There were whites only restaurants, whites only hotels, white section of the hospitals, whites only and non-whites ambulances, etc.

There were embarrassing situations particularly when black personalities and celebrities that were invited to compete in South Africa came to visit. They could not be accommodated in the whites only hotels because of their colour. This forced the regime to create a category that would accommodate the visiting non-white guests.

To resolve the predicament of where to accommodate the distinguished black guests the system created a category that it referred to as 'honorary-white-status'. The visiting black guests, having been granted 'honorary-whites- status' would then earn the right to be accommodated in hotels reserved for whites only.

In a desperate attempt to break the stranglehold of the boycott by the international community, the regime lucratively rewarded those who embraced its campaign of wooing and bringing personalities to South Africa. These celebrities and personalities were attracted by money and broke a worldwide campaign to isolate apartheid South Africa.

The artists were from different backgrounds including singers such as Percy Sledge, Brooke Benton, The Staple Singers, and boxers such as Curtis Cokes, Ruben Carter and many others,. There were others in other sporting codes as well.

Several artists took a principled position and refused to have any association with the regime. Barry White, Mohammed Ali were among those who refused to perform in South Africa.

The 'honorary status" was also granted to South Africans of Asian origin such as the Chinese who were considered by the system as being neither black nor white enough to qualify for any of these categories.

My friend Andre' van Niekerk (the only white friend, I had)

Apartheid policies guaranteed that South Africans, black and whites, lived separately and had different lifestyles.

On the one hand, whites were left alone in the suburbs to indulge in their comfort, to enjoy wealth and a privileged life. Their huge houses with swimming pools and well- groomed gardens were little havens. The system of white minority governance guaranteed this superior quality of life. On the other hand, blacks who were on standby to provide services to the comfort of their masters were tucked a safe distance away in deplorable surroundings, to forage for food and eke out a living. They were only allowed to come to the white environs when their services were required. The colour of one's skin defined this distinction and determined one's location and place of abode.

White politicians, religious leaders, and apologists of this shameful discrimination, scrambled to whitewash the embarrassing mess through vigorous propaganda campaigns.

Politicians explained it away as an arrangement preferable to both blacks and whites that given the choice would rather co-exist with their own kind to avoid an adulteration of their culture, tradition, or their accustomed way of life. At the same time, religious leaders scrambled to find justification within the scriptures, attempting to legitimize the status quo.

The paths of blacks and whites never crossed except only as employers and employees or perhaps masters and servants. It was unthinkable to contemplate a friendship that developed across the colour lines. Therefore, my friendship with Andre van Niekerk was one of those extremely rare ones. The day he was born, his colour secured a sheltered, privileged life preserved for the few. I, on the other hand, unfortunately belonged to the overwhelming, underprivileged majority, and considered, by white supremacists, to born on the 'wrong side of colour'.

Rev Dick Morgan, an American Missionary and a white priest that taught us religious instructions at high school introduced me to Andre. The system was designed so that only black teachers were responsible for the education of black students. Similarly, the same situation pertained for white students for they too were taught by their own colour. The only exception that was made was to allow white teachers or priests to conduct religious instruction to the black communities. Since the law did not allow both blacks and whites to be in each other's residential areas without permission, these teachers or priests required a special permit to be allowed to travel to and from the black communities.

Reverend Dick Morgan travelled once a week to teach the Word of God to the young, rebellious black youth that were becoming increasingly resentful of whites in general and priests were no exceptions. Although we were not violent towards the priest, his presence amongst us, meant to calm us down, ironically enraged us even more. We saw it as a repetition of the tactics deployed by imperialist England, designed to rob our ancestors and to confiscate their land. We had learned in history that the missionaries were the first to be dispatched to our countries; their roles were to pacify the natives before soldiers with guns moved in to complete the conquest.

Despite our prejudices then and now with some maturity, I do not believe in the least that Rev. Dick Morgan saw his role as being that of subduing militant black youth to be more accepting of their oppressive and miserable conditions. He was a God-fearing, honest man and in his own way, genuinely intended to make a meaningful contribution and play a role in ending the injustice caused by white supremacist policies.

He faced serious challenges trying to persuade a disbelieving congregation that with increasing awareness and consciousness of the oppressive environment, was becoming more-and-more disdainful and less inclined to be accommodative of persuasions that called and appealed for tolerance and forgiveness. Every time in his lessons the holy Reverend faced a barrage of questions such as, "If it is true that we are all equal before the eyes of the Lord, why is it that God allowed a situation where whites became privileged and chose to leave blacks to suffer the indignity of poverty and modern slavery?"

To his plea that we must be peaceful and reject any retaliation, we responded in no uncertain terms that we were tired of having to give the other side of our cheeks repeatedly without any improvement of the conditions we found ourselves in. I always admired Rev Dick Morgan's patience. He would listen as we rumbled on in our anger at the system and then tried very hard to counter the arguments we presented.

On one of his visits, the Reverend approached me with an invitation to select nine other students that plus myself would constitute a group to attend a birthday party of one of his white students in the 'Roodepoort' suburban area where he lived. I approached some of my friends quietly. They were all excited at the prospect of our very first visit to a white neighborhood to mingle with students of our age across the colour line.

The Saturday of the birthday we were collected by the Rev and driven in his Volkswagen mini bus to Roodepoort. A group of young white boys and girls were waiting patiently for our arrival. Initially there was a tense encounter as we did not know what to make of each other, but in a little while we warmed to one another and began gibbering excitedly as if we were old acquaintances.

In the excitement and the discussions that ensued I met Andre. For most of the evening we sat separated from the rest of the group and engaged in serious discussions about everything. We bonded and established a link that was to continue long after the birthday party.

I was to become a regular visitor to the van Niekerk's. Rev. Morgan collected me from Soweto and brought me back for every visit. At Andre's place we played table tennis and other games. At no stage, during all my visits to van Niekerk's, did I ever feel discriminated against.

At some point, Andre and I decided that instead of the usual weekend visits to his place, we would spend some time together in the city centre. One Saturday morning, at an agreed time we met at a location in Johannesburg and toured the city, going to places of interest. After a while, around lunchtime, Andre' suggested we look for a place to eat. I reminded Andre that as far as I knew, there was no restaurant in the whole of Johannesburg that permitted whites and blacks to wine and dine together. I suggested that we looked for separate restaurants catering along colour lines in accordance with the prescribed law and then meet later after lunch.

"Nonsense," retorted Andre in disbelief, "There must be a place where we can sit and eat together. Come with me." And so we began our search for a place to have our lunch together. It was frustrating and humiliating that every place we went to, with Andre leading and asking the question "Is it permitted for my friend and I to come in and have lunch?" the answer invariably, expressed differently at each eating place we approached, was "You can come in and have a seat sir, but the boy must wait outside". We stormed out in anger and searched for the next eating place with no better results.

We repeated this until we came to one of those open space restaurants at the base of the Carlton centre building in the city Centre. The little restaurants had see- through windows and tills where orders and payment were made. The tables were neatly laid out in an open space outside the room, visible to people behind the tills and those serving inside.

"Seat here! and I will go and order our lunch" Andre' suggested, pointing to a table, and moving hurriedly inside the room to place the order. I sat down with a big sigh of relief and was pleased that I could rest my feet after the long hours of crisscrossing the city. It took me a while to notice that all the people around were staring at me. It was clear that without making a sound, I was disturbing the peace. Upon scrutiny, it dawned on me that all those seated at other tables around mine were exclusively white.

Just by sitting there I had encroached in other people's area and comfort zone. Many of the whites stretching their necks and looking in my direction were either curious, cynical, while some were downright angry and felt insulted. "Who is this arrogant black that dared to challenge established procedure and encroach into their space?" Andre and I assumed that because the tables were in an open space, there would not be a rigid application of the discriminatory laws. We were wrong.

The black youngster cleaning around and wiping the tables assessed the situation and assumed that I was a visitor from an African country up north and was probably unaware of the severe punishment meted out to those who defied the law. He came quickly to me and very politely inquired in broken English, whether I was a South African: "Where coming, '*Mnumzana*' (Sir)?" he politely asked.

Upon discovering that I was a South African, he switched from English and speaking comfortably in Zulu he cautioned me, "It is not allowed for blacks to sit here sir; this place is reserved for whites, '*Baso ku bopha, Mnumzana*' (you will be arrested sir," he added.

"Oh! I was not aware," I replied in Zulu, at which point, I looked through the glass panels of the restaurant and saw that at the till inside the shop, Andre was being questioned by the restaurant owner about my presence there. The shop owner had seen Andre and I arrive together.

I stood up slowly, afraid to disturb the peace any further, and moved away meekly – my actions deliberately intended to demonstrate that I was submissive and that it was not my intention to cause trouble - akin to a dog that once taught a lesson would move away whimpering with its tail between its legs. I was frustrated, but above all I was

217

ashamed and humiliated.

Andre was equally angered and embarrassed. As a white youngster, the system had concealed from him the extent to which race or religion was manipulated to perpetuate the crudest and barbaric form of discrimination. He was leading a decent, honest God-fearing life, and was never exposed to the ugly side of the reality in Apartheid South Africa.

When he realized that I could be arrested, we quickly left the place carrying with us the food he had bought. We walked the streets looking for a suitable spot to have lunch till we eventually found a public place where we could sit, as two friends and share a meal together.

We looked around and came across the long, round concrete pillars at the center of the building that are built to hold and reinforce the roofing. We perched ourself on the concrete support of one pillar, placing the food on the floor between us and began to eat. Even at that, black and white passers-by were surprised at our audacity and stared at us as they passed. They understood that this was not the usual master and servant relationship.

I remain truly indebted to the van Niekerk family. Their conduct and acceptance of me for who I am, across the colour line, changed the perception and generalization I had then that all whites were racists and oppressors.

My acceptance of Ntate John Nkadimeng's education of an ANC philosophy of a South Africa that belongs to all who live in it that we were all skeptical about when we joined the ANC in Swaziland, was made easier by the interaction of people like the van Niekerks, Joe Slovo, Ronnie Kasrils, Albie Sachs, Wolfie Kodesh, Michael Lepsly, Eli and Violet Weinberg. and others. It took some educating and a real journey of political understanding indeed, to appreciate the assertion that it is not necessarily the colour of people that is oppressive, but the system that creates conditions for racism to flourish.

The new democratic South Africa is creating what Bishop

Desmond Tutu described as 'The rainbow people of God,' against the background of hate and bitterness, the campaign to build a strong and egalitarian South Africa continued. This was no easy feat; whatever progress made so far must be sustained through structures and institutions that will perpetuate our success, education should be the backbone of this agenda.

Transforming our educational system will bring about the integration of our different races. We have had differing attitudes that have persisted since the invasion of colonialists from 1652 up to 1994. We have had decades of this oppression, and so it will not all go away in one day, one year or even one decade. The walls of social, economic, and moral divide between the whites and the blacks are gradually being dismantled through appropriate legislation.

The fight against Apartheid was an economic and class struggle, where race was projected, used to exploit and accumulate wealth. Africa fought against colonialism and Apartheid; the principles of these have merely shifted ground to a new turf. We are now faced with economic apartheid and a widening gap between the rich and the poor. Looking back through my life, the early struggles against deprivation and resentment; the years of exile and back-alley lifestyle, all diminish in worth when placed side by side with the glory and hopes of my current experience and that of black South Africans.

Time brings with it healing, but also has a strange way of re-enacting evil. What I have learnt over the years, through experiencing loss and challenges, is that it is not time that brings healing; rather it is what we do with time that facilitates the healing.

I fear that the new theatre of Apartheid will not find ample grounds for fierce resistance because as they say, "The water that sinks the boat is the water that has entered into the boat and not that around it." The theatre of the 'rich and poor' divide has favoured privileged Africans enormously. Escaping poverty is now a 'rat race' without rules. Corruption and other forms of illegality are largely unquestioned in this race because the majority of the people are uneducated and therefore, unconcerned. The Portuguese phrase 'a luta continua' which played a vital role in encouraging the FRELIMO Movement during the Mozambique's war of independence comes to mind at this time. Indeed, the struggle must continue and victory can only be real when the material and the socio- economic conditions of the poor and marginalized improve substantially.

CHAPTER 17

HIGH COMMISSIONER
TO THE REPUBLIC OF ZIMBABWE

"Zimbabwe is a jewel of Africa, rich in culture, history and natural beauty."
Julius Nyerere

The ANC sent me out to Zimbabwe again, and as we were now heading home, I was now focused on shutting down the Mission. It was a transitional period and we were now going to join government and prepare for elections that would transform the country from an apartheid state to a democracy. Our last-born son, Tawanda Sean Mamabolo, was born during this period in Zimbabwe.

Marshalled on all fronts the struggle had yielded results; negotiations with the Apartheid regime began and the resulting 'one person one vote' led to the ANC winning most votes and thus being mandated to govern the country.

The ANC has always maintained that the South African struggle was waged on several fronts. Nelson Mandela put it aptly in his message smuggled out of Robben Island after the SOWETO uprising of 1976 in which he stated,

> *"Unite; Mobilize! Fight on! Between the anvil of united mass action and the hammer of armed struggle we shall crush apartheid"*

In addition to mass action and armed struggle, other fronts were the ANC and people's underground activities and the international campaign to isolate the regime.

Ready to govern

We were going back home after many years exile, while some had spent many years in prison. Many comrades had a lot energy and were determined to deliver services to the people; it was an opportunity to put into practice all the theories we had learned regarding the revolution and transforming society. South Africa was the last colonial state to be liberated. Many people assumed we would govern so much better than other nations because of the experience the ANC had gained from witnessing mistakes made by liberated countries in Africa who having attained their freedom, had faltered, and fallen short of addressing the plight of their people. We were determined not to repeat the same mistakes.

Negotiation implied compromise; a Government of National Unity (GNU) was formed. I joined the Department Of Foreign Affairs. The ANC ranked its cadres according to their experience. The highest ranked, were comrades such as Lindiwe Mabusa, Billy Modise, Jackie Sedibe, Welile Nhlapo, Jerry Matjila, and George Nene. I was truly honoured to be considered amongst them, glad to be able to use the wealth of experience gained from having been a representative of the ANC in various countries and international institutions.

The New South Africa and Africa

The remarkable conflict resolution leading to democracy in South Africa placed heavy onus on the country. There were great expectations that the stature of the new democratic country and of its first president would be an asset in the resolution of conflicts on the continent. The experience gained in the negotiations to dislodge apartheid and the country's commitment to fight against human rights abuses wherever they existed placed South Africa in the driving seat in the quest to make Africa and the world a better place to live in.

South Africa immediately got involved and attempted to mediate in several conflicts on the continent, preferring the role of a peacemaker rather than being a peacekeeper. The country's cabinet considered several policy options defining South Africa's involvement in peacekeeping missions on the continent. Amongst these was the need for a clear mandate before getting involved because it was also considered that the country needed sufficient means to participate in any peacekeeping mission and must also be assured that there was a clear entry and exit strategy.

The first real challenge to determine the influence South Africa can exert was provided by Nigeria with the execution of Igbo activists, Ken Saro Wiwa and eight others. These men, then referred to as the Ogoni 9, were protesting the environmental health hazards and the little benefits to Igbo communities generated by the extraction of oil by multinational companies in the east of Nigeria. They were sentenced to death by the Abacha regime. In addition to the Ogoni nine, Abacha had also arrested two military Generals, Shehu Shagari and Olusegun Obasanjo, who were accused of plotting a coup. Mandela sent his deputy, Mbeki, to beg for the stay of execution of these men and for the release of the Generals.

Mbeki's delegation received a positive response from Abacha who pointed out that he could not interfere and stop the judicial processes, but committed to pardoning the men should they be sentenced to death. It therefore came as a surprise when Ken Saro Wiwa was executed. Mandela was snubbed and infuriated. He responded by condemning the Abacha regime for the violation of human rights, and calling for Nigeria's expulsion from the Commonwealth family.

The response from Mandela and South Africa split Africa into two. There were those who respected Mandela as a human rights icon and supported his stance on the issue, but there were also many who felt that his response would be pleasing and be like sweet music in the ears of imperialists and our former colonizers. The latter group were also opposed to what they perceived as the marginalization of a sisterly African country.

I was in Zimbabwe as South Africa's High Commissioner at the time and the strained relationship between Nigeria and South Africa impacted the Africa Group of Ambassadors. The Nigerian Ambassador, Lamine Metteden, and myself both of us representing our countries, went toe to toe in an attempt to win the support of the group. Despite our collision on policy issues, Metteden and myself remained friends and to this day he has my respect as one of the best diplomats that Nigeria has produced.

Head of Mission

Nelson Mandela appointed me as South Africa's new Head of Mission to Zimbabwe. I was going back to a country where I'd spent more years than any other in my entire life in exile. I had served the ANC in that country in various capacities and eventually as the Head of Mission. It was a familiar stomping ground where I was well known and was familiar with lots of people, Ministers, government officials as well as President Robert Mugabe.

The ANC understood that forming a unity Government with representatives of the racist ruling party of South Africa (The Nationalist Party) was not going to be easy. It entailed issues of transformation that we had to contend with. On the employment of the South African Missions were employees that had for years served the racist regime where their loyalty to the Government was demanded and not taken for granted. I knew some of these employees in Zimbabwe from the time I served as ANC's Chief Representative, operating in the same space we had crossed paths on many occasions. I was convinced that most of them hated my guts, especially those who believed the regime's propaganda that we were all just a bunch of terrorists. It was therefore awkward for them and to me that the 'terrorist' was now taking over as the head of the Mission.

I arrived with my family at Harare airport for the umpteenth time. We had left just a few months before after closing the ANC Mission. It felt like we had just gone to South Africa for a holiday and were now coming back. Zimbabwe had been home to my family for many years. We were met at the airport by members of staff of the South African Mission. They were formally dressed, and lined up orderly to greet us on the tarmac before we were taken to the VIP lounge.

We were driven to the official residence that was now elevated in accordance with the status of the diplomatic relations that South Africa and Zimbabwe enjoyed.

Before then, Zimbabwe did not have diplomatic relations with South Africa, but instead had what was referred to as a "Representation of Economic Interest.' I was, therefore, the first Head of Mission of South Africa to Zimbabwe.

This was a moment to savour, for my appointment as High Commissioner for South Africa was history-making in process and a bitter sweet moment given the memories the country held for me and my wife. My comrades and I were making our own history just as South Africa itself was making history. I was not alone. There were other comrades such George Nene, our first High Commissioner to Nigeria, Lindiwe Mabuza our High Commissioner to the UK, Welile Nhlapo our first Permanent Representative to the OAU and many others. At the time, of course, the biggest history that was made and received worldwide attention, was the inauguration of Nelson Mandela, a former political prisoner of the racist regime for twenty seven years, as the first black President of the Republic of South Africa.

At the mission, I inherited a staff that was wholly white, except for black Zimbabweans who were employed for supportive roles, such as serving tea or cleaning the toilets. We were in a black, African country and most of our locally recruited personnel were whites. Indeed, even the secretaries were white South African women who were married to Rhodesians. Justification for this most obvious racist approach was given as concerns for security. The Mission at the time was conscious not to recruit black Zimbabweans, presumably because of the fear that Mugabe's security would seize the opportunity to infiltrate its agents.

I immediately realized that my priority would be to transform the Mission for it was inconceivable that an African mission serving in a black country could consist largely of white people. For me, it was imperative that the composition of the Mission reflect the population demography of the country. Naturally I faced some resistance and the process was not smooth, but ultimately we achieved our objective.

CHAPTER 18

ETHIOPIA

"We see a new Ethiopia, a new Africa, stretching her hands of influence throughout the world, teaching man the way of life and peace."
Marcus Garvey

The Birth of the African Union (AU)

In 1999, President Mbeki appointed me as South Africa's Permanent Representative to the OAU. I was to replace Comrade Welile Nhlapo, our first representative of a democratic South Africa to the continental body. This appointment opened a new chapter for me. It was the beginning of my involvement in continental politics. I was also honoured to serve at a time when the Organisation of African Unity was giving way to the African Union.

South Africa was at the time basking in the honeymoon of our remarkable journey of transition from an Apartheid pariah state. The country was highly regarded and so were its leaders and diplomats. The ANC and Nelson Mandela were the toast of Africa. In Addis Ababa, the capital of Africa's political unity and integration, there were very high expectations of what the newly democratized South Africa could deliver.

Nelson Mandela and Thabo Mbeki, after him, led the way. We relied on the soft power the country was bringing in our ability to resolve conflicts through negotiations. The democratization of South Africa and the defeat of Apartheid provided evidence of this soft power.

Addis Ababa was a hype of activities, debates were in full swing, discussions and consultations to which South Africa was central were plenty. There were frenzied negotiations on what should constitute articles of the envisaged Constitutive Act of the proposed new continental body that was to replace the OAU. I felt highly honoured to have been given the opportunity to lead South Africa's interface with other African countries in Addis Ababa at this critical period in the history of our continent.

The 1999 OAU Summit held in Algiers, being the last before the new millennium, became a precursor to the decision of Heads of State and Government to establish a new continental body. There was a high turnout with most of the leaders attending. The newly elected Nigerian leader, Olusegun Obasanjo, and South Africa's Thabo Mbeki were in attendance and so were veterans like Togo's Gnassingbe Eyadema and Gabon's Omar Bongo, both of whom had been in power since 1967.

Libya's Muammar Gaddafi, who had not attended an OAU meeting since 1977, as well Egypt's Hosni Mubarak, who had also been absent from continental Summits since Islamic gunmen tried to kill him in Ethiopia in 1995, were in attendance. There were other leaders in attendance such as Ethiopia's strongman, Prime Minister Meles Zenawi, and the Eritrean President, Isaias Afwerki, whose countries were at the time embroiled in a bitter war over territory. Present also were Zambia's Frederick Chiluba, Zimbabwe's Robert Mugabe, Uganda's Yoweri Museveni. Two founding members of the OAU, Mwalimu Julius Nyerere and Ahmed Ben Bella attended as special guests.

Preparations were different from what was customary in the Summits of the OAU. Leaders used to come to the Summit to read prepared statements, but this time around the Secretary General, Salim Ahmed Salim, had proposed that the Algerian Summit be organized according to various themes on the challenges facing the continent at the moment.

The context of the Summit on the verge of the new millennium reflected and took stock of the achievements of the OAU and began mapping the path for the future of the continental body. Present at the summit were three heads of state that had come to power through a coup. This prompted a discussion and an agreement was reached that a warning be issued to such countries and that a program be introduced to assist these countries to bring them back to civilian rule.

The consequence of the discussions was that the 35th Summit of the OAU decided that future Summits of the Organisation should bar from attendance leaders who came to power through unconstitutional means. The Summit also addressed the vexing problem of terrorism, the distribution of small arms in Africa, the reduction of armed conflicts and the use of children in armed conflict.

The biggest issue to be addressed by the leaders was globalization and its impact on the continent. Mbeki was asked to lead a discussion on globalization amid a consensus that Africa had not recovered from what many described as the lost decade (1980 – 1990). The continent exhibited symptoms such as negative growth, collapsing economies, civil wars, failing states and crumpling state structures. The Summit also discussed the vexing question of Africa's debt. Mbeki's brilliant presentation not only focused on globalization in general, it also drew attention to a serious problem confronting Africa, the illicit flow of capital from the continent.

The Libyan leader Colonel Gaddafi proposed a Summit to review provisions of the OAU Charter, and an agreement was reached that Libya would host it. This was the beginning of the birth of the AU. The review of the Charter led to the Constitutive Act and the formation of the new organization, the African Union.

There was a feeling that the process of political, economic, and social integration of the continent was proceeding slowly. It was argued that the slow pace was disadvantaging the continent's efforts to compete with others in the race for economic growth and development.

Globalization was seen to be benefiting other continents at Africa's expense. There was never a debate about the urgent need to unify the continent. The difference, similar to disagreements reflected in the old age debate that started 1963 with the formation of the OAU, was in the method to be deployed to achieve such unity.

In preparation for the Summit, Ambassadors of various countries that were based in Addis Ababa travelled frequently to attend various meetings in Tripoli. In accordance with AU procedures, Ambassadors would meet and whatever proposals they made would then be validated by a meeting of the Council of Ministers before endorsement by the Summit.

In Tripoli the preparations were not easy given the fact that Gaddafi was determined to enforce his vision on the rest of the continent. He produced a document that had a number of controversial proposals that were presented for scrutiny. Most of his proposals were rejected by other member states, particularly South Africa and Nigeria that envisioned a different approach.

From 1963 when the OAU was founded to date, debates on the integration of the continent evolved around two essential questions:

Whether declaration of a united and integrated continent can be immediately declared or it is necessary to avoid short cuts and base the integration on a gradual building block approach, by first strengthening sub -regional economic blocs that will ultimately be merged.

In 1963, an accompanying issue for the debate was the issue of whether as part of integration, consideration should be given to delinking borders and relinking new states as agreed upon as opposed to strengthening the inherited colonial boundaries.

Gaddafi's position, like that of Kwame Nkrumah in 1963, was for the immediate integration with the formation of a Central Government whose Headquarters would be based in Libya.

Gaddafi also advocated for dissolution of national armies and the creation of one army for the continent, again with the HQ in Tripoli.

Gaddafi's pronounced that his 'United States of Africa' (USA) would also abandon the IMF, the World Bank and similar institutions and opt instead for the creation of Africa's own financial institutions.

Gaddafi went to great length to achieve his goals. He splashed Libya's wealth accrued from oil and used the cash to lobby and bribe other countries to support his positions. Countries that were in arrears in paying for the OAU's membership fee had their debts settled by Libya if they committed to voting in favour of Gaddafi in the debates that ensued.

Gaddafi envisaged the shape of the cabinet of his proposed African Government, and he began approaching certain individuals promising them Ministerial positions. My own Minister, Dr Nkosazana Dlamini - Zuma was approached and promised the portfolio of the continental Ministry of Foreign Affairs, an offer that she turned down.

When the Heads of State and Governments descended on Libya for the Summit that had been agreed upon in Algiers, the country was in a celebratory mood. There were posters of Colonel Gaddafi accompanied by slogans everywhere. I recall seeing a poster with a slogan referring to Gaddafi which read, 'Hail the Mayor of Africa.'

The brother leader as he was commonly referred to, was clearly positioning himself to lead the "United States of Africa' as he'd envisaged it. It was known that he preferred to be called 'Leader' or 'Guide' and not President, as this was to denote that he had the responsibility to lead the entire continent. He believed that the term 'President' confined the authority of the person within national boundaries, whereas 'Leader' would be all encompassing.

The brother leader had an interesting understanding of what leadership was all about. In one session the leaders debated the prolonged rule of some African leaders. When it was his turn to contribute to the debate Gaddafi was of the view that a leader's term of office should not expire. He made the following observation, "A leader is not some medication in a pharmacy that expires after a period."

Gaddafi had also made extensive preparations for what he perceived to be a possible shift of the continental's HQ from Addis Ababa to Libya, a proposal that was bitterly opposed by Prime Minister Meles Zenawi of Ethiopia. A beautiful, massive infrastructural building with various offices was built in the city of Sirte. These were to be donated by Gaddafi to become the new HQ of the continent. Observers commented that these were bigger and better looking that the United Nations Headquarters in New York.

The Summit eventually adopted the Sirte Declaration after huge debates in which there was clearly a push back on some of Gaddafi's positions. The Sirte Declarations outlined a road map towards the Constitutive Act and the formation of the AU as the successor to the OAU. Gaddafi pushed for the adoption of the Sirte Declaration to be on the 9th of September 1999 (09/09/ 99) a date of National importance to Libya.

The Sirte Declaration announced decisions to:
- establish the African Union
- speed up the implementation of the provisions of the Abuja Treaty, to create an African Economic Community, African Central Bank, African Monetary Union, African Court of Justice and Pan-African Parliament, with the Parliament to be established by 2000
- prepare a Constitutive Act of the African Union that was expected to be ratified by 31 December 2000 and become effective the following year.
- give President Abdelaziz Bouteflika of Algeria and President Thabo Mbeki of South Africa a mandate to negotiate for the cancellation of Africa's indebtedness
- convene an African Ministerial Conference on security, stability, development and co- operation (This was the beginning of the establishment of the Africa's continental security architecture)

In preparation for the Summit, Gaddafi provided free accommodation and food to all the delegates, and dispatched Libyan planes to collect delegates throughout the continent. In addition, he sent a plane to collect military platoons from several African States.

The intention was to have an exhibition of a military parade that would showcase the envisaged united African military force. The brother leader believed that if the army command is centralized, the conflicts in the continent would come to an end. He occasionally asked his colleagues, the other heads of State, "Why do we need our own little national armies?" He rationalized that having national armies led to countries fighting each other. This would not happen if individual countries did not have armies.

Various artists from the continent, Miriam Makeba amongst them, were ferried to Libya for performances. Just before the Summit, Gaddafi had summoned most of the traditional leaders of various countries of the continent, who at the meeting hosted in Libya, declared that Gaddafi was the 'King of Kings'.

Many African leaders whilst fully in conformity with the notion of the continent's political and economic integration totally rejected most of Gaddafi's positions. Leaders such as Thabo Mbeki and Olusegun Obasanjo who were holding positions similar in many ways to those of Julius Nyerere in the debates on the union of the continent in 1963, preferred a unified Africa that would emerge from the strengthening of the regional economic and political communities. They argued that a mechanical declaration of unity would be superficial and not substantive. They were most definitely opposed to the idea of centralizing the army under the command of the brother leader in Libya.

The Group Of Five

Preparing the Constitutive Act entailed a lot of work. This was in part driven by the urgency required that countries should be on alert and not allow some of Gaddafi's wild machinations to take root. Like-minded countries banded together to negotiate the articles of the Act. Five countries formed what was later known as the Group of 5 (G5), an informal grouping consisting of Algeria, Ethiopia, Mali, Nigeria, and South Africa. The G5 met at Ambassadorial level in Addis Ababa and other places reporting to Ministers and Head of States. The G5 worked assiduously to craft the articles of the Constitutive Act, and lobbied other countries to support the position of the five countries.

The Summit in Libya that produced the Sirte Declaration was followed by summits in Lomé, Togo in 2000, when the Constitutive Act of the African Union was adopted, and in Lusaka, Zambia in 2001, when the plan for the implementation of the African Union was adopted. The first session of the Assembly of the African Union was held in Durban on 9 July 2002 while the inaugural session of the Pan-African Parliament was held in March 2004.

The first Chairperson of the Commission was the former Malian president, Mr. Alfa Konare. The choice of a person of such a caliber and status as that of Konare, and we lobbied for him, was deliberate. The G5 leaders reasoned that the continent needed to demonstrate seriousness of purpose by having a chairperson who can be respected and taken seriously globally. This demonstrates how seriously regarded the birth of the new continental body was; if it is the beginning of a coordinating governance of Africa, its representation should look the part.

There were fierce debates as well with the establishment of the New Partnership for Africa's Development (NEPAD), the African Peer Review Mechanism and Africa's Security and Defence Pact discussed in subsequent Summits of the AU, and eventually the African Peace and Security Architecture.

The NEPAD is a strategic socio-economic framework of the African Union that is intended to map a path towards the eradication of poverty, promote sustainable growth and development, and to evolve a program that will ensure the integration of Africa in the world economy, while also accelerating women's development.

It is in fact a merger of the Millennium Partnership for Africa's recovery Programme (MAP), a brainchild of the former President of South Africa, Thabo Mbeki and the Omega plan that was put forward by the former President of Senegal, Abdoulaye Wade. The merger was named New African Initiative (NAI), it was reworked further until NEPAD was born.

African Peer Review Mechanism (APRM)

During this period, the AU Summits were full of interesting debates, one such debate was around a kind of a peer review mechanism that should be put in place. There were debates on whether membership to the mechanism should be voluntary or whether its provisions should be obligatory to all members and should determine membership of the Union as is practiced in the European Union. It is common knowledge that membership of the EU is not obtainable if the candidates do not meet certain requirements.

The APRM, launched in 2003 by Heads of State and Government, is described as innovative and ambitious. It is a specialized agency, self-monitoring and peer review tool that is intended to promote good governance and it is voluntarily acceded to by member states.

The APRM considers its core mission to be *"The deepening of democratic practices through, inter alia, the review of national policies and practices against established standards of governance."* It further states that its mission is to identify deficiencies as well as practices and development of tools and methods by which deficiencies would be rectified, and the best practices disseminated and replicated across the continent.

> *"The ultimate aim of the APRM is to encourage and foster the building of transformative leadership and continuing constructive national dialogue through inclusive and participatory self-and peer- assessment processes."*
>
> *(APRM Strategic Plan 2016-2020)*

235

When the APRM was conceived, there was a big debate on the timing of the operationalization of the mechanism. Some member states argued that the mechanism should be operational only when two thirds of the countries ratified the instruments of the protocol. This is usually the practice with accreditation to membership of institutions and bodies of the AU.

The committee of sixteen Heads of State and Government appointed and representing the five regions of the AU charged with the finalization of the APRM debated the issue of the operationalization extensively. In a meeting of the Committee in Abuja, President Abdelaziz Bouteflika led the charge of those arguing that the mechanism can only operate if two thirds accede to and ratified it.

This came as a surprise to his other colleagues of the group of five such as Mbeki, Obasanjo and Meles, who in their understanding had reached an agreement that pushing the decision of a two thirds majority vote should be rejected because waiting for all the countries to ratify will render the mechanism to become stillborn. They argued, instead, that in the event there were even five countries ready to embark on the peer review processes the mechanism must be operationalized and those member states should be allowed to proceed.

Leaders such as Mbeki and a few others that urged for the speedy establishment of the peer review mechanism were determined to remove all the loopholes that could create an opportunity for those with dictatorial and undemocratic tendencies to take advantage and undermine this noble effort, making it unworkable through technicalities, including the inability to reach the two thirds membership.

In their view, the envisaged newly created APRM would constitute the beginning of the 'good boys club' central to which is the adherence to principles of good governance. They concluded that leaders that were reluctant to join would eventually be put under pressure by their own masses who would need an explanation as to why their governments were not counted amongst the progressive forces.

The debate in Abuja was won by those who advocated for the quick establishment of the mechanism. Today, at the time of writing, almost all members of the AU have acceded and ratified it. In the interest of good governance and assisted by Africa's experts in various fields, the mechanism does a remarkable work of pointing out discrepancies in countries and serves as the primary Continental Early Warning System. Its objective is stated as being "to promote the adoption of policies, standards and practices that leads to political stability, high economic growth, sustainable and inclusive development and accelerated economic, regional and continental integration through sharing of experiences and the scaling up of best and successful practices".

The creation of the AU in the new Millennium provided an opportunity for a rethink of the continental policies and the best minds set about to put forward ideas. The debate on the Non-Aggression and Common Defence Pact also generated heated debates. The debate centred on the principle often used in such pacts that an attack on a member state, a signatory to the pact, is an attack on all others and therefore all are obligated to come to the defence of the attacked country. G5 countries were careful to steer the debate away from just the simple notion of coming to the defence of the member state, but to lay emphasis on the lead of politics in decision-making and therefore the primacy of negotiations and peaceful resolution of conflicts.

After Summits in Togo and Zambia, South Africa was honoured to be the first country to host the first Summit of the AU in 2002. It was held in Durban. I was appointed Deputy Director General responsible for Africa and had to come back from Ethiopia to operate at the HQ in South Africa to help with the preparations for the Summit.

South Africa organized and prepared well for the Summit. The coordination and protocol arrangements were overseen by Ambassadors Billy Modise and Kingsley Makhubela.   Almost all the   Heads of   State   and Government from all the corners of Africa, including VIPs such as Julius Nyerere, who was no longer the President of the United Republic of Tanzania, and the United Nations Secretary General at the time, Mr. Kofi Annan, were in attendance. Colonel Gadaffi made a dramatic entrance, bringing with him, all the way from Libya, his own armoured car for use in South Africa.

President Mbeki had assigned cabinet Ministers who, with the assistance of protocol officials, were to receive the Heads of States as they arrived at the Durban International Airport. The Ministers received the guests and then accompanied them to a location where Mbeki would then welcome them. Gadaffi was received by the Minister of Defence at the time, the late Joe Modise.

Since Gadaffi had brought along his own armoured vehicle, Modise had to jump in to accompany the brother Leader. Modise was later to narrate that he was taken aback when Gaddafi's entourage took a different route from the one that was officially designated to transport the visiting guests.

After travelling some distance, the car stopped and Gaddafi stood up through the roof of his bullet proof car that had an allowance to open at the top. Out of a nearby bush a crowd of young South African blacks came out carrying placards with slogans that read amongst others 'Hail Muammar Gaddafi, the Leader of Africa'.

The shocked Modise later stated in his narrative that Gaddafi who was standing up through the opening, waved back at the motley crew of individuals that were waving and shouting slogans.

He glanced at Modise, who was standing next to him whilst struggling to take in all that was happening before his eyes and commented, "You see! People will always recognize and know who their leaders are!" It was clear that the whole show was arranged by the diplomatic Mission of Libya in South Africa.

238

It is important to note that when the AU was established, there was an unwritten agreement that the big countries, that are obliged to pay more money in the assessed contributions, should not occupy key positions such as the Chairperson and Commissioner for Peace and Security etc. Many argued that if this was not observed it would be tantamount to, an example given, the USA demanding the position of the Secretary General of the UN because she makes most of the financial contributions.

To enable the organization to function, member states annually contribute financially. The Equitable Assessed contribution is determined in accordance with the GDP of the countries. Countries said to be in the upper ceiling, such as South Africa, Nigeria, Egypt, Algeria, and Libya, were therefore, in terms of the understanding, not expected to challenge for the highest positions.

In 2001 I applied for a post to become the Deputy Director General responsible for Africa. I emerged as the preferred candidate after facing a panel of Ministers and Deputy Ministers chaired by Dr Nkosazana Dlamini Zuma. I worked with a team of dedicated colleagues who were Chief Directors heading different sections, the likes of Mxolisi Nkosi, Tselane Mokouena, Sonto Kudjoe, Jersy Duarte, Kingsley Makhubela and others. I served under several Director Generals including Jackie Selebi, Sipho Pitjane and Ayanda Ntsaluba. It was also an honour to work with other DDGs such as Ndumiso Ntshinga, Mo Shaik, Anil Suklal, Professor Eddie Maloka, Ronnie Mamoepa and others.

Immediately after my arrival at the Africa branch, I arranged to meet the entire team in the Africa section. As they gathered in the main hall, I immediately noticed a familiar face in the crowd. Katrina (not her real name) was an employee in one of the sections. The last time I had seen Katrina was in a court in Zimbabwe where she was charged with spying for the Apartheid regime and received a twenty-five-year sentence. I was shocked and taken aback to see her again now. This was the last place I expected to see an apartheid spy.

It soon became clear that the regime had used this lady and with the changes that were taking place, they no longer had any use for her and literally dumped her in the Department of Foreign Affairs.

In 1987 Katrina had been sent to infiltrate the ANC in Zimbabwe and report to Pretoria. She was a young college graduate, the daughter of a doctor father and an artist mother and she joined the spy trade duped into thinking that she was serving her country. She had been brought up being told that the ANC, which was the largest guerilla group, was the enemy. Like many white people of her generation living in South Africa, she grew up receiving the regime's propaganda of the 'Swart Gevaar' (the black danger) that was always drummed into her.

Her mission, and she chose to accept it, was to infiltrate the ANC posing as an anti-apartheid activist. We put her up in one of our residences in an area called Sentosa in the capital city, Harare where she stayed with other comrades whilst awaiting to be send to other destinations. She made attempts to communicate with her handlers, but she must have been poorly trained because it is the way she tried to send her reports to Pretoria that got her arrested.

She would write her reports, put them in an envelope with South African addresses and request the police guards whom Mugabe's regime had placed there for our protection to post them for her. Conscious that we were at risk of an attack, the Zimbabwe Government had deployed security guards to all ANC residences. Katrina pretended that these were letters she was sending to her parents back home. She was obviously very naïve to believe that the guards were foolish enough to fall for her tricks. It is not mentioned in records but some of these security guards were very likely trained intelligence officers and not just ordinary policemen and -women.

The suspicious security men and women went along, and each time Katrina gave them an envelope to post they took it promising to deliver to the post office. The letters were opened immediately she was out of sight. All the messages intended for the agents in

Pretoria were collected and a case was built with the evidence later used against her in court. In one message that was being dispatched, she drew a diagram of the entire structure of the house, with all the rooms indicating locations of bedrooms of the comrades she was staying with. We could only assume logically that this was to help the regime to locate who is where in the event of an attack.

I attended when Katrina appeared in court in Harare. She claimed that whilst held captive she had been whipped, starved, raped and water-boarded by the security men who interrogated her. On 1st November 1990 she was sentenced to 25 years by a Zimbabwean judge. Her sentence was later reduced to 12 years on appeal and consideration of her claims of torture, and she finally served six and a half years.

Eventually Katrina was released when Mandela and the negotiators for a democratic South Africa appealed to all governments that persons who had earlier been arrested for spying for the Apartheid regime should be released wherever they were as part of a fresh start in alignment of the change that was taking place in South Africa.

During the time Katrina worked for me, she and I never referred to her previous role as an Apartheid spy. The team were unaware of her history. I was in a privileged position where I could have made her life miserable, but I chose to keep quiet and let her go about her work without impediment. Towards the end of my period working with her, I received one day a bouquet of flowers and some chocolates from her, delivered to my office. My assistant asked me, in puzzlement, why she had sent these to me. I shrugged it off and said maybe she had enjoyed us working together. Clearly she had already suffered greatly for what she had done and I did not feel it was my place to reveal her past.

CHAPTER 19

SPECIAL ASSIGNMENTS ACROSS AFRICA

"Not everyone is allowed a complex identity. Throughout history, individuals and entire communities have been systematically stripped of their personhood and idiosyncrasies, often to make them easier to demean, denigrate and subjugate - and in some cases, eradicate. Being able to define yourself openly and fully is a privilege; it is a grace many take for granted."
Dipo Faloyin

Sierra Leone

Whilst serving as the Permanent Representative of the country to the OAU, Salim Ahmed Salim, Secretary General of the OAU appointed me to be his envoy to the Mano River Basin and the conflict in Sierra Leone. Travelling with my assistant, Mr. Jimmy Adissa of Nigeria, we crisscrossed the west African region consulting stakeholders such as the governments of the region and the warring factions.

Sierra Leone is a country in West Africa on the Atlantic Ocean that gained its independence in 1961. The capital city, Freetown, is beautiful. There is a scenic view of the range of hills at the harbour that gives an appearance of an image of a lion in repose. The country owes its name to the 15th century Portuguese explorer, Pedro de Sintra, who came up with the name "the Lion Mountains".

The country commemorates the nation's slave trade history with the Cotton Tree landmark and King's Yard Gate. Both were known as places of refuge for returned slaves in the 18th and 19th centuries. It is rich with diamonds that were later, in the 20th century, acclaimed worldwide as "blood diamonds". Unfortunately, the diamonds discovered in Sierra Leone became more of a curse, condemning the country to perpetual wars and poverty.

In 1997, the country became embroiled in a bitter conflict that was characterized by brutality that had the international community decrying the abuses of human rights. The ragtag rebels of the Armed Forces Revolutionary Council (AFRC) and the Revolutionary United Front (RUF) wreaked havoc and fear amongst the community. They were known to have enjoyed the support of the notorious warlord, the former President of Liberia, Charles Taylor who has since been convicted by the International Criminal Court (ICC) for gross violation of human rights.

These were terrorist groups that were reinforced by the recruitment and use of child soldiers. They raped women and had little regard for human life. Young girls were conscripted as sexual slaves or were forcibly married to the Generals. The rebel groups recruited children because they could be easily manipulated, knew no fear, and can be trained to be more loyal and obedient than adults.

The groups utilized inhumane methods of terrorizing the community, such as cutting off people's hands. They would force their victims indicate their preference on how their hands should be cut and the choice was between cutting at the sleeve or having only the hand removed. When I arrived in the capital, Freetown, I got to talk to a lot of people who narrated scary stories of how the rebels moved from one house to the next and amputated limbs, of people who felt trapped, and were unable to escape. There was no doubt that the citizens had been severely traumatized.

The RUF indicated that it amputated people so that it could prevent them from voting for what it considered to be the wrong leadership. There were other explanations given, amongst which were that they were trying to stop soldiers from carrying guns that according to them were used by the army to point at their 'brothers and sisters'. Even more ridiculous was a claim made by some of the rebels that the amputations were meant to prevent people from mining because the proceeds of the diamonds were used to finance the Government of the day. Hundreds of thousands had their limbs amputated making that the rebels' signature of terror against the populace.

On a personal level, two events remained etched in my memory for a long time. One was eight-month-old Mari Koroma whose hand was cut by the rebels when she was only 3 months old, that I saw when visiting a refugee camp for amputee victims of the civil war. It was difficult to imagine that there exist people in this world that are so heartless and are capable of such cruelty.

The second event was a visit I undertook to the front-line of the conflict area and where it dawned on me that I had placed myself in the line of fire. In an attempt to have an understanding of the conflict, I requested to be sent to the front-line. This was at a state bordering Liberia where the rebels and government forces faced - off in continuous battle. The rebels operated from a so-called liberated territory.

When Jimmy and I arrived, we were fetched by a taxi driver, who, whilst driving us to the hotel, pointed to a location a distance away which was an area occupied by the rebels and considered by them a "liberated area." He informed us about the war that was ensuing and of repeated attacks from across the terrain by the rebels. Something he mentioned caught my attention and had me shivering with fear and that was a report he gave about cannibalism. The driver informed us that some of the rebels were of the belief that if they were to eat parts of brave and historic leaders, they would in turn, inherit the courage or wisdom of such leaders.

That evening the hotel's electricity was cut due to power failure, it was hot, and I could not sleep a wink as I imagined that there could be an attack under the cover of darkness. I sincerely wished that I had not displayed such bravado as there had been no need for me to expose myself to such danger. The taxi driver had been explicit in his description of alleged attacks by the rebels. He stated that in one incident he saw an RUF member holding a human liver in his hand and looking for salt. I was terrified to say the least.

Long after I had left and was now in safety, I tried to establish the veracity of the story of the taxi driver by talking to others. For all I knew the narrative by the driver could have been a fabrication, particularly the bit about cannibalism. Unfortunately, hard as I tried, I could not find any emphatic assurance that the story by the driver was just a figment of his imagination.

Much as they were disorganized, the rebels were a handful to the government of the day. In May 1997, military officers of the self-proclaimed Armed Forces Revolutionary Council (AFRC) dethroned the government of President Ahmed Tejan Kabbah. However, the member states of the western African region refused to entertain an unconstitutional transfer of power in their region. Power in Sierra Leone was again restored to the constitutionally elected government, by the intervention of the regional military forces, the Economic Community of West African States Monitoring Group (ECOMOG)

However, the continued challenge to constitutionality and power by the rebels was reinforced by the support received from the Liberian warlord, Charles Taylor. The situation was also not helped by the fact that the United Nations operated under a UN Security Council (UNSC) resolution that made the contributing military forces of various countries under the UN become impotent and unable to intervene effectively.

The rebels had fierce commanders like Samuel Sam Bockare, widely known as Mosquito, who was a ruthless killer and known to boast about the adrenaline rush and excitement that he experienced when killing people, comparing this feeling to reaching orgasm. These killers were closely aligned to Charles Taylor and operated mostly from Liberia. Addissa and I travelled a lot to Liberia to consult with Taylor and to seek permission from him to meet the rebels many of whom were in his territory. In our interventions, it became clear that their motivation for the terror attacks on the people was the control of the diamonds that were sprawled in the country.

> *In one of our visits in May of 2000, we arrived in Freetown to reports that more than 300 UN troops had been taken hostage. The Chicago Tribune of May 6, 2000, reported that according to a UN spokesperson, "The soldiers had their weapons taken away from them and they were stripped of their clothes. About a dozen armoured vehicles belonging to the Zambian contingent of the UN forces were confiscated and were now being driven by the rebels, according to reports from the field.*
> *"Another contingent of more than 100 Nigerian peacekeepers was stripped of weapons and then released," said the spokesman, Fred Eckhart. The newspaper further quoted a Western diplomat in the capital Freetown who stated that, "The 8,300 member UN force, composed mainly of African and Indian troops, was rapidly losing confidence under the assault."*

The attitude from the contingents were not because the troops could not fight, but this was the resultant consequence of the constraints emanating from the resolution of the Security Council. It was problematic that rebels were able to capture weapons from forces of the UN, who were there to intervene with the intention to calm the volatility of the situation. The situation was worsened by the fact that these weapons, seized from UN forces were in turn used against the Government and the people.

In Sierra Leone, I worked closely with the UN Under Secretary General (USG) and representative of the Secretary General, the former Foreign Minister of Nigeria, Ambassador Oluyemi Adeniji. Although the OAU was in involved in resolving conflicts, in those yesteryears the UN was always in the lead and the OAU played only a supportive role, the situation has since changed.

I had the privilege of consulting with leaders of the region on the conflict in Sierra Leone. The OAU played a role and gave momentum to the complex peace process in that diamond-rich nation.

My role as envoy was to engage regional leaders such as Charles Taylor in Monrovia, Liberia, Nigeria's Vice President Atiku Abubakar, National Security Advisor, Gen Aliyu Mohammed, the Executive Secretary of ECOWAS and others in the region. My mission covered Nigeria, Liberia, Guinea and Mali, which were considered to be playing a crucial role in the efforts to bring peace to Sierra Leone.

São Tomé And Principe

In the early morning of July 2003, soldiers seized key sites in São Tomé, including Ministries, radio station and telecommunications. The Prime Minister and some cabinet ministers were held captive. The rebels who participated in the coup claimed that they were protesting in response to the social and economic crisis engulfing the country. The soldiers were also concerned about the deplorable living conditions and bad diet in the barracks where they lived. It transpired that the leaders of the coup were fourteen soldiers who had just returned from South Africa after they had been released from service in the South African Defence Force. The coup plotters had served in Namibia and South Africa where they fought in the service of the Apartheid regime, and had been members of the notorious 32 Battalion.

In the 1970s, the Apartheid Government in South Africa created a mercenary unit consisting mainly of refugees from Portuguese-speaking African countries. The Battalion popularly known as the 32 Battalion (Sometimes nicknamed the Buffalo Battalion was from members of the defeated 'Frente Nacional de Libertação de Angola' (FNLA). Some of the recruits of the battalion came from Mozambique and the islands of São Tomé and Principe.

With the advent of democracy in South Africa, these nationals from various countries in Africa were offered South African citizenship by the Apartheid regime and were incorporated into the defence force. Fourteen of those who had come from São Tomé and Principe opted to go back home. These became the core and leadership of the coup in São Tomé and Principe.

South Africa was invited to participate in the mediation in São Tomé and Principe because of the involvement of these members of the 32 Battalion, men who considered themselves South Africans after being granted citizenship by the regime. These men had themselves demanded that South Africa should be part of the mediation.

President Joaquim Chissano, who at the time was Chairperson of the African Union, requested President Mbeki to dispatch a unit that was to join other mediators in São Tomé and Principe. Mbeki put together a team that consisted of his Head of Security, Billy Masetlha, a colleague from military intelligence, General Tony Nyembe, South Africa's Ambassador to Gabon, Mr. Mokgethi Monaise and I represented Foreign Affairs.

Immediately upon our arrival, we pulled the former members of the 32 Battalion aside and began discussing with them, asking them what their motive was in orchestrating such a coup. The men had an interesting story to tell:

After they were recruited by politicians in the opposition to the ruling party, they left their country fleeing from the socialist policies and dictatorship of the then President Manuel Pinto Da Costa (1975-1991) who had been in power since independence. In exile they parted ways with their political leaders whom they accused of exploiting their naivety to benefit their own greedy ends. Using makeshift dinghy boats, they navigated the rough seas and landed on the enclave of Walvis Bay in Namibia that was under occupation by the Apartheid regime. On arrival they were immediately detained as illegal immigrants. After spending a year in prison, the regime gave them a choice, they could either continue staying in prison or they could be freed if they agreed to join the new military unit, the 32 Battalion. They opted to join the unit.

The new unit was used by the regime to fight cadres of SWAPO in Namibia and the ANC in Angola. With the advent of independence in Namibia, the 32 Battalion was dissolved, its members, the Portuguese-speaking Africans from various countries in the continent, were taken to South Africa, given citizenship and integrated into the national army.

The notorious battalion is known to have committed numerous crimes, killed refugees and innocent civilians including women and children in a series of attacks in Angola. There were also allegations made that during the so-called 'black on black' violence in South Africa just before the advent of democracy, these men were used as the third force that was utilized effectively to create confusion and to kill citizens, thus, magnifying the perception that it is black people killing each other.

On arrival, we found the team of international mediators led by the Congolese and Gabonese Foreign Ministers, Messrs. Rudolphe Adada and Jean Ping respectively, already at work. It was fascinating to see the interest, to quickly find a solution to problems of such a tiny country, shown by the international community. I could not help making comparison and reaching a conclusion that other small countries such as Burundi or the Comoros would not attract the same kind of attention.

It was clear that the oil deposits and the potential that São Tomé and Principe has to become a wealthy country is responsible for the appeal that attracted so much attention. The team of International Mediators was led by two Ministers from Congo and Gabon, and included representatives of The Community of Portuguese Language Countries (CPLP). Other countries represented were Nigeria, the United States of America, and of course, South Africa.

This was the second attempt by the military to remove a democratically elected government, the first attempt was in August 1995. When the coup of 2003 occurred the President of the country was visiting Nigeria at the time. The negotiation immediately focused on ensuring the safe return of the President and restoration of constitutional order.

Considering that the rebels had asked for the South African team, it became easy to quickly convene the coup plotters separately and got them to commit and sign an agreement that was crafted during the negotiations with the international team. The negotiations were made easy by assurance by the rebels that they were not contesting to take over power. Their intention was only to draw attention to the deplorable conditions in the barracks and in society in general.

The agreement negotiated addressed among others, the release of the Ministers held in captivity, the safe return of the President, Mr. Fradique de Menez. Parliament was asked to approve an amnesty law and the National Assembly endorsed a law on the use of resources and management of the oil sector. All parties concerned agreed to the return to constitutional order and there was also to be the establishment of a monitoring mechanism to oversee compliance with the constitution and the principle of the division of powers.

The agreement was signed by the coup plotters and was forwarded to the President who had moved from Abuja to Libreville to await the signing. The President was returned to São Tomé aboard a Nigerian plane and in the presence of President Obasanjo to guarantee security. Obasanjo jokingly described how the President of the country insisted on him disembarking first when the doors opened on arrival, and literally pushed him (Obasanjo) to the front.

Soon after the return to constitutional order and as part of our contribution to the stability of that country, South Africa dispatched a shipment of non-military items to help with the improvement of conditions in the barracks. The South African mediation played a huge role in the resolution of the conflict. I was impressed with the leadership of Masetlha who immediately took charge as we interrogated one after the other, the former fourteen members of the 32 Battalion. We convinced them that we would ensure that their grievances were attended to.

Equatorial Guinea

On 7 March 2004, the Zimbabwe and Equatorial Guinea governments arrested mercenaries in their respective countries. The mercenaries in both countries belonged to one group of people who were plotting a coup d'etat to overthrow the government of Equatorial Guinea led by the President Mr. Teodoro Obiang Nguema Mbasogo, and replace him with the opposition leader Mr. Severo Moto Nsa, who was exiled in Spain. The financiers of the plot included the son of Margaret Thatcher, the former British Prime Minister. Mr. Mark Thatcher initially denied involvement, but eventually confessed his role in the attempted coup and was fined thousands of British pounds.

The group of mercenaries led by the British mercenary, Mr. Simon Mann, had made a stopover in Harare on their way to Malabo to execute the coup. They made attempts to buy military equipment under the pretext that the purpose of the purchase was to protect diamond mines in the Congo.

According to Zimbabwean authorities, the mercenaries had made an order of 61 AK 47 riffles, 150 hand grenades, 10 rocket propelled grenade launches (100 RPG shells) and 75 000 rounds of ammunition. The Zimbabweans did not buy their story and rounded all the men that were in the 727 aircraft that was waiting on the tarmac, destined for Malabo and had them arrested.

There was an advance party of 15 suspects in Malabo led by the ex- member of the 32 Battalion military unit (Buffalo Battalion), Mr. Nick du Toit. After being alerted by the South African and Zimbabwean secret services, the authorities in Equatorial Guinea acted swiftly to nip in the bud this dangerous plot that could have had dire consequences.

In addition to Simon Mann, there were also 20 South Africans, 18 Namibians, 23 Angolans, 2 Congolese and 1 Zimbabwean involved in the plot. In the trial that ensued, the plot revealed that the coup plotters were duped by Zimbabweans and were made to believe that they could acquire weaponry from the Zimbabwe Defence Industry whose Director was Colonel Tshinga Dube, an old friend of mine. If they had succeeded in acquiring the weapons, Mann and his group would have arrived from Zimbabwe with the weaponry and in Malabo the President would have been lured to come to the airport under the pretext that he would have received gifts and donations. The President and many other influential people would have been ambushed and executed.

The coup failed and the President publicly accused Spain of being behind the plot. The appearance of two Spanish warships close to Equatorial Guinea's coastline reinforced the allegations made by the Equatorial Guineans. The accusation was quickly rejected by the spokeswoman of the Spanish Government who categorically denied any involvement by her country declaring that "…there are no ships, we deny any kind of involvement". This was somehow contradicted by the statement made by the Minister of Foreign Affairs, Ms. Ana Palacio, who declared that the warships "were not there on a mission of war, but one of cooperation". This was, undoubtedly, a diplomatic blunder on the part of Spain.

In Malabo the crackdown was fierce, many foreigners were rounded up and attacked. There were many foreigners working in Equatorial Guinea, mostly from the neighbouring countries such as Cameroon, Gabon, Nigeria and Ghana. The author, Adam Roberts, writes in his book, *The Wonga Coup*, that "gangs of xenophobic youth threatened migrant workers in the streets and demanded their papers". He states further that "on 13 March addressing a meeting, Obiang said that "the coup plotters planned to turn our city into a blood bath". He told his people to be suspicious of outsiders and ordered 'operation clean-up "to expel illegal immigrants".

Nick Du Toit and his team were rounded up, arrested and imprisoned at the notorious Black Beach Prison.

I led a delegation of officials of the South African Government sent by the President to convey a message to the authorities in Malabo.

We were received warmly by the President, and arrangements were also made for us to meet official of various ministries to discuss cooperation and the way forward. Our mission was to make it clear that the South Africans, members of the Executive Committee and former soldiers of the defunct 32 Battalion, did not act with the approval of the Government of South Africa.

Judging from the warm reception that our delegation received and considering that the South African Secret Service were among the first to raise alarm, we were confident that we would not encounter any hostilities. We were, however, taken aback when in one of the meetings of officials, an old man raised his hand and asked a question directed at me, "Can you tell me, why are you, South Africans, trying to kill us? Is it because of the oil?" Why don't you just request us? Maybe we will consider sharing it with you. It is not our fault that we are endowed with all the oil reserves; this is a God-given gift and not of our making," the old man continued.

After negotiations with authorities in Equatorial Guinea we were obliged to visit the detained South Africans and engaged the authorities to ensure the wellbeing and welfare of our citizens. Masethla, Monaise and I made several visits before the men appeared in a court of law. We also counseled their families who came to visit.

Whenever we visited them, the men, Du Toit, Allerson, Boonzaier, Cardoso, Domingos and Schimdt told us harrowing stories of torture and deplorable conditions. We noticed that we were never taken to the prison to visit them. Instead, arrangements were made for the men to be escorted to the nearest police station that had been designated as our meeting place.

They claimed that they were made to sleep with their hands cuffed tightly behind their backs. They also claimed that they were made to stay long periods without taking a bath. Although they were allowed to bath and given lotion, dressed in clean clothes each time we paid a visit, the indelible marks left by the tight cuffing were undoubtedly visible. They also indicated that for ten days after their arrest they were burned with cigarettes, beaten with rifle butts and hung upside down. Adam Roberts also reports that "one of the guards stamped on Nick's foot so hard the toenail came off…The inmates eventually referred to this abuse as the 'Malabo manicure".

The prisoners were kept in a big hall where they were mixed with criminal elements. They reported that one day without any explanation, a woman who was arrested was thrown into their cell. We could not understand the rational of putting a woman in a men only cell, a strange occurrence never heard of anywhere in the world. We warned the inmates to keep a distance from the lady as it was most likely a ruse intended to entice the men to have sex with her.

Simon Mann, Nick Du Toit and others were found guilty by a court in Malabo and were sentenced to 34 years. They served only five years of that sentence after they received a Presidential pardon from Obiang Ngema Mbasogo.

Mann later apologized for what he did, and still maintains that although he cannot consider himself a freedom fighter, he was convinced at the time that a coup against what they described as a relic dictator was in the best interest of the people. What Mann was not saying was that if this 'violation of human rights or the dictatorship' had taken place in any other small country such as Burundi or the Comoros, that is not bestowed with mineral wealth to the same extent as that of Equatorial Guinea, his benevolent gesture would have come to naught. Clearly if he and his little band of mercenaries had succeeded in executing their plan, their irresponsible action would have turned the country into a blood bath with thousands of innocent people killed.

The Democratic Republic Of The Congo
As earlier mentioned, from 2007 I was South Africa's envoy to the Great Lakes. Our focus was the resolution of the conflict in the DRC. The whole region was embroiled in an ethnic conflict that pitted the Hutus against the Tutsis. There is, a horrific history of

genocide underpinning the ongoing conflict in the region. The Rwanda genocide is still fresh in many people's minds.

The conflict in the DRC is clearly resource-driven and characterized by a history of colonial greed contingent upon the huge demand of the crucial mineral resources available in that country. As has been the case in most African countries, the availability of such natural and mineral resources, instead of being wealth that must be celebrated and utilized to benefit the people, became a curse that condemned the population to poverty and perpetual enslavement and continuous war. The minerals extracted from the bowels of the earth in Africa are remodeled to create luxury and a better life for citizens of other continents.

There has been many phases of the conflict beginning with the colonial greed, plunder and terror of King Leopold and Belgium that resulted in the massacre of thousands of Congolese.

This is described well in Adam Hochschild's book, 'King Leopold's Ghost' that informs how Leopold's greed was first exposed by a trusted employee of a Liverpool shipping line, a subsidiary of the company that had the monopoly on all transport cargo to and from the Congo Free State as it was then called. The employee, Mr. Edmund Dene Morel, was sent to Antwerp by the company to supervise cargo to and from the Congo on behalf of King Leopold, the only human being that was allowed as an individual to colonize and own a whole country.

He immediately noticed and was shocked to observe that "at the docks of the big port of Antwerp, he witnessed his company's ships arriving filled to the hatch covers with valuable cargoes of rubber and ivory. But when they cast off their hawsers to steam back to the Congo, while military bands play on the pier and eager young men in uniform line the ships' rails, what they carry is mostly army officers, firearms and ammunition."

He immediately concluded that there is no trade going on, that very little or nothing is exchanged, and realized that there can be only one explanation for their source: slave labour. Morel was later to mount campaigns throughout the world including in America drawing the attention of everybody to the cruelty of the genocide committed by Leopold and his greed.

The Congo was also subjected to a CIA-inspired assassination and coup of the people's Prime Minister, Mr. Patrice Lumumba. The CIA and Belgium helped to install the puppet, Mobuto Sese Seko, into power. He was the leader of the coup who later became the most corrupt president in Africa, and whose riches made him counted amongst the wealthiest in the world. Mobuto was himself toppled by a rebel leader Laurent Kabila who in turn was later assassinated. Nelson Mandela and South Africa got involved and assisted in negotiating the transition from Mobuto to Kabila.

The current conflict in the DRC began in 1998, and it is estimated that over 4.7 million people have been killed by fighting, starvation and disease. In the east of the DRC alone, there are around 120 armed groups and close to 4.5 million Internally Displaced People (IDPs). Essentially the conflict is a continuation of the ethnic divide between the Hutus and the Tutsis that was responsible for the genocide in Rwanda. Rwanda accuses DRC of harboring and allowing the Hutu-based Interahamwe to launch attacks from the east of the DRC. Similar accusations are leveled by Uganda that points to the fact that in the Northeast of the DRC, the Lord's Resistance Army of Joseph Kony has survived and thrived.

Apart from the problem of ethnicity, the war is compounded also by greed for the mineral wealth. The DRC is richly endowed in, among others, Gold, diamonds, Copper and Coltan (Mineral used in mobile phones).

There had been reports of charlatans exporting gold from the Ugandan side of the border where there is no existence of gold mines.

In retaliation to the perceived DRC's support for the Hutu rebels Uganda and Rwanda backed the establishment of the 'Rassemblement Congolais Democratie' (RCD), a rebel group that was bent on overthrowing the Government of the Congo. Some SADC countries couldn't tolerate the situation and became drawn into the conflict in support of the DRC. In no time the conflict in the Great Lakes threatened to engulf the entire continent and break out into a full-scale war, at the time pitting Angola, Zambia, Namibia on the side of the DRC against Rwanda and Uganda on the opposing side.

The situation on the ground was a reflection of the lack of effective governance, a mixture of violent crime, displacements and land-based conflict exacerbated conditions.

South Africa's involvement in the DRC was based on the need to contribute to the greater African vision of a united and prosperous continent. We recognized that there are countries that could be described as giants on the continent because of the wealth and mineral resource they have available. Potentially if capacitated and enabled, these countries can be the driving force towards Africa's prosperity on the continent.

The President, Thabo Mbeki, referred to such countries as locomotives. South Africa recognized that the African countries with such a potential are Egypt in the North, the Sudan and Kenya in the East, Nigeria in the west and the DRC and South Africa in the central and Southern Africa. We were convinced that these countries possessed a potential that if realized could lead the economic recovery of the continent.

The DRC alone has so much to offer, a scoping report produced in 2005 concluded that "The Democratic Republic of the Congo (DRC) has one of the richest natural resource endowments in the world, with mining and forestry offering enormous growth potential. The DRC also possesses Africa's most extensive network of navigable waterways and has vast hydroelectric potential most of it remaining untapped." In fact, the Inga hydro- electrical scheme has the potential to supply electricity not only to the DRC, but also to most countries in sub- Saharan Africa.

The South African Government committed and did whatever

possible in her intervention in the DRC, considering the challenge posed by the interests of the major western countries for this specific sphere of influence. The country was considered by many to be punching above its weight. Mbeki was convinced that Africa had to do the utmost to take leadership in turning the situation in that country around. When President Mbeki visited for the bi-national meetings in the DRC he took with him a number of his cabinet Ministers. Some even joked that Mbeki could easily have held his cabinet meetings in the Congo on some of those visits.

All envoys from the world descended on the DRC, we formed a pool and worked together to facilitate the process. I got to know other envoys such as the Americans, William Lacy Swing who was the Under- Secretary General for the UN Organization Stabilizing Mission and James Swan, the US Special Envoy at the time. Together with the Canadian, the Netherlands, the European Union and other African countries we established a structure that came to be known as Friends of the International Conference of the Great Lakes Region (ICGRL).

Despite the humongous efforts put in by countries, the AU, the UN and other international institutions, sadly for close to twenty years since the elections that were meant to end the war and bring about constitutionality and democracy, the DRC is still very much embroiled in conflict. Rebels in the east of the county still run amok and foreign exploitation still marks its landscape.

At the time, with the momentum of the agreements that were reached with the parties that were signatories, we ran around with UN experts trying to figure out how to implement the Demobilization, Disarmament, and Reintegration (DDR) of the rebel forces. We deliberated on the best way to effect the Security Sector Reform (SSR) and talked about the ownership of the process by the country and people. Surprisingly, the same discussions are still held twenty years later and counting.

Burundi

From 1993 to 2005, DRC's eastern neighbour, Burundi, that also shares a border with Rwanda, was embroiled in a civil war. The conflict, sparked by the assassination of the democratically elected Hutu President, Melchoir Ndadaye, spiralled and resulted in a death toll of more than 300,000 people. South Africa, together with the international community, rallied to negotiate a peaceful resolution of the conflict in the region.

The tiny landlocked Republic of Burundi, with a population of about 12 million people received attention that included, at one stage, mediation by iconic leaders such as Julius Nyerere, Nelson Mandela, Yoweri Museveni of Uganda and Benjamin Mkapa of Tanzania. The persistence of Nyerere and Mandela eventually produced results and an agreement between the warring parties, known as the Arusha Accord, was reached. Unfortunately, not all committed to the agreement; the military wing of a Hutu rebel group, the Phalephehutu FNL, did not sign and opted to continue the armed struggle.

The mediation in Burundi was in phases; in 1999 President Nelson Mandela was appointed facilitator of the Burundi Peace Process (BPP) by the Great Lakes Summit Initiative for Burundi chaired by Uganda with Tanzania as the Vice Chair. His efforts led to 19 political parties of that country signing the Arusha agreement. The only discrepancy with the accord was that the main political parties namely the CNDD–FDD and the Phaliphehutu – FNL refused to sign, remained outside the peace process and continued the armed struggle. With Mandela's support Mr. Pierre Buyoya and Mr. Domitien Ndayizeye became President and Vice respectively, during the transitional arrangements. Buoyed by the progress achieved, the African Union deployed a peace mission in Burundi that was known as the African Mission in Burundi (AMIB).

Deputy President Zuma continued the efforts of former President Mandela, and his facilitation of the process led to the signing of three additional important agreements. On 8 October 2003, the Pretoria Protocol on Defence and Security Power sharing in Burundi and on the 16 November 2003, The Forces Technical Agreement (FTA) were signed. Ambassador Welile Nhlapo assisted the facilitation of both Mandela and Zuma. Eventually in 2004, the United Nations Security Council approved the deployment of a peacekeeping Mission; the United Nations Operation in Burundi (ONUB).

After a nation-wide referendum, Burundi held elections to elect their government in 2005. The Burundi also endorsed a new constitution by an overwhelming majority. However, despite the progress made, all was still not well, the Phalepehuitu FNL rebel group refused to be part of the changes that were taking place and continued a bitter war that resulted in numerous killings. Its leader, Agathon Rwasa, remained a mystery. He was said to be operating from the bushes in neighbouring countries, and was widely known but very few people in the country had actually seen his face. South Africa was entrusted with negotiations to bring the last rebel group led by Rwasa into the fold.

Envoy To The Great Lakes Region
I had just been appointed South Africa's envoy to the Great Lakes of Africa when a former South African Parliamentarian by the name of Jan van Eck approached me and informed me that he was the advisor of the Palipehutu FNL. He also informed me that the rebel group was ready to negotiate and that he had advised the group to indicate to the Heads of State of the East African region that their preference for a mediator was South Africa.

With van Eck's assistance arrangements were made for me to meet with the representatives of the rebel group in Kenya. Accompanied by an official from the desk, we spent the whole day at a hotel in Kenya with the spokesperson of the party, Mr. Pasteur Habimana, and his delegation, trying to understand the standpoint of the party.

Three weeks after my meeting with Habimana, President Jakaya

Kikwete of Tanzania, who at the time the was Chairperson of the East African Region, came to South Africa on a working visit. Kikwete forwarded the request of the region, appointing South Africa as mediator in the quest to bring the FNL into the fold. Mbeki appointed his Minister of Safety and Security, Comrade Charles Nqakula to be the facilitator, and I was to assist.

Negotiations were tough. There was an instance when the FNL threatened to withdraw, alleging bias on the part of the facilitator. Another incident saw a representation of the group approach Nqakula demanding that I should be replaced as his assistant. Nqakula rejected their request, stuck to his guns and kept me on as his assistant. It transpired later that the request of the FNL was at instigation of some members in our team who felt that I was keeping too close an eye on the finances. We were receiving funds from the European Union and other organizations and it was imperative to account for it properly.

It became apparent that part of the delay in finalizing negotiations and reaching was due to the various messages that were conveyed to the warring factions. The one person who fell out of favour was Mr. Jan van Eck while we were still hailing the role he played in linking South Africa with the mediation process. We soon realized that he was not working with us to end the negotiations and we got the impression that he was using his position as an advisor to the FNL to encourage the party to reject some of our proposals. We attributed van Eck's behaviour to an attempt to prolong the negotiations for whatever reason.

The process was also stalled by the parties' lack of understanding that negotiations are a give and take, a win-win situation. The FNL refused to barge or entertain any compromise in what they believed was the correct position. Pasteur was accustomed to saying that "the peasants will not understand if we compromised" whenever they were required to bargain with the Governing party.

We had to stop the negotiations and solicited Vasu Gounden

and his African Centre for the Constructive Resolution of Disputes (ACCORD) to help and give basic training on what negotiations are all about. A selected group of members of the parties locked in negotiations came to South Africa for training. This also afforded an opportunity for the negotiators to work together in an informal setting and helped ease the tension and help them, foster greater understanding of each other.

The Facilitator's team also sought to minimize interference by others and kept people away from the negotiations which became counterproductive. We discovered that after each session, daily, some of the negotiators were invited to Missions of western countries where they would, over dinner, be quizzed on what transpired in the negotiations and also received advice that sometimes went contrary to messages of the Facilitation team.

To help address this challenge Nqakula followed the example of other peace processes by establishing a Group of Special Envoys for Burundi (GSEB), these included representatives of the African Union, the European Union, the United States of America, and the United Nations.

By pulling together everybody we ensured that the same message was being conveyed. Following that manner a ceasefire agreement was finally signed by the parties.

The GSEB reached a common understanding on the following points that were expected to arise in the course of implementing the Comprehensive Ceasefire Agreement:
• Power sharing
• FNL transformation into a political party
• FNL dissidents
• Political prisoners
• Civil society
• Rewriting history
• Forces technical agreement
It took some time to persuade the Palipehutu FNL to change its

name. All concerned pointed out that it would not be acceptable in the new dispensation, whose healing process was to strive for the unity of the nation, to accept the existence of a party that advocated ethnic exclusivism. Eventually the party conceded and agreed to do discard mention of Phaliphehutu (Hutus only) from their name and that they would henceforth be known as the FNL.

'In consultation with Burundi's regional and international partners, a Programme of Action was developed to help ensure the full implementation of the Comprehensive Ceasefire Agreement (CFA) between the Government of Burundi (GOB) and the Palipehutu-FNL (FNL). The Program of Action addressed, in a comprehensive manner the political, security and socio-economic reintegration dimensions of the peace process, to ensure the early resumption of the process as well as prevent its collapse in the future.

The Program of Action comprised two phases that enabled the safe return of all FNL leaders and combatants to Burundi and their political, economic, and social integration in that country. The process of integration was closely monitored to ensure that the security of returning FNL members was assured and that systems that would cater for their integration were properly defined and put in place.'

In 2007, Nqakula established what we called 'Political Directorate,' and appointed me to Chair. The Political Directorate was to be based in Bujumbura and comprised of the following:
- A representative of the Facilitator (Chair)
- The Special Representative of the African Union in Burundi
- The Executive Representative of the Secretary-General of the United Nations for Burundi
- A representative of the Government of Burundi
- A representative of the Palipehutu-FNL
- The Ambassadors in Burundi of Uganda, Tanzania and South Africa
- A representative of the European Union

The Political Directorate addressed political obstacles that arose during the implementation of the Comprehensive Ceasefire Agreement. It served as a "listening forum" and promoted trust between the parties. The Directorate facilitated dialogue between the two parties, including on political arrangements aimed at the inclusion of FNL into the national institutions within the framework of the Constitution. It monitored and assisted the parties in implementing these arrangements. The Directorate communicated and kept all partners informed of developments in the peace process.

The Group of Special Envoys for Burundi (GSEB) supported the work of the Political Directorate. The Group met every three months to review progress in the peace process. Agathon Rwasa and other FNL leaders returned to Burundi in May to be part of the peace process and began the work of transforming their organisation into a political party. It was hoped that the roadmap chartered would be key in ending close to two decades of civil conflict in Burundi.

The return of Rwasa and his colleagues from exile in Tanzania raised hopes that the 15-year civil war that has seen the demise of about 300 000 people would come to an end. Nqakula and I were in the flights that brought Rwasa and the leadership of the FNL from Dar es Salaam to Bujumbura, in part this was also the guarantee of security and to give assurance to the FNL. At this stage the party was distrustful of the Government in power and the FNL cadres harboured fears that there could be foul play.

Rwasa had been away from the country for 20 years, and although he remained popular inside the country many did not know how he looked like. On our arrival at the airport, there were thousands of people at the airport and lining the streets from the terminal to the city, many eager to set eyes on Rwasa.

There was a light moment when our South African Ambassador, Mr. Mdu Lembede's car came to the airport, flying the flag to fetch him, and to be in the convoy. Mdu had been actively involved and was part of South Africa's mediation team. The convoy was arranged such that Nqakula and Rwasa travelled together in the car provided by the mediation team. Mdu and I jumped into the ambassador's official car.

As the cars moved slowly through the crowds that were lining the street, we soon noticed to our amazement that the crowds excitedly mobbed and cheered the Ambassador's car and in particular crowding on my side and waving. It became clear that the many who had never seen Rwasa before, had immediately assumed that the man with a big frame seated next to the Ambassador was their FNL leader. I took in the situation, flabbergasted at the turn of events but soon began enjoying the attention and discreetly waved back. We all had a good laugh later.

CHAPTER 20

MY TOUR OF DUTY
AS HIGH COMMISSIONER OF NIGERIA

"Nigeria is often called the "Giant of Africa."
This name comes from the vastness of its land,
the diversity of its peoples and languages,
its huge population (the largest in Africa),
and its oil and other natural resources."
Anon

As shared earlier in the book, I served as the South African envoy to the Great Lakes Region during which we successfully mediated and facilitated the comprehensive ceasefire agreement between the Government of the Republic of Burundi and the Palipehutu – FNL.

Thereafter, it was time to move on. I reached an agreement with our minister for Foreign Affairs, Dr. Nkosazana Dlamini Zuma, that the next posting would be to Nigeria.

With that, she recommended me to be appointed High Commissioner to Nigeria and I, patriotically, accepted the appointment. Nigeria is not only important to South Africa, the two countries have several things in common.

The two nations are members of the Commonwealth of Nations, the political alliance of fifty-six member states, most of which are former colonies and territories of the British Empire. Secondly, both countries are ranked among the largest economies on the continent and therefore, leaders in their respective regions.

In addition, relations between the two countries are unique because of Nigeria's stance against Apartheid and her unparalleled support of our liberation struggle. Nigeria was in the forefront in opposing the oppressive, racist white minority government and chaired the Anti-Apartheid Committee at the UN. They also mobilized many others to oppose the racist regime by highlighting its atrocities.

Further, the Nigerian government established what was popularly known as the Mandela Tax. This was a tax that the citizenry were made to pay to support the liberation movement in South Africa.

In addition, Nigeria gave scholarships to many South Africans, particularly at the university level, which contributed greatly towards an educated workforce at independence.

Having provided so much support to South Africa and because of their readiness to combat Apartheid, Nigeria lobbied for recognition as one of the Front-line states. In essence, front line states are those states that border South Africa. Nevertheless, the Nigerian government felt that they had earned the right to be considered among those closest to South Africa, albeit not geographically.

In recent years, economic diplomacy has taken center-stage in relations between nations. Given their political history, South Africa and Nigeria should be enjoying economic and social relationships that supersede many others on the continent. They both have products and services that the other needs. We could have forged stronger ties that might also have been beneficial to the continent. Nonetheless, there is still room to do so.

Of course, every coin has two sides. There were some challenges that I tried hard to look into and to resolve as best I could. The first was to do with visas for Nigerians wanting to go to South Africa. They felt that South Africa was not open to business whereas Nigeria had opened her doors wide to South African business.

The feeling was exacerbated when one senator travelled with his entourage to South Africa and unfortunately did not have the mandatory Yellow Fever vaccine card. He was turned back in what became a diplomatic incident of gigantic proportions. The sentiment that South Africans do not like Nigerians was the prevailing one through Social Media. I had a meeting with the Minister for Communications and as we left her offices, the doors were opened to an onslaught of the media who were unrelenting about the anti-Nigerian sentiments. With calm and diplomatic poise, I defended my country's position while trying to smooth the ruffled feathers.

Another incident that threw a dark mark on relations with Nigeria happened following the brutal and tragic shooting of a well-loved South African musician celebrity. Lucky Dube was followed in a park in Johannesburg and shot dead in a robbery attempt which went wrong. The security officers were quick in arresting the criminals who were then arraigned in court.

At the time, the lack of a good banking system between the two countries, resulted in many wealthy Nigerians coming to shop in South Africa with cash in hand. They were compelled to declare the money in their possession which in most cases ran into thousands of dollars, The information they had to give when declaring which included the hotel they would be residing in, exposed them and made them vulnerable to crime.

Instead of their love of shopping and taking holidays in South Africa becoming a boom to the South African economy, criminals made it a nightmare for our Nigerian visitors. Many of these visitors proudly wore their Nigerian attire which made them easily distinguishable.

Lucky Dube was a young, popular, reggae celebrity and he lived the part, dressing in designer clothes and driving an expensive car. The criminals who shot and killed him mistook his identity and thought they were robbing a wealthy Nigerian who was most likely moving with a lot of cash. In court, one of the alleged criminals said, "I saw the dreadlocks and I thought he was a Nigerian…" obviously making reference to more than the dreadlocks. He thought Lucky had to be a Nigerian because of the display of wealth.

The uproar from that statement was thunderous and reverberated all the way from South Africa to West Africa. It was very unfortunate, to say the least, and did nothing for the strained relations between the citizens of the two countries, government relations notwithstanding.

All the above notwithstanding, my experience was that Nigerians are, culturally, very hospitable people. I was impressed at how food is an experience rather than just a meal. When they entertain, they go all out and really make you feel at home. I loved the fact that everything is done with a great deal of attention and fanfare. For instance, if a Nigerian official invited you out to a meal, it was bound to have the makings of a party with everyone close to him being invited to welcome you. Their generosity is second to none which was evident in the quantity and variety of food served and drinks that flowed even at what was meant, in my mind, to be a simple meal. It is one country that I felt most at home in and that I really enjoyed the cultural experience.

On a positive note, the role the two countries played together regarding the formation of the African Union was phenomenal. During my term as Ambassador to Ethiopia, I saw first-hand, the hard work, effort and vision of former Nigerian President Olusegun Obasanjo and former South African President Thabo Mbeki. That joint effort carried out by two of Africa's eminent statesmen and their teams is a testament to what can be achieved by strong relationships between our countries and all others on the continent.

CHAPTER 21

PERMANENT REPRESENTATIVE
TO THE UNITED NATIONS

*"The United Nations is our one great hope
for a peaceful and free world."*
Winston Churchill

At ten fifty-five in the evening of May 16, 2015, the Etihad Airline proceeding from Abu Dhabi touched down at the Dhaka International Airport. The weather was slightly humid which made me little concerned as I contemplated how hot it would be the following day at midday if it was already so warm at that time of the evening. Bangladesh is so hot and humid that on several occasions people, particularly the elderly, die due to heat strokes.

On our way to Dhaka, sitting in the comfort of the business class, I closed my eyes and for some time savoured the progress I had made in life. It had been a journey from a freedom fighter, sometimes labelled a terrorist by most western governments, to being the respected South Africa's Ambassador to the United Nations and on this trip carrying the additional title of 'President of the Group of 77 plus China' (G77 and China). The Group is a forum providing 134 member states of developing nations a platform to present a unified and coordinated position in the on-going negotiations at the United Nations, focusing mainly on socioeconomic and developmental issues.

On this trip to Bangladesh, I was accompanied by a few ambassadors and officials, all members of the G77 and China, representing their specific countries. We left New York, transiting through Abu Dhabi Airport in the United Arab Emirates, all of us very excited and awestruck by the significance of the task ahead of us. Most of us were visiting Bangladesh for the first time at the invitation of our friend, His Excellency Dr Abdul Momen, who was the President of the High-Level Committee of the South- South Cooperation and Ambassador/Permanent Representative of Bangladesh to the United Nations.

We were attending a meeting on South-South Cooperation and Triangular Cooperation focusing specifically on the Post-2015 Development Agenda: Financing for Development and Technology Transfer.

At this point in history we were placed, as Ambassadors to the United Nations, at the thrust and in the leadership of our countries' negotiations for a Global framework that we envisaged to be transformative, ambitious yet achievable that was to be known as the post-2030 Sustainable Development Agenda or Sustainable Development Goals (SDG's). The SDG's succeeded the Millennium Development Goals (MDG's), a product of intergovernmental negotiations agreed to in 2000 and whose time limit was the year 2015.

As I looked around at some of the colleagues fussing over me, the Ambassador of Lebanon, Nawaf Salam, strolled over for quick last chat before we disembarked. (In 2024 he was to be appointed President of the ICJ and went on to become Prime Minister of Lebanon.) I also overheard someone advising a fellow official, "I think you would be better off discussing this issue with the President" (referring to me) – I could not help but be smug. I was in charge. Who would have imagined that the 'kid' emerging from the dusty streets of Soweto, out of the crucible of the fires that characterised the battles of the townships against the mighty arsenals of the powerful white minority regime of South Africa, could one day be entrusted with such huge a responsibility. I was humbled indeed.

At the meeting in Dhaka, I shared the podium with the Prime Minister of Bangladesh, Honourable Sheikh Hasina, the Finance Minister Abul Maal Abdul Muhith and other dignitaries. Speakers emphasized that the overarching goal of the Global agenda that we are negotiating is to have a world free from the curse of hunger and poverty by 2030, improve longevity, improve school enrolment and stop the spread of diseases.

The meeting also discussed the proposed technology implementation mechanism.

The meeting in Dhaka and many others were preparing countries of the South for the High-level dialogue scheduled to take place in July of that year in Addis Ababa (Ethiopia) on Financing for Development (FFD) and the Summit in New York to be held in September, on the Post 2015 Development Agenda.

2015 was a glorious year for South Africa: we chaired the Group of 77 and were therefore in the leadership of a number of history-making processes, including the much-anticipated Financing (FFD), the 2030 Sustainable Development Agenda and the Conference on the Environment. The 2030 Sustainable Development Agenda adopted by the Heads of State and Governments in September became the embodiment of the Global aspirations for the coming fifteen years.

The Agenda consisted of seventeen goals and one hundred sixty-nine targets. The Agenda represented an ambitious plan of action that speaks to people, planet and prosperity. The Agenda is also committed to the eradication of poverty in all its forms, leaving no-one behind.

I was very proud and grateful to President Zuma for having given me this opportunity to contribute and play a leadership role on behalf of South Africa and the African Continent. As I saw it then, the young men and women under my leadership in New York, were simply flying the flag that signified Africa's active participation rather

272

than being handed down policies to follow. It was, indeed, a new dawn.

My Office

I arrived in New York at the beginning of 2013 and virtually hit the ground running. Upon my arrival, the President of the General Assembly, Mr. John Ashe, appointed me together with the Ambassador of Ireland, Her Excellency Anne Thompson, to co-facilitate the outcome document of the Millennium Development Goals (MDG's), which document was to set the negotiating road map for the Sustainable Development Goals (SDG's).

Over a period of two and a half years, I was involved in a number of facilitations for the General Assembly including persuading one hundred and ninety-three member states to agree to a United Nations Nelson Mandela Award that recognizes selfless contributions of personalities in the area of reconciliation, forgiveness, conflict resolution and freedom. I also facilitated the declaration of the Decade of People of African Descent 2016 to 2026 and in 2014 was appointed and chaired the State Parties to the Law of the Sea, followed by chairing, on behalf of South Africa, the Group of 77 plus China (G77 + China) – a group consisting of one hundred and thirty- four member states.

These were remarkable achievements by any stretch of the imagination. I received a lot of accolades from fellow diplomats, many of whom acknowledged that it is rare that one diplomat gets the opportunity to do so much in such a short time. Many Ambassadors come and go without having had the opportunity to facilitate even one resolution. The results of my achievements were enough for any diplomat to get the nod from his bosses.

I drew on the maturity gained through the years in the struggle whereas we had served because we believed in what we were doing. Besides, I had been in very good company of many great sons and daughters of South Africa who contributed and molded many of us.

There was the legendary Johnny Makhatini who gave such sterling leadership of the ANC's international relations in exile. The first Foreign Minister in the Nelson Mandela's first democratic administration was Alfred Nzo; Nzo was for many years the Secretary General of the ANC. The department was also led by Madam Nkosazana Dlamini – Zuma who later also led the African Union Commission. I should add to these leaders, the Director General of DIRCO at the time, Dr Ayanda Ntsaluba. All these and many others were great leaders who in various ways left a legacy we are all proud off. I felt honoured and privileged to have been led and guided by these stalwarts of our struggle.

The Mission in New York was not always a bed of roses, nor was it only progress and achievements. We were operating under different conditions, and some of the new recruits of the ANC, most of whom found themselves suddenly in positions of leadership, were all about self- preservation. At workplaces we rushed to outstrip each other to win the favorite privileged spot and to gain the attention of the Minister. In many cases backstabbing, backbiting and mudslinging were the order of the day and sadly, the once revered missions became a dog-eat- dog environment.

During our Chairing of the G77 and China New York, we worked under extremely difficult conditions. For instance, experienced experts who were supporting me were pulled out from the Mission in the midst of very important operations without explanations and replaced with new, inexperienced ones. It appeared is if there was a deliberate intent to sabotage the Mission.

Unfortunately, leadership cannot always be good. On occasion, there is bad leadership as well. I strongly believe that during my tenure in New York, the Department was under the grip of a terrible and nightmarish leadership at Headquarters. Many of us who were steeped in ANC politics that taught us to reject notions such as racism and tribalism were shocked to see these tendencies practiced and displayed openly with the support of the higher echelons in the

Department of International Relations and Cooperation (DIRCO).

At some stage in the Department, an environment of 'us and them' along tribal lines was created, 'you are either with us or against us' environment prevailed. The department was under a dark cloud, and those who could not be acquiesced to endorse and support the openly tribal tendencies were targeted. I believe I was one of those, and consequently a number of people worked to ensure that I did not succeed in my Mission. They failed dismally because not only did I complete my term, I also successfully raised the flag of South Africa at the United Nations that I joined after serving the Government and people of South Africa as a diplomat for twenty-two years.

I was honoured by the National Parliament of Argentina ('Camara de Deputates') in Buenos Aires and also in the State of Mendoza for my role in the leadership of the G77 and China, and for the support and role I played in the negotiations of resolution on Debt Restructuring. Many other members of the developing countries were grateful and openly expressed their gratitude.

I was due to return home. My term was coming to an end, and considering the clashes I had already had with the tribal leadership back home, I knew I was destined for a hostile reception. I weighed my options, requested President Zuma to release me as I felt I could serve the country better by joining the United Nations. Zuma gladly gave me his blessings and I applied and joined the UN, appointed by Secretary General Ban Ki-moon and Chairperson of the AU Dr Nkosazana Dlamini Zuma, to head the Hybrid Mission of the AU and UN in Darfur, Sudan.

CHAPTER 22

DARFUR

"Always bear in mind that the people are not fighting for ideas,
they are fighting to win material benefits,
to live better and in peace,
to see their lives go forward,
to guarantee the future of their children."
Amilcar Cabral

Serving in the Sudan was an experience in the atrocities men are capable of, on the one hand, and the resilience of human beings, on the other.

The conflict in Darfur gave rise to thousands of Internally Displaced People (IDPs), hundreds were killed leading to many in the international community accusing the Al Bashir regime of genocide.

In the IDP camps, whilst there was security offered inside, the women were sometimes forced by circumstances to leave the camp in search of firewood. More often than not, they were raped. Sadly and undoubtedly, rape had become a weapon of war. I visited the IDP camps regularly to meet the leadership of the displaced people, and got the opportunity to chat with these women and listen to their tragic tales.

In most cases when I asked why their menfolk, husbands or brothers, did not accompany them when they went out to gather firewood, their answer was always chilling. Many would report that

"If the men escorted them or went to get the firewood, they would get killed" According to them, they as women, were "only raped and were still able to come home." What a choice these women faced!

As if that was not enough, the country is prone to natural disasters such as flooding which would engulf a whole area, forcing more people to be displaced and lose all their possessions. Desertification resulted in a wide raging conflict for fertile land. The Bashir regime was forcefully taking land from the farmers, mostly of African origin of the Fur clan and encouraging nomads, of Arab origin, to take occupation.

The recurring problem was the conflict between the nomadic tribes who were herdsmen and the farmers. There were designated routes on which the nomads would traverse the land looking for food for their animals and of course, the farmers crops were a boom in this semi-arid region.

The small flames of quarrels needed very little to ignite them into full-blown raging fires.

I cannot forget a worrying incident that caused a serious conflict that occurred at a café just outside the IDP camp. A man, called Nassir, went out of the camp and visited the café. He ordered a cup of coffee and sat down to wait. A nomad of Arab descent, called 'Ali', walked in right after him and ordered a cup of tea. There was only one waitress serving both men. Whilst the coffee was brewing, she decided to serve the tea first to save time.

When she brought the tea to Ali, Nassir got really furious and accused her of playing favourites. She tried to explain her rationale for serving the tea first, but Nassir was having none of that. Ali tried to reason with Nassir and that infuriated him so much that he pulled out a knife and stabbed Ali who died instantly. Nassir, fearing that Ali's clansmen might retaliate, dragged Ali's body back to the camp.

Later that night, we got information of an impending attack on the IDP camp by Ali's angry clansmen. The attack was going to happen in the midnight hour. On receiving the information about the impending attack, I send our forces to protect the IDPs. I realized that we were going to need re-enforcement and woke up General Mohamed Hamdan Dagalo (widely known as Hemedti) to assist, and he did. Without his help there would have been a tragedy of unimaginable magnitude.

The attacks on displaced persons or refugees were always brutal, it is difficult to imagine how human beings can be so cruel to their own kind. We witnessed this brutality after the aftermath of these attacks where intervention did not happen on many occasions. We knew what to expect if the attack had been successful. More often machetes were used, and in some cases without hesitation the whole camp would be set on fire, with many women and children being burned to death. In this incident UNAMID's and Hemedti's intervention brought a huge relief. Hemedti explained that it was difficult to restrain the clansmen; he knew Ali personally as they belonged to the same clan.

Hemedti was an enigma, not so long ago the man had been in charge of the Janjaweed, translated "Mad men on horses". He had been really notorious as head of Bashir's killing machine. When it became clear that Bashir's government was not sustainable, he broke away, saying that he could not go against the will of the people and was seen as the saviour of the people.

He played a key and important role in the transitional government from Bashir's Islamist regime towards a new constitution and democracy. In the alliance formed during the transition, he became the No. 2 in charge of the military and the government. This was a transition during which the interim government would prepare the nation for the popular vote.

I look back as the circumstances prevailing during our peace-keeping mission against the backdrop of what was going on now in 2023, and I know for a fact that unless the international community intervenes, we are going to have a bloodbath in the Sudan. The situation is dire for its citizens, most of whom have never known peace and stability.

278

The current war in the Sudan between Hemedti's Rapid Support Force (RSF) and Sudan military supremo General Abdel Fattah Al-Burhan that has brought untold suffering and resulted in hundreds of deaths of innocent civilians, has got nothing to do with the interest of the people. These are two military men hungry for power and whose greed will see them trample across thousands of bodies if needs be, just to usurp power.

The United Nations, African Union Mission To Darfur (UNAMID)

As early as 2007, the African Union Peace and Security Council (AUPSC) and the United Nations Security Council (UNSC) deployed the United Nations-African Union Hybrid Operation in Darfur (UNAMID) to address a conflict between the Government of Sudan and rebel groups. At the time the conflict led to conditions that some characterized as a genocide because so many people were killed. The UNAMID initial deployment to Sudan comprising an authorized strength of nearly 20,000 troops and more than 6,500 police, was the largest peacekeeping operation in the world at the time.

About the time I left, when a decision was taken by the Security Council to end the Mandate of the Mission, there were less than one quarter of that force remaining, concentrated largely in the Jebel Marra area.

With 1.6 million internally displaced persons (IDPs), a deep humanitarian crisis exacerbated by the COVID-19 pandemic, and rising levels of violence, Darfur in 2020 was far from being a stable place as UNAMID – locals and peace-loving people the world over lamented the fact that the AU and UN's most important crisis prevention tool on the ground – appeared set to depart.

When I arrived in 2016, Darfur continued to experience intermittent inter-communal conflict right across the whole region coupled with pockets of conflict between the Government's forces and the Sudan Liberation Army – Abdul Wahid (SLA/AW) rebels in the Jebel Marra area. Armed criminals, including Arab nomads and former Government-allied militia roamed the countryside and committed serious crimes.

Local conflicts between farmers and nomads continued to arise over scarce land and dwindling natural resources, especially water, amidst rising human and livestock populations, thus reducing livelihood opportunities.

In its resolution 2363, the Security Council defined UNAMID's mandate to cover the protection of civilians, facilitation of humanitarian assistance, mediation between the Government and non-signatory armed movements based on the Doha Document for Peace in Darfur (DDPD) of May 2011, and support for mediation of inter-communal conflict.

These core areas of responsibilities have remained relatively the same over the past 4 years, with some modifications over time, dependent on Sudan political developments.

The DDPD and a number of high-level initiatives sought to address the root causes of conflict and its consequences to include aspects such as power sharing arrangements, wealth sharing, human rights, justice and reconciliation, compensation and return, and internal dialogue amongst others.

In this time, I wore two hats, firstly as the Joint Special Representative (JSR) - Head of Mission, and additionally as the Joint Chief Mediator (JCM) as part of residual functions from the Doha process. Thus, in my double- hatted role, I was involved extensively in coordinated mediation and diplomatic negotiations and engagements with various stakeholders and parties to the conflict whilst simultaneously heading the Mission.

At the start of my tenure, the DDPD held precedence as the main guiding political document which provided the framework for UNAMID's mediation efforts. Thus, the implementation of the DDPD, in collaboration with other initiatives such as the Thabo

Mbeki-led African Union – High-Level Implementation Plan (AU-HIP) Roadmap and other mediated peace talks in this time, became the mainstay of the peace process in Darfur, Sudan. The AU-HIP Roadmap was agreed upon by the Government of Sudan and the armed movements, included the signing of cessation of hostilities and humanitarian assistance arrangements amongst various parties.

For both the DDPD and the AU-HIP Roadmap, key parties to the conflict remained as non-signatories despite constant encouragement for them to sign without delay. During this period, my energy was expended towards fostering international, regional and national efforts to revitalize a peace process that was becoming moribund.

The latter part of my tenure coincided with the overthrow of Bashir through a series of civil society-led protests. President Omar al-Bashir, who came to power in a coup d'état in 1989, was overthrown by the military in April 2019, following a protest and resistance movement which began in December 2018 and which placed mounting pressure on the government to address the rising commodity prices, a free-falling Sudanese pound and a pervasive economic crisis. The people of Sudan took to the streets to peacefully protest for better conditions. After the military overthrew President Bashir, the Transitional Military Council (TMC) attempted to govern the country, to the exclusion of civilian leadership, and without implementing the demands of the civilian protesters. Thus, despite the removal of President Bashir, demonstrations continued from April to June 2019. The stand-off between protestors and the security forces unfortunately turned violent with security forces killing as many as 127 protesters in the capital of Khartoum in June.

This forced the short-lived junta to include civilian leaders in a new transitional government as part of a power-sharing agreement. This arrangement was formalized by the Political Agreement that was signed between the TMC and the civilian protesters, represented by the Forces of Freedom and Change (FFC) on 17 July. The Political Agreement was complemented by the Draft Constitutional

Declaration, which was signed by the FFC and the TMC on 17 August.

The TMC was dissolved and the Sovereignty Council was created on 20 August 2019 with Abdalla Hamdok, a technocrat, appointed as Prime Minister on 21 August 2019, a development which was expected to usher in a 'comprehensive peace process' from 1 September 2019.

I started my service with UNAMID at a time when the peace talks had stalled, and the parties were not engaged in any internal or external negotiations. In this context the AU had charged President Thabo Mbeki of the African Union High Implementation Panel (AUHIP) with the task of resurrecting the talks. He initiated a series of meetings in Addis Ababa to this effect, and at my first attendance had thrown me squarely into the mix. He assigned the talks on Darfur to me while other colleagues handled the issues related to the Two Areas (South Kordofan and Blue Nile). Hence, I found myself in the role of a mediator for Darfur.

The talks at this stage were characterized by deep mistrust between the Government of Sudan and the Darfur armed movements, a problem exacerbated by the Government's insistence on using the hitherto signed DDPD as the basis for any future negotiations and the movements mounting severe opposition to this. Eventually the intervention of President Mbeki and myself was not enough to surmount this impasse. This led to a period of inactivity in the Darfur political process.

In the meantime, the armed movements got involved in the conflict in Libya where they are said to have been involved in mercenary activities at the behest of General Khalifa Haftar, who was fighting the UN-recognized government in Tripoli. The vacuum created in the peace talks was soon filled by the German Berghof Foundation, which initiated what was coined Pre-negotiation Talks in Berlin. I was invited to facilitate these talks, which culminated in the signature of a Pre-negotiation Agreement on 6 December 2018.

The agreement was meant as a precursor to the substantive talks that would have started in Doha in the following weeks.

However, the non-violent revolution, characterized by sit-ins, that emanated from inflation and hiking prices of bread and fuel took over the political space in Sudan at the beginning of 2019. The persistence of the Sudanese, especially women and youth, was to seal the fate of the Bashir regime and equally foreclose the advent of talks in Doha.

With the fall of the regime, and the formation of a Sovereignty Council and eventually a Transitional Government of Sudan (TGoS), the prospects of talks in Doha became a far cry as the Emirates seemed the preferred venue for the Generals in power as well as for some of the armed movements, especially Minni Minawi. However, the Emirates failed to get the talks into track. The Government of South Sudan immediately stepped in and started organizing talks which eventually culminated in the signature of a Juba Peace Agreement for Sudan on 3 October 2020, involving both Darfur and the Two Areas. The Chief Mediators, representing the President of South Sudan, Salva Kiir, enlisted the logistical assistance of the United Nations and UNAMID who were tasked with providing this support. While these talks were conducted in an unconventional manner, the change in tone and attitude, and the trust between the parties was the harbinger for success.

The Darfur peace process and the national and regional politics that encapsulated them have epitomized and defined my tenure as the DJSR and JSR of UNAMID. I should state with the benefit of hindsight, that the inability to craft an inclusive or all-encompassing peace agreement hinged on deep distrust between the central government led by President Bashir, and the several armed movements in Sudan's peripheries. With the fall of this regime and the onset of the TGoS, a change in attitude and approach was enough to clinch a new agreement that looks more promising than most of its precursors. However, without consistent and sustained financial support, the parties will not be able to implement this ambitious agreement, leading it into the catalogue of failed accords in Darfur and Sudan.

Further, I acknowledge that our own internal bureaucratic rigidity became an obstacle to decisions and actions that could have resolved inter-communal conflicts in a quick and effective manner. In a break from this tradition, I initiated projects in Um Tajok for the construction of water pumps along the grazing routes, and this was enough to permanently resolve a longstanding and lethal conflict between farmers and herders in this area. Targeted and timely actions of this nature, rid of bureaucratic constraints and peripheral considerations, are more effective in resolving conflicts with immediacy.

Another instance where fast-forward thinking was required was the landslide incident which occurred in Alfekhei Suleman Village, in the Tarba area of East Jebel Marra on 7 September 2018, when rocks and debris fell over households. It was established that 20 people from the same household (comprised of 5 families) died and 4 survived the incident with minor injuries. 4 people belonging to one family were still trapped under the collapsed mountain and the community agreed that they should be declared as buried at the scene. This catastrophe also killed livestock and damaged agriculture, with the value of damage estimated at 17.5 Million SDG. The same incident occurred in adjacent villages of Tuguli, Khina, Wadi Amulu and Wadi Adu, but there was no loss of life or damaged properties.

On 18 September, I dispatched a joint team comprising of 6 persons (4 UNAMID civilian staff members (POC, ODO, UNDSS) and 2 UNCT staff (OCHA and UNHCR), escorted by 70 UNAMID military peacekeepers, 2 police personnel, 2 military observers, as well as 30 Special Forces and six doctors departed to the affected area. The assets of the Mission included 1 Cargo Carrier, 1 Water Tanker, 1 Recovery Truck and 1 APC ambulance supported by 3 APCs. It was supplied with 7-day food ration and water,

10 tires and fuel and carried 100 Non-Food items including 200

Jerrycans, 100 plastic sheets, 200 plastic nets, 100 kitchen sets for cooking, 200 blankets provided by UNHCR, as well as 200 mosquito nets provided by IOM.

This prompt intervention saved further loss of lives and an onslaught of misery that would have visited the affected communities. Our engagement attracted praise to the Mission from the Government of Sudan and even from our traditional critics like Abdul Wahid Nour (SLA Abdul Wahid).

Another crucial intervention to protect civilians occurred in the famous Kalma IDP camp in Nyala, South Darfur. There was no government presence in this camp due to the IDPs consistent refusal to engage with and even recognize the authorities. The Government had long maintained that the camp was under the influence of hardline SLA/AW commanders and supporters, who brought arms into the camp. Against this backdrop the Government threatened to dislodge these forces and root them out of the camp.

I measured the danger involved in such an intervention and therefore broke with diplomacy to oppose any Government action in the camp. This action prevented potential confrontation between the Government and the IDPs. However, the threats began to resurface when the government embarked on a weapons collection exercise throughout Darfur, with its intention to extend the exercise to IDP camps, including Kalma. I engaged the Government on the foregoing, calling for caution in the implementation of this plan in Kalma IDP camp.

I suggested a tripartite modality of the GoS, IDPs and UNAMID, for this exercise and for ensuring security in IDP camps, including Kalma. In this context the Mission maintained presence and responsibility in the IDP camp and prevented an escalation of violence.

However, crucial interventions in conflict-related incidents and information gathering patrols were more often than not denied or given at a time when it was already inconsequential. The GoS has maintained the argument that the presence of UNAMID in Darfur and the semblance of conflict and instability that it gives is a constraining factor to international and local investments. The GoS has all along believed that the exit of UNAMID, with its Chapter VII mandate, and the deployment of a peace-building mission would augur well for its politics and socio-economic development.

Finally, UNAMID was mandated by the Security Council to exit Darfur while about 1.6 million IDPs were still in camps, unable to return to their places of origin or to other places. No one was happy with the decision, least of all the people of Darfur. Pressure for the Mission to exit was from the new Transitional Government that wanted to be seen to be in control but the lack of trust in anything-government among the IDPs was a serious cause for concern. There was hope that the Juba Peace agreement would pave way for peace and constitutional arrangements leading to elections and a new democratic dispensation.

The other reason for the abrupt exit of the Mission, was the inward-looking attitude of the Trump Administration that had won elections in the US which meant that America was cutting down on financing peace-keeping missions. The Secretary General of the UN was adamant that he was not going to prolong the life of a mission if he is not afforded resources. The US is the biggest contributor for maintenance of Peace-keeping Missions. Donald Trump with his ' America First ' slogan had no appreciation as to why the US should be making a financial contribution to stop conflicts thousands of miles away.

I belive that our mission at UNAMID was to a very large extent successful. I am grateful to a number of people who made a contribution. I am not able to mention them all here, but one I should particularly thank here was my personal assistnat, Arijeta Shporta who did so much to introduce me to UNAMID and the environment.

EPILOGUE

HIGH COMMISSIONER TO THE UK & NORTHERN IRELAND

"Africa's story has been written by others;
we need to own our problems and solutions and write our story."
Thabo Mbeki

I went back to South Africa and soon after was appointed the High Commissioner to the United Kingdom and Northern Ireland. This is a very dynamic mission because of the ties between South Africa and the UK which include a shared language (English) and cultural links, similar systems of law and finance, and a shared passion for the same sports as well as a common interest in promoting trade and a rules-based international system.

When I first arrived at the South African High Commission in London, Her Royal Highness Elizabeth II was Queen of the United Kingdom and other Commonwealth realms which she had been since 6 February 1952. I was to present my credentials to her, but unfortunately she passed away on 8 September 2022. She had been Queen regnant of 32 sovereign states during her lifetime and remained the monarch of 15 realms by the time of her passing.

I therefore presented my credentials to His Royal Highness King Charles III soon after he took office. A short time thereafter, I had the privilege of hosting my President, His Excellency Matamela Cyril Ramaphosa, who was invited by the King for a State visit.

London, as a city, has lots of history that is linked to the liberation journey of many African nations. It is also home to a host of Africans who are in the Diaspora and a dynamic trading partner.

Living in London is in itself an experience, spanning the museums that host a wealth of national and global heritage, the opera to Kew, the exceptional Royal Botanical Gardens.

Of particular interest are the Kew Botanical Gardens which were first founded in 1840 and have grown to become one of the most famous gardens in the world. Located in southwest London, they have been designated a UNESCO World Heritage site because they host over 50,000 unique plant species. We, in South Africa, do have botanical gardens that we can truly be proud of. Among them are the Kirstenbosch National Botanical Garden which grows only indigenous South African plants. The Kirstenbosch estate covers 528 hectares and supports a diverse fynbos flora and natural forest. The cultivated garden (36 hectares) displays collections of South African plants. Even older than the Kew Botanical Gardens are the Karoo National Botanical Gardens that were originally established in 1921 near Matjiesfon.

London is also known as the birthplace of the Beatles and of Shakespeare, the English playwright, poet and actor who is considered "the greatest writer in the English language and the world's pre-eminent dramatist".

Home to the capital of the United Kingdom, London, is indisputably, a globally influential centre of finance, culture and higher education.

It is a great city to visit.

My focus as High Commissioner has been to ensure that South Africa and the United Kingdom create new impetus in the strengthening of the historically deep and strong bilateral relationship by elaborating on existing cooperation projects and identifying new areas. To achieve this, the following overarching themes have been identified to guide the substantive engagements:

- Trade, Investment and Inclusive Economic Growth (including infrastructure investment)
- Climate Change and Energy
- Health
- Education and Skills Development
- Science and Innovation
- The Mission's strategic objectives include:
- Strengthening economic cooperation with the UK in support of our government's programs aimed at growing the South African economy through the promotion of trade and investment.
- Intensifying cooperation in the field of infrastructure development and resilience by building on gains already made and by consolidating UK support for investment in South Africa's infrastructure development programs.
- Focusing on the need to address unemployment through increasing South Africa's ability to enhance skills development and strengthen collaboration in the fields of education, science and innovation.
- Ensuring that the UK's support for the Government's efforts in improving the healthcare system, including through investment into health infrastructure and in developing skills and capabilities for the establishment of the National Health Insurance.
- Highlighting the Just Energy Transition

South Africa: On Deep Reflection

I cannot complete the book without a remark on the goings-on in South Africa. We are facing many challenges as a nation. There are many reasons for this and for the fact that we have not achieved the mandate we set out to attain post-1994 especially after such a brave and brilliantly executed liberation journey.

However, we must remember that Rome was not built in a day.

In comparison, the US has had over 200 years of independence and they are still struggling with what would seem to be very basic issues such as racism. However, while we must not be too hard on ourselves, let us take stock with the help of books such as this one and many others that have been published on the true history, the struggle, and the vision for our nation. Let us own our mistakes so that we forge a future that will be a testament to our foresight, and our commitment to generations to come.

To comprehend the essence of South Africa's transformation, we must journey back to the pre-1994 era, a time when the sun struggled to pierce through the shadows of apartheid. Envision a nation ensnared in the clutches of a discriminatory system, where society's fabric was woven with threads of segregation and oppression. The air was thick with the palpable weight of injustice, a darkness that shrouded the aspirations of a nation.

Apartheid, more than a policy, was a systematic dehumanization of the black majority. It was a structure meticulously built on the foundation of institutionalized racism; a sinister tapestry that denied basic human rights based on the colour of one's skin. The scars of this dark era are not just etched into history books, they linger on in the collective memory of a nation that bore the brunt of inequality and injustice.

The impact of apartheid resonates in the pain and suffering of millions of South Africans who endured a reality where equality was a distant dream. Families torn apart, communities segregated, and lives stifled under the weight of a system designed to perpetuate discrimination — this was the harsh and painful reality that defined the pre-1994 era.

Many sacrifices were made by men and women for South Africa's future which is our present. The masses inside the country bore the brunt, facing the enemy armed with rudimentary weapons such as stones, many were arrested and spent years in prisons and thousands more were uprooted from their families and exiled for years. Let us honour those sacrifices by leading and living with integrity that is borne of patriotism and the spirit of Ubuntu.

My story is one of daring youth, of sacrifice that we did not imagine as we set out from Soweto through present-day eSwatini into the many countries that gave us refuge and the opportunity to regroup and win the fight for liberation. It is a story of unity, of friendships with people in many countries who so graciously hosted us and made us feel at home.

It is a clarion call that as human beings we must never settle for less than we know we can be; that evil cannot triumph over good. It also underscores the acceptance of the responsibility to make a difference because, "if we don't do it, then who will?"

For me, writing the book has been cathartic, a period of deep reflection, of appreciation for the grace of God who sustained us through the most difficult time in our lives, personally and collectively. It has been a time of remembrance of all the comrades I served with, some of whom paid the ultimate price. It's definitely been a time of musing over some hilarious moments and also of awe at our daring and our escapades as only young people can undertake.

With all the sacrifices that were made, the vision that drove us to fight for our freedom, the fact that we are part of the African continent that is characterized by resolve and desire for a better future for its people and our place of leadership in the world, I believe we shall overcome. We shall get through this winter season of our lives as a nation and as a continent, break the chains that seem to hold us back, and together, build ourselves up to what we aspire and know deep down, we can be and that future generations can be extremely proud of!

The early '90s marked a seismic shift in South Africa's history, a time when the shackles of apartheid began to loosen. The journey towards democracy was not a linear progression, but a tumultuous process of upheaval and reconstruction. It was a path paved with the bravery of those who dared to challenge the status quo. The ANC and its leaders, such as Nelson Mandela, Oliver Tambo, Walter Sisulu, Albert Luthuli, Joe Slovo, Chris Hani and many others were household names and recognized as those who individually and collectively delivered the dream of freedom.

Since the advent of democracy there has been some achievements. Commemorating the tenth anniversary of the death of one of the heroes of our struggle Nelson Mandela, our President HE Matamela Cyril Ramaphosa made the following observation:

> *"Since the advent of democracy, access to health care has improved. Many more South African households live in formal dwellings and have access to basic services. Social grants support around 18 million poor and vulnerable people.*
>
> *Today, mineworkers and other vulnerable workers have rights that those who came before them were denied. These include the right to be compensated if they are injured or become sick on duty; the right to organise, to full protection of our labour laws and to safe working and living conditions.*
>
> *Today, not only are all schools open to all races, but millions of learners from poor households attend no-fee schools. Every day 9 million learners receive a meal at school.*
>
> *Today, through the National Student Financial Aid Scheme more than 700,000 young people from poor, working class backgrounds are being funded for tertiary studies."*

Indeed, substantial progress in the ongoing battle to roll back the man-made, poor conditions confronting our marginalized and impoverished communities has been achieved. These are some of the fruits of democracy.

And yet, despite these achievements, and as every South African knows, there is still much more work to done.

As South Africa celebrates its 30th year anniversary of democracy, poverty, unemployment and inequality still define the lives of millions of our people.

Our country has been hit by a global financial crisis; political, social and economic shocks; worsening natural disasters; and the most severe global pandemic in over a century."

These setbacks have made the devastating apartheid legacy of inequality worse. The country is also now counting the cost of years of under-investment in electricity, water, rail and port infrastructure. One of the biggest setbacks has been the damaging effects of state capture, corruption and concerted efforts to weaken public institutions. The state-owned enterprises are in a sorry state and are unable to contribute to the alleviation of the miserable conditions that exist.

It is apparent as South Africa heads for the next election that it is still not yet Uhuru. A humongous amount of work remains to be done if the country is to face, in earnest, the task of tackling the three challenges of poverty, unemployment and inequality. I have no doubt that comrades genuinely committed to serve and fight for the people will be asking the question, "What happened to the organization of Nelson Mandela, Walter Sisulu Albert Luthuli Oliver Tambo and all those, believing in the vision, made incredible sacrifices to see it become a reality?"

A lot of work remains to rid the people's organization of opportunistic and corrupt elements that have moved centre stage and done a lot, in a short time, to taint and damage the good brand. The people of the new democratic South Africa are resourceful, creative, however, and they are more than capable of overcoming adversity. There can be no doubt that in time they will be able to ensure an inspiring and prosperous and future for this remarkable nation.